C0-AXB-892

THE SENSE OF HISTORY
Secular and Sacred

THE SENSE OF HISTORY

Secular and Sacred

by

M. C. D'ARCY, S.J.

BBfUL

GREENWOOD PRESS, PUBLISHERS
WESTPORT, CONNECTICUT

0424187

103547

Library of Congress Cataloging in Publication Data

D'Arcy, Martin Cyril, 1888-
    The sense of history.

    Reprint of the 1959 ed. published by Faber and
Faber , London.
    1. History--Philosophy. 2. History (Theology)
I. Title.
D16.8.D25 1974   901   73-16797
ISBN 0-8371-7230-6

——

IMPRIMI POTEST J. D. BOYLE, S. J., PRAEP.
PROV. ANGL. SOC. JESU, DIE 23 MARTII 1958.
NIHIL OBSTAT JOANNES M. T. BARTON, S.T.D.,
L.S.S., CENSOR DEPUTATUS. IMPRIMATUR E.
MORROGH BERNARD, VIC. GEN., WESTMONAS-
TERII. DIE 15A DECEMBRIS 1958.

© Martin Cyril D'Arcy 1959

All rights reserved.

Originally published in 1959 by Faber & Faber Ltd.

Reprinted with the permission of Faber & Faber Ltd.

Reprinted in 1974 by Greenwood Press, Inc.
51 Riverside Avenue, Westport, CT 06880

Library of Congress catalog card number 73-16797
ISBN 0-8371-7230-6

Printed in the United States of America

10 9 8 7 6 5 4 3 2

CONTENTS

0424187   103547

INTRODUCTION

This book owes its origin to the choice of subject I made when in 1938 I had to give the presidential address to the Oxford Society of Historical Theology. The subject, 'A Christian View of History', had for some years interested me, and, without consulting the views of others, I had formed a private view of my own. (The address is embodied in one of the chapters of the present work.) Once started on the subject, however, I was tempted to develop it at greater length, and during the years since then I gathered intermittently material for a large work on what would be called a Christian Philosophy of History. Too late I realized that the same kind of subject was attracting or tempting a host of writers. I was constantly coming across reviews of new books which dealt, in one way or another, with the same theme. It seemed waste of time, therefore, to add to the spate of criticisms and appraisals of the numerous distinguished philosophers and historicists who have written on the subject.

I have felt, nevertheless, that there is room for a book which considers certain preliminary problems connected with history, historicism and Christian theology, and if the title were not too long, I should like to call this book 'Prolegomena to a Christian View of History'. I include 'history' and 'historicism', because there are current discussions of their possibility and nature, which seem to me to be both full of interest and provocative. History has suffered by being taken for a serious and 'scientific' subject long after the physical sciences had established themselves and taken over the field of knowledge. Philosophers, too, with their strict standards as to what constituted knowledge, have been chary of admitting the pretensions of history. (I can remember a meeting of the Philosophical Society at Oxford twenty-five years ago, when the philosophers, after listening to a paper by an historian on the nature of history, decided its claims were bogus.) The physical scientists, too, have been tempted to compare the methods used by historians with their own strict techniques and to find the historical methods wanting. The historians have not, perhaps, with some exceptions like Collingwood, taken sufficient care to separate themselves off from the scientists and justify their own approach. In a former work, *The Nature of Belief*, I pleaded for a genuine activity of the mind, called 'interpretation', which enabled us to find patterns and unities, especially in human affairs. The word, 'patterns', however, is suspect these days when positivists are in the saddle, and the historian fears that he may be accused of doing what his *bête noire*, the historicist is supposed to do, namely, indulge in large patterns and groupings of the past.

There is, therefore, still need for a discussion of the nature of history. The historicist—and by historicist I mean a philosopher of history—is much worse off than the historian. The historian has won his spurs, whereas the very possibility of writing a philosophy of history is vehemently denied by many historians and philosophers. Before, then, the question of a Christian philosophy is raised, something must be said about the credentials of any proposed form of historicism. But even if these preliminary problems can be cleared out of the way there are special difficulties connected with the Christian faith which have to be faced. Christianity has been called an unworldly religion, and, even if this adjective be ambiguous, all Christians accept a distinction between faith and reason. Faith, though it does not in the most traditional interpretation of it abandon or abrogate reason, has for its content truths revealed by God, which are beyond the comprehension of human reason. Whatever, then, be the credibility of Christian teaching about the supernatural order, it is open to question whether Christianity has any decided view about secular history or the development of human culture.

These and kindred problems are my chief interest and are discussed in the main portion of this book. In order, however, that they should have a proper setting I have had to go over well-trodden paths and show the lines along which the philosophy of history has developed. Amongst past thinkers I have picked for a longer explanation and criticism those who both threw light on the issues I have in mind or challenged the mind by opposition. Amongst modern writers the reader will notice many omissions. The reasons for this are various. I have not wanted to overburden this book with references or synopses and criticisms. Again I have been unwilling to interrupt the thread of my own thoughts or to have to show that a view which might seem similar to my own was in fact different. My silence, however, about one writer might lead to misunderstanding. Mr. Christopher Dawson has written with great distinction and authority on Christianity and history, and even while writing this Preface I have received a copy of a book, called *The Dynamics of World History*, edited by Mr. John J. Mulloy, and containing a selection of his essays on such themes as 'The Movement of World History' and the 'Dynamics of Culture'. From these titles it might appear at first sight that I have been attempting to cover the same ground; but I do not think that I trespass on his territory. He would prefer, I think, to be regarded as an historian rather than as an historicist, and his reflections on the variety and progress of cultures are those of a scholar and a Christian. The purpose, on the other hand, of this book is to inquire into the possibility of any form of historicism, that is, any philosophy of history,[1] and then, on the supposition that not all forms are ruled out, to suggest, by appealing to the Bible and theology, the kind of contribution Christianity can make to a philosophy. Where so much is still dark these suggestions can be at most tentative. Appeal is made to doctrines, which are accepted on faith and lie, therefore, outside the domain of the historian. In a philosophy of history, history is interpreted; keys are used to open doors which are closed to the historian, keys such as karma or sin and punishment or evolutionary progress or Yin and Yan. Christian truths are, therefore, not argued in these pages; they are taken for granted and introduced to see what light they may be able to throw upon the human scene. They are to be judged by their success.

M. C. D'ARCY

30th September 1957

---

[1] I use the word 'historicism' as identical with a philosophy of history. In Italy the word is associated with the views of Benedetto Croce and his school of Idealism.

11

Chapter I

NATURE OF HISTORICAL KNOWLEDGE

The Middle Ages inherited from the Greco-Roman world a body of knowledge which included histories as well as philosophy, ethics and rhetoric. For reasons which need not detain us the more speculative studies became the main subject of interest. At the universities the trivium and the quadrivium did not include history or the empirical sciences. Metaphysics and logic were pursued at first ardently, but by the time of the Renaissance they had almost dried up for want of sustenance. It was natural, therefore, despite the return of so many able minds to classical models, that refreshment should be sought in a study of the world now opening out in every direction. The discovery of mathematical methods which could be used to extend and test the evidence of the senses was decisive in settling the way in which knowledge would advance. Nature now took the place of the reality beloved by the metaphysician and sciences of nature rapidly developed, helped on as they were by the startling successes gained by the methods and techniques employed. Gradually it came to be accepted that the one sure form of knowledge was that obtained by the empirical methods of the physical sciences. The seventeenth and eighteenth centuries may be said to belong to them. The nineteenth century saw even greater discoveries, but a new element had by now begun to enter in. It was that of time, and with the realization of the importance of time history, too, began to catch up with empirical science and demand recognition as an important branch of learning. This is not to deny, of course, that many influential works of history had already been written. Man is always interested in the past. Gibbon and Hume and many others in England and on the Continent had started modern history, and what is more Vico and Voltaire and Hegel, a contemporary of Niebuhr and Ranke, had attempted to give a rationale and philosophy of it. But it was only gradually that history became accepted as a partner and equal of science in practice. I say "in practice" because after the historical method had been accepted by the sciences and the sciences had benefited by this aid, and after historical studies were in full spate, then the question was asked with steady misgiving: on what grounds can history be called a science at all?

This question was bound to arise, and in a form determined by the long sway of the physical sciences. They had run ahead and come to be accepted as the only sure and correct way of approaching facts. History had lagged behind, and for a long time had had no clear shape and no scientific pretensions. It had grown to look like a science almost by accident as able writers struggled to free themselves from prejudice, to disentangle fact from fiction and give a sensible and convincing account of the past. Their work made the place and function of time in the processes of nature apparent to the scientists. Gradually this notion of time and development penetrated science so intimately that there was danger of taking the genesis of a fact as a complete explanation of the fact. Before the end of the nineteenth century evolution as a primary and co-ordinating hypothesis had become firmly established, and the future as well as the past was envisaged in terms of inevitable progress. With reason then has the last hundred years been said to be directed by the new star of history.

With his usual prescience Newman seems to have divined the coming importance of the historical approach to knowledge. In his *Essay on Development* he tried to formulate certain principles of development in theological doctrine, and long before he wrote *The Grammar of Assent* he spent three years pondering on the nature of the historical judgment, how it was formed and on what grounds it was justified. He was to see before he died the break up in many parts of Christendom of the old hard and fast beliefs in immutable truth. Time came to be accepted as a factor in the growth of hitherto assumed absolute truths. Metaphysics turned into a process, knowledge became pragmatic, and in religion liberals and modernists held the field. Without knowing it, however, many of the thinkers most under the influence of historical relativism assumed one absolute principle, and that was the truth of continual change and development. History without realizing the fact was intent on murdering its own claims to truth. If all be relative the very statement of this truth becomes relative, and historical theorizing is built on shifting sands. Most historians were not themselves philosophers and therefore they were not themselves aware of their own serious predicament; nor were they able to offer a well-considered and balanced defence of historical knowledge. They were not trained to meet those who challenged the historical method as inherently vicious and they had no philosophical knowledge to call upon when attacked by philosophers who trusted no other forms of knowledge save deduction and induction. This was indeed a situation which has continued even to this day. The philosophical thinkers by their trade, which was as old as Plato and Aristotle, held in respect metaphysical or at any rate logical truths, and they knew by heart the steps which had to be taken for any new metaphysical or logical knowledge to be acquired. They had been habituated for centuries, also, to the methods of the physical sciences, and though there was no complete agreement as to how induction worked, they acknowledged the legitimacy of scientific inference. But they could make nothing of the claims of the historian to have knowledge worthy of the name. The application of a general principle to a particular case they could understand, and what fell under observation and experiment. These could be grouped under the traditional treatment of concepts and perception. But how could they admit as a form of genuine knowledge a so-called science which had no basis in immediate experience or *a priori* truths?

The embarrassment of the philosophers will be better appreciated if we recall the vagueness which has for centuries lain around words like belief or moral certainty. When a man said that he was morally certain, this meant as a rule that he was not really certain, but prepared to bet heavily on his opinion or belief. In old books on Epistemology three types of certainty were often enumerated: metaphysical or mathematical, physical or natural and moral. The first is obvious, the second was meant to cover truths such as 'arsenic is poisonous' and 'oil is heavier than water'; the third seems to be a store-house for what could not be included in the first two. The word 'moral' was appropriate for moral intuitions and judgments and could be extended to unquestionable political principles and ideas.

But then other 'truths' were slipped in. It was undeniable that Queen Anne was dead, that there were islands in the Pacific, and it was taken for granted that education was worth-while, that I shall die, that virtue is its own reward, that we have had parents, that Plato wrote with a serious intent, that the Bible has been a formative influence in the West. These and many other beliefs which could be cited, would by all, or at least by large groups, be taken as certain. How different they are one from another can be seen at a first glance. Then there is the matter of belief. It is strange, when we consider what a vital word it is in the Christian religion, that fixed meanings were not hammered out. What seems to have happened is that the theologians took under their wing the subject of belief and thought and wrote about it as it interested them. This meant that they explored the Christian teaching of faith and were attracted to more general problems only in so far as they bore upon the nature of the supernatural act and habit. Faith in the Catholic theology is defined as an act whereby we believe without doubting whatever God has revealed. It is an act of the mind directed by the will, and it is reasonable, free, certain and supernatural. From this it is clear that faith is no ordinary act of belief and its special character may well mislead those who are seeking for the general definition. What it has in common with belief as it is more vaguely understood is that it does not rely on direct perception or intuition of any kind but depends upon the word of another. This is expressed in ordinary language when we say: 'I believe you.' The evidence in other words is not observed directly but reported. Now from the beginning of recorded history men and women have been living on the evidence of others, and almost everything we think about and talk about is somewhere or other dependent upon the evidence of other people. Nevertheless far less time and trouble have been given to the analysis and assessment of the nature of belief than to other forms of knowledge.

History has for its subject matter the past, and the past comes to us by verbal or written tradition and the evidence left by the work of man. Our knowledge, therefore, is by belief in the words of others, and just because the nature and value of belief have been so disregarded by thinkers, we are faced with the paradox that while history rides the intellectual world it has not yet won its spurs. In recent years, it is true, thinkers have been making up for lost time. Those who belong to the Idealist and more specifically to the Hegelian tradition of thought have adopted history as the most significant activity of mind. Marx, for instance, takes over the dialectic of Hegel and applies it to the economic changes which, as he thinks, determine history. Croce, on the other hand, keeps Hegel's doctrine of spirit, but removes the static and purely logical element in the dialectic by identifying all history with contemporary history, the living actual present historical judgment. The more positivist philosophers have tried to keep away high-flown ideas and make of the past a series of facts which can be verified and treated by empirical hypotheses. Both schools have, however, met unsuspected difficulties.

To the ordinary reader history does not present any peculiar difficulties. He reads of the past and uses his own judgment to decide whether some recorded facts are likely or unlikely. He feels that he knows the difference between legend and a sensible story. He is prepared to accept the sensible story if it comes to him from one whose judgment and knowledge are trustworthy. If challenged he will instinctively appeal to the facts. Facts are the visible stones on which truth can be built, and to find the facts all that are needed are time and trouble. If he is told by a competent authority that on a certain issue or about a certain period the facts are not yet known, he is quite content to wait. He does not for a moment believe that uncertainty or ignorance about one area of history entails uncertainty about all the past outside his personal experience. Nor is this state of mind due entirely to that credulity or taking for granted what we are told, which Walter Bagehot, in criticizing Newman, suggested was native to man. We are most of us hazy about much that we learnt in history textbooks at school, but certain past events, either out of necessity or through interest, have become familiar and taken shape like a honeycomb in the mind. Most of us have our favourite periods and persons. About these we read avidly, and in the process we pass from opinions to firm beliefs. If we are not too prejudiced in favour of our own country or some person like Mary, Queen of Scots or Oliver Cromwell, we take our view from the facts as presented to us in histories and memoirs, and we become increasingly confident in the truth of our judgments. As in a trial in court or in a detective story the facts are not isolated; they form a series of clues which enable

17

us to understand both what happened and why it happened.

Such is the straightforward explanation of how we learn about the past. Is then the sceptical philosopher creating false difficulties and making mountains out of molehills? Unfortunately his doubts and complaints are not so easy to brush aside. Facts themselves are a rock of offence to some. For, first, how do we know when a fact is a fact? We are apparently often mistaken. And, secondly, facts to be of any use to the historian have to be significant. A fact out of context has no more meaning to us than the name of a person of whom we know nothing whatsoever. Again when facts jostle each other or run along in a series without intelligent comment, they may provide the material of history, but they are not history. History is a late growth in the evolution of man. The past has been kept alive immemorially by word of mouth, by story-telling and ballads and annals. The deeds of great men were an inspiration to the race of which they were the ancestors, and as a consequence all that was remembered of them was handed on. Early tales use the simplest narrative form; there are no involved sentences, no intrusion of explanations; the word 'and' is sufficient to join one sentence with another. When a writer has learned the art of writing picturesquely and of selecting what is of most human interest, the story may become excellent reading. Unfortunately when this happens the writer is inclined to sit lightly to truth, and to become far too credulous. The listeners sit like the boys in the well-known picture at the feet of an old sailor listening to a good yarn. So the next stage is to be wary and critical, to test what has been said and written by independent evidence, by asking questions about the author's integrity and experience, and by watching one's own temptation to credulity and prejudice. This dose of scepticism is invaluable, but clearly it is not enough. One must do more than cross out statements in a record or chronicle which are unsupported or appear fantastic. Scientific history or history proper does not arise until the series of human events takes on some form. A writer like Thucydides differs from the chronicler by pointing the issue, by reflecting on his material and seizing on what was significant in the events which he described. The historian now begins to know what he should look for; he gathers together the evidence and has a theme with dominant motifs, and he learns progressively how to sift the true from the false, the accurate from the exaggerated. Raw facts are now being formed into a significant structure.

Such an account, however, in the eyes of philosophers, may make matters only worse for the historian. We have not been told how we know past facts, and even granted that they exist and can be known, they cease to provide the solid basis for historical knowledge. Apparently they have to be significant, to be interconnected, and some can be ignored while others are constitutive.

In this age of account-keeping and committee-findings, science, as well as history, has been asked to produce its credentials. There is no universal agreement about either the subject matter of scientific inquiry or its methods of procedure. Many distinguished works have appeared within recent years, varying from complete disbelief in the correspondence of scientific concepts with reality to an unbounding confidence in the adequacy of science to explain everything. Doubts about the truth of history could not go further than Hans Reichenbach's assertion in *The Rise of Scientific Philosophy* that 'we have no absolutely conclusive evidence that there is a physical world and we have no absolutely conclusive evidence either that we exist'. Karl Popper in his *The Open Society* tries to define the working limits of the physical sciences. The methods of science, he tells us, serve by enabling the scientist to unify, explain and predict. As an example of the method he takes the breaking of a thread. An explanation of why it breaks is given when we ascertain that the thread is capable of carrying a weight of one pound and no more. It had broken because a weight of two pounds had been placed on it. The law here is simple and universal, *scil.*, that whenever tension on a thread surpasses a certain maximum for this kind of thread, it will break. Here in the very explanation we have both a law, however trivial that law may be, and also a prediction. In the pure sciences we are interested in the making sure of the universal law or hypothesis, and we test it by examples. In the applied sciences, such as in the building of a bridge, it is the concrete example which is of importance and the law is just a means. Popper goes on to contrast the precision of the process in the physical sciences as compared with what happens in an historical investigation. The historian is unable to unify and predict, and he is faced with an infinite subject matter. In place of universal laws he has to play with easy generalizations, such as 'men are ambitious' and 'bigger battalions win'. To make any use of his subject matter he has to select points of interest, such as social or political development, moral ideas or conflicts of parties. He then turns to facts which have to be worked up into a case. This makes history to some extent arbitrary, and Popper somewhat cynically holds that what is meant by history is in fact the record of political power-seeking and the use of that power. History is a feeble subject for knowledge because, in contrast with science, the historian can never isolate his facts and subject them to the test of multiple experiment. A team of scientists working in different places and at different times on one type of experiment should arrive at exactly the same result, if the experiment be performed correctly. A team of historians working together on the same subject would have no more unanimity than a jury faced with the evidence produced before them in a law court.

If the methods of the physical sciences are the one standard for describing the real world, as Karl Popper seems to suggest, then history is at a great disadvantage. To rescue it Mr. W. B. Gallie has argued that history is closer to the biological than the physical sciences. The genetic sciences look for some kind of continuity between one or a number of temporally prior conditions and a subsequent event. They do not claim that they thereby are enabled to predict with certainty; they provide sufficient conditions, and there is always a one-way traffic in time. Not that some geneticists do not fall into the fallacy of equating their explanation with that of the physicists and so treating the explanation as a prediction. They say, for instance, that the length of the neck of a giraffe is explained by the advantage it gives in food-getting, whereas we do not know how and why such a condition might not have been disastrous. The same fallacy is present in some economic and sociological generalizations, and it invalidates much of the Marxist presentation of pre-history. History has something in common with this genetic approach to past events. The historian is not concerned with a mere concatenation of facts, one following the other; nor, as Popper thinks, does he rely on a number of common-sense generalizations of a predictive character. He is in the position of one who knows certain antecedent facts, and in the light of them, and with a sense of the drift or direction of the story contained in these facts, he interprets what follows. This means that he must get the 'hang' of the group of events he is investigating, infer motives, and make a consistent and, at the least, a plausible story of his material. In other words, he is looking for 'an intelligible whole'.

Mr. M. C. Blake in 'Can History be Objective?' agrees with Mr. Gallie in distinguishing scientific and historical statements. The ideal scientific statement is a closed deductive system, whereas historical writing is fluid and adapted to human habits of speech. One should not expect finality in the answering of historical questions, for there are different ways of saying the same thing and usually alternative explanations. As there are working canons of history accepted by all for determining the accuracy and reliability of sources and evidence, all that is needed in history is good judgment, and in any particular discussion of historical events the relevant distinction is that between objective and subjective appraisal of the events. Carrying still further this line of defence Mr. P. H. Nowell-Smith, in 'Are Historical Events Unique?' argues that we distrust history only because we are still too infatuated by the successes of the physical sciences. Before Hume, he says, it was assumed that an explanation to be called rational must proceed by deductive steps from *a priori* premises. Once this was shown to be too narrow induction was given its imprimatur, and it has proved so successful that it has usurped the place of authority, as the exercise of reason *par excellence*. But if induction be rational, though it is not deductive, then there is no reason why other methods should not be at least tolerated. 'To say that, deductive systems apart, the only legitimate criteria must be those recognized by natural scientists is to be as arbitrary as it is to condemn inductive methods for not being deductive.' The neglect of this truth is responsible for so many attempts to assimilate history to the physical sciences. In fact history has its own methods, suited to its subject matter, which offer their own justification. They differ from the methods of the sciences in two respects. Scientific explanation is often said to be based on regularities. This view, the 'regularity theory', is in accord with the modern positivist trend in scientific thinking and in philosophy. The old idea of cause is abandoned, and instead the regularity with which events succeed one another is put in its place. An event of a type A is found to be regularly connected with an event of the type B. 'I invariably feel queer after eating strawberries.' This particular statement becomes a causal statement of science when it becomes one about types of events. But lest it be thought to be no more than an empty explanation that so and so always happens a theory is constructed, and the conjunction of events is brought under 'the deductive umbrella of a well-established theory'. It is this 'umbrella' which is the object of interest to the scientist, for we then pass from a regular occurrence, such as that of spring tides at new and full moon, to a theory which appears to tell us why there is this conjunction of events. We are dealing with universals which enable us to predict what will happen invariably. The discovery or refutation of such generalizations is the way in which science advances.

Now historians do not search for such regularities, as human events do not fall into classes or types which can be used for infallible predictions. As compared with the physical scientist they deal with particular or, as I should prefer to say, the quasi-particular instead of the universal. The scientist may want to know the habits of the bee or the beetle, the bee, that is, as a universal; the historian deals with the story of man. The scientist wants to discover what happens *whenever p*, the historian what happened *when p*. The one applies a general truth, the other is concerned with a particular series of events, such as the French Revolution. The French Revolution can, indeed, be compared with other revolutions, and a statesman soaked in history may be better able to judge a probable course of events than the ill-read man. Human nature, be it masculine or feminine, has something *varium et mutabile* in it, and though mass movements do have some recognizable features and have their periods and rhythms, they are never just specimens of a type. The events which the historian studies await an explanation, and they are at first open to many explanations, which in time may be reduced. The actions, for instance, of a Robespierre can be attributed to 'his patriotism, his arrogance, his bloodthirstiness or his timidity'. We know antecedently that human actions are motivated and we look at the evidence in order to decide which motive was predominant. This implies that we are already in possession of a number of truths about human nature, and there is no mystery about their acquisition. Human people live together; they read about others, and they learn to interpret other persons' actions in the light of the general behaviour of human beings. The pertinent problem for the historian consists in making the right attribution of what he knows to the particular person and action he is studying. Nowell-Smith gives us a rule for the historian that 'roughly the strength of the evidence required to make an explanation acceptable' should be 'proportional to the strength of all those vague, inarticulate generalizations about the conduct of human beings with which the explanation would, if true, be consistent'. Later, in his paper, Nowell-Smith likens historical explanation to the construction of a jigsaw or pattern into which the discovered facts 'have to be fitted to form what is, in some sense or other, an intelligible whole. Science is a pattern of concepts, history a pattern of particular events or facts'. To illustrate what he means he takes the very topical question of the relation of cigarette-smoking to cancer. To ascertain this the scientist looks first for a statistical correlation between the two. If a significant correlation but not an invariable conjunction be found, then the hunt will turn to finding one factor which 'is present in all cases of cigarette-smokers who contract cancer and absent from all cases of cigarette-smokers who do not; with the isolation of this factor it will be said that a cause of cancer has been discovered'. In history, on the other hand, we form a picture and look to see whether the particular facts fit in with it. If they do, they are then illustrations of a point of view and not instances supporting a generalization. Clearly what is important in the historical approach is the selection of significant data. We try to show that our picture leaves out no important fact, and at the same time gives the most likely or the only intelligible meaning to all the facts.

From all this we can draw some important conclusions. One is that history differs from science, and is none the worse for that. Secondly, history is concerned with the particular or quasi-particular in contrast to science which is satisfied with types. Thirdly, history uses interpretation; it seeks for an intelligible pattern or whole. Nowell-Smith is surely right in claiming for the historian the right to practise a way of knowing different from that of the scientist. Were it not for the preponderance of science in the modern world such a claim would be accepted without question. The distinction, too, between the kinds of question which science and history ask is obvious. Nowell-Smith insists that the historian is concerned with the particular, the particular event or person. The examples he gives, however, show that it is not so much the particular as the particular related to some pattern or intelligible whole. The historian looks for some meaning in an historical episode; there are various individuals who play their part in it, and if we wish to know its significance we must interpret their motives and their concerted actions. They are playing their part in a public act, and it may be that their actions will change the course of history. A Julius Caesar is judged differently by a Livy, a Cicero and a Mommsen. Caesar happens to be such a complicated and mysterious figure that we are tempted to set history on one side and meditate upon his personality. But the historian wants to know about his character only in so far as it exercises its influence in the course of events. That is why I have suggested that it is more correct to say that the historian is interested in the quasi-particular, and this distinction I shall take up again later. The pattern is, as Nowell-Smith makes clear, what is all important for the historian, and it is pleasant to find a philosopher of the Humian tradition coming out openly in favour of 'an intelligible whole'. The weakness of so much discussion of history today comes from the unwillingness to allow for anything beyond empirical data and a verifiable succession of events. As the scientist has ostracized cause and replaced it by regularity of succession in events, so too the empirical philosopher commits *hara-kiri* by refusing to treat historical events except in terms of sense-data. Nowell-Smith does not behave like a Gallio, who 'cared for none of these things'; he admits that human nature has some characteristic ways of acting, and that we ought to look in the objective world around us for 'an intelligible whole'. He does not, however, pursue these hints, and as a result we are left, at the end, somewhat uncertain as to the nature of historical knowledge, its validity and justification. If there are no laws to be found which will enable the historian to predict, and if his judgment must be a subjective one, how can we speak of certainty at all?

An answer to this is *solvitur ambulando*, and historians have succeeded in bringing enough order into the past to make the record infinitely precious and valuable to the living in innumerable ways. Aristotle warned us that we should not translate the methods suitable to one subject-matter to another indiscriminately, nor ask the same kind of questions. It is only perverse prejudice which insists that the methods suitable to science are alone right. We must expect that human action has need of a different treatment from that of dead matter. If we examine our behaviour and our attitude not towards the past but in the present we can see that our judgments have many different strings and we are not nonplussed because persons do not behave like things. When the lift or our motor-car fail to work we are sure that something has gone wrong with the mechanism, as we know how it ought to behave. When, on the other hand an acquaintance fails to keep an appointment we do not react in the same way. We know that he is not an automaton. But that does not prevent us from passing judgment on his conduct. If he is a dependable person we wonder whether he may have met an accident or be ill; if we know him to be undependable we shrug our shoulders. That is to say we act as if we had enough knowledge to form an opinion on his behaviour. The running of buses and of trains depends upon the will of human beings; nevertheless we have no hesitation normally in planning a journey. If we learn that there has been a strike, we may feel that we know enough to be almost sure why the strike has occurred. The daily newspapers give for the most part up-to-date news. That news is of varying importance and trustworthiness. Most of us are confident that we can weigh it and if we are doubtful, that means we have not yet the wherewithal to test it and arrive at the truth. All day long we are passing judgment on our friends, on public characters, on the events of the day, national and international affairs. None of this subject-matter belongs to the world of nature; it is what will become, with the passing of time, history. What we do now spontaneously and with reflection the historian will do at a future date, and is at the moment doing with regard to past human events. There is, therefore, an accepted way of looking at human behaviour, one which we have no hesitation in accepting, and the fact that it is different from the knowledge we have of physical events does not usually trouble us. If then we are capable of arriving at some truth about the present, what stands in the way of our knowing something about the past?

It may be said that the present is under our noses, whereas the past is gone and there are no certain means of bringing it into the present. The historian might retort that the scientist also freely uses the past, that he is dependent upon a knowledge of experiments and explanations made before living memory, and again that some of the sciences such as archaeology and palaeontology are specifically concerned with ages which precede even the earliest historical records. Some also make the point that memory can make a bridge between the present and the past, that we can cover up to a hundred years in this way, so that by talking with some still living, who in turn talked with eyewitnesses of incidents of the Crimean War and the Great Exhibition of 1851, we ourselves can have first-hand evidence of what is long past. But this appeal to memory, while it serves to remind critics that past history is not like Mahomet's Tomb apparently unattached to the earth, does not of itself safeguard the past. All learning, be it scientific, philosophic or historical, has to make use of memory. That is certain. To fasten on a similarity, to mark and identify, to follow a series of experiments, to make use of one's reading, more often than not require the use of memory. Without it we are not only in blinkers, we have no past or successive experience. Memory is, therefore, a pillar of truth, but that is not to say that alone it can support the whole building. As we all know to our cost memory is an unreliable guide. We are, for instance, sure that we remember a place, and yet when we return there we discover that it is different from our memory of it; we retail a past experience, which is still vivid, and are intensely embarrassed when friends point out that our story cannot be wholly true. Memory must in its first tapping at our door be authentic, but what we recognize across intervening experiences is not always the original. Even in the first sense-experience of which now we have only the memory, the seeing and the understanding built it up into the framework of our thoughts, and this global apprehension or interpretation, as I have called it elsewhere, is liable to error. It may be, too, that in the first impression some element in the whole struck us subconsciously and more forcibly than the rest, and this, in the process of time and in the recurrent memories, serves to distort the original experience. Be that as it may, memory needs to be tested and to be confirmed by other evidence before it can be accepted as a certain witness of the past.

Memory then needs itself to be supported by confirmatory evidence and other tests, and even then it does not take us a long way back in History. There are centuries for the know-

26

ledge of which we have to rely on other criteria, written accounts, traditions, art-remains and coins and tombs. The evidence of eyewitnesses is the most welcome of all; then contemporary accounts and the considered judgments of a later writer, who shows that he is critical and well informed and has used first-hand sources which are now lost to us. This is the equipment with which the historian, in lieu of observation and experiment, approaches the past. Some philosophers think that the result can be only uncontrolled guesswork. 'Your guess is as good as mine', but mine fits in better with contemporary ideas and outlook. Burckhardt in the modest and ironical claims he made was not far removed from this scepticism. History is for him 'the record of facts which one age finds remarkable in another'. It is futile to look for more, to hope to see the past as those who lived in it saw it or to draw together into one system or under unifying principles the various movements of which there are records. All that we can do is to bring on to the stage what interests our own age and to preserve our continuity with the past thoughts and actions of our fellow men. The past now belongs to us and if we cut ourselves off from it we neglect what is vital to our present culture and happiness. We lose the sense of our own significance if we do not keep the past, the present and the future before us, and therefore the work of the historian is to safeguard this continuity and consciously or unconsciously to look at the past in the light of our present predominating interests and estimates. Modern positivists, like Dr. K. R. Popper, are more ruthless than Burckhardt. Burckhardt was a great humanist, and, however inconsistently, permitted himself reflections on culture, religion and democracy and other such subjects. Positivists for their part think such moralizing a waste of time, and, indeed, dispense with such a meaningless general subject as history in itself. What is known as history splits up into a number of diverse activities whose value and method depend upon the nature of the subject-matter investigated. What is common to these subjects is that unlike science proper they have each a particular result in view. We do not ask the architect or the engineer to do more than help directly or indirectly the making of better buildings. The expert in political or economic or social history does not engage in science, that is to say he is not concerned with the abstract or with general propositions; his ultimate aim lies with the concrete and the

27

0424187

103547

practical. Up to the time of the modern positivist history, so it is now said, had been thought of in false terms, as a theoretical activity concerned with a bogus subject-matter. But, let it be said in answer, so long as there is human nature there will also be a kind of history which is more than engineering. The positivists deny its existence and would expel it. But though you expel nature with a fork, it will always return.

The late R. G. Collingwood, the outstanding English theorist on history, surprisingly denied the identity of human nature through the ages. As he handicapped himself further by denying that there were any unalterable facts of the past, he does not appear to be the kind of defender the practising historians would woo. Collingwood was no doubt influenced by Croce and he belonged to the idealist tradition. He was not, therefore, inclined to swear by hard facts or adopt that line of defence. So far from this he underlined the two main weaknesses of the historian, that facts are worthless unless they are significant, and that the past is beyond observation and experiment. As an idealist he emphasized the view that facts have to be thought of and expressed in ideas, but whereas the Hegelians tended to treat ideas as static realities, he held that in history the past only comes alive in the ideas expressed in the living judgment we here and now make. The past is not like a treasure waiting there to be discovered by our digging; if that were so we could never reach it, for such a past could never be a present. But this solidifying of past thinking, this turning of it into a thing, is, as Bergson also saw, a bad habit of the mind. It is like identifying a continuous movement of music, whose nature it is to be in a process of becoming, with the static figures on a score which help us to follow it. Now the historian lives again the thinking of those he meets in history; he relives their thoughts, and for this reason history is a genuine form of knowledge, perhaps the most genuine of all, and certainly far superior to physical science. The scientist has to deal with sensible reality, whose characteristics he can study best by means of a mathematical technique. This reality remains always mysterious and alien; whereas in history thought meets thought, and by reliving others' thoughts we are in direct contact with them and enjoy truth.

One of the peculiarities of Collingwood's view is that in reliving the past we relive only its thoughts, and by reliving he means re-thinking. Whatever others may try to do, this is the function of the historian proper, and consequently Collingwood excludes from the task of the historian much that we take for granted formerly happened. No doubt he wished to insure the truth of historical work and to give it a status which the philosopher could recognize. Past experiences which are not the expression of thought he considered to be so fugitive and unreal that they are in the strict sense of the word unknowable, and historians by clinging to them were only defeating their own claims. He admitted, and this was a large admission, that he meant thought as expressed in action. In so far as past human behaviour was an expression of thought it could be made present to us now by our re-thinking it. On a first impression many might agree that this was a plausible account. In a sense we do seem to grasp what Wolsey or Chatham or Wellington had in mind in their actions. But what of the actions which are left undone when they should have been done? Furthermore the view will look much less plausible if it is maintained that we are able to identify ourselves with these men and actually think as they thought. Yet this is what Collingwood claims that historians do and must do. So one is the historians' thought with that, say, of Abelard, that the distinction between Abelard and the historian as two different persons, living at different periods of history, can be ignored. By power of intuition which transcends the difference of past and present, of human person and human person, thoughts are made one and the same. Now if we turn to our own experiences, which we know best, all of us will remember occasions when our affection for and sympathy with another can be such that we almost share their joy or suffering and can, so to speak feel what they are thinking. The word 'sympathy', like the word symbiosis in another reference, does correctly and almost scientifically, express this experience. It comes near to an identification of two persons' feelings or thought, but on analysis we should never say that it is a real identification. We break down one wall of partition and know much more intimately what another person is like. We are attuned and sing together, but the word 'together' implies a recognition that we are still apart. When Eugénie de Guérin writes to her brother: 'I have a pain in my brother's side', the very exaggeration makes the expression more poignant. And if this sympathy be a mode of fellow-feeling rather than an intuition and identity, re-thinking can still less accurately be called an identity. It is true that when I work out a simple geometrical problem I am re-thinking the thought of the author of it, in the same way that mathematical and other obvious truths can be thought of by innumerable people and in identically the same way. They have become impersonal; they have so far as we are concerned no author. But of what was in Pericles' mind when he made his most famous speech in Athens, of what Caesar was thinking when he dined with Cicero, of what Wellington thought before and during the battle of Waterloo, I have no such intuition. Imagination, sympathy and a deep understanding of their lives and their period may lead me to a confident interpretation of their thoughts, but that is as far as I can go. These three persons, chosen as examples, lived at different epochs, and of all of them we have much evidence. Not only that, they are close enough in culture for their actions to seem intelligible to us. But we have only to think of a Stalin or a Mao to realize that the thoughts of men of a different culture and set of ideas are not easily open to us, and that the difficulty of interpreting, still more of intuiting, the intentions of an Attila, a Montezuma II or an Iroquois chief are perhaps insuperable. There are behaviourists who would dismiss the distinction between action and thought as unwarranted, and Professor Ryle has recently in his *The Concept of Mind* given support to this position. This is not the place to discuss whether such a position can be more than a clever parlour game. Without the distinction the labour of an historian would be greatly simplified; it would also become fiction. Language, it has been said, was given to us to deceive, and the same might be said of human action. The villain and the saint alike can smile; it will be to our cost if we take the smile at its face-value and identify it necessarily with the mind's intent. In the record of men's actions in the past we are continually at a loss to know the intention which lay behind the action. How simple it would be, for instance, if we could pass from the actions of a Charles I or Cromwell to a knowledge of their intentions and their policies. But just because both these characters were complex and hard to understand we are faced with many problems in the history of the times and with different answers. Part of the interest in historical research is precisely the reconciling of actions which appear inconsistent, some of them according with our formed conception of a man's character, others not. We are not satisfied until the conflicting evidence comes together to make a pattern, until, to return to the examples given, the inconsistencies of Cromwell or Charles are made intelligible by a convincing interpretation of their inner and outward lives.

Collingwood's explanation of history, therefore, omits too much of what is accepted as history and at the same time asks too much of the historian. That is not to say that his view does not contain valuable suggestions. He himself in various places of his writings supplied his own correctives. No historian can reach eminence who has not some power of reliving the past. He has to pass beyond the limits imposed by his own private experience and by his own time and make himself contemporary with the period he is studying. Just as the judgments of explorers and missionaries about primitive peoples are not worth the paper they are written on unless they enter into the ways and habits of those among whom they are living, so too the historian has to enlarge his mind to grasp the significance of an age whose culture and traditions differ from his own. Conscious of this necessity, Wilhelm Dilthey singled out this power of living through the experiences of the past as the differentiating mark of the historical sciences. The physical scientist has to use imagination as well as observation and experiment, but his subject-matter has no life which he can relive. Mankind, on the other hand, form a society of shared experiences; they communicate with one another, exchange thoughts and come together in fellow-feeling and emotion. History is concerned with human experience and therefore it can and should make use of this way of knowing which is beyond the compass of the natural sciences. In so emphasizing this special characteristic of history Dilthey did much to elucidate its methods. It was a pity that he spoilt his success by upholding the same extreme view as Collingwood about the intuition of and identity with the past. He denied that we reach our knowledge of the past by any form of inference. Some might agree with this, but few would follow him in asserting that we know the past directly; that is to say, that in reliving the past we are in direct contact with it. He supposes that when we 'live through' the experiences of Charles at the scaffold we have an identical experience ourselves, and when we think of Cromwell we are similarly affected as he was. There are some whose imagination is so strong that they cannot bear reading of tragedies and they may even feel sick owing to their vivid realization of past tortures or of concentration camps. A great poet, like Shakespeare, does more than re-create; he creates a secondary figure more real to us than the original. He gives us a Macbeth and a Richard the Second who almost take the place of the historical person. We, who are not great poets, do not know what Macbeth was like, and so far Richard remains an enigmatic figure. We know more about Henry VIII, and St. Thomas à Becket seems a relatively simple character. Nevertheless I do not think it necessary for the historian to relive by direct personal experience the varied marital emotions of Henry, and I doubt if it would be easy to feel the same ecclesiastical passion as the saint.

One other writer, one of the most outstanding philosophers of history, must here be mentioned. This is Vico (1668–1744); Vico's place is among the philosophers. If he had been listened to the emphasis on scientific truth as the solitary possession of man would have been modified and the relations between science and history improved. Vico regretted that the influence of Descartes had diverted thinkers from history to science; he marvelled that 'the philosophers should have bent all their energies to the study of the world of nature which, since God made it, He alone knows; and that they should have neglected the study of the world of nations or civil world which, since men had made it, men could hope to know'. Whether Vico proved by the success of what he called the New Science that he was right is another matter. That he had made a distinction which was well worth considering is indubitable. That the physical world can be made to unfold some at least of its secrets is proved by the innumerable material inventions with which we are now surrounded. On the other hand modern scientists are very modest in their claims to knowledge about the ultimate nature of the physical universe. Moreover, as Collingwood pointed out, we cannot read our own minds in nature, we cannot even read its thoughts. There is no mind in nature to be understood, no thoughts to be relived. Vico long before Collingwood realized this and had the temerity to argue in a scientific age that as man had made history he ought to be able to understand it. Within the human mind are already present all the principles and all the means requisite for the comprehension of man's deeds and works. We are at home with history as we cannot be with nature; it is our own affair. *Mutatis mutandis*, it is as if an Englishman who had been exploring the rock formation in a far-off island suddenly came upon a game of cricket. The rocks may have baffled him, but the rules of cricket were made at home and he has played the game himself. When then Vico says that the 'world of human society has certainly been made by men' and that we have only to look within ourselves to find its principles of explanation he gives a much-needed charter to the science of history. In every-day life we have no difficulty in understanding and interpreting most of the human actions which fall within our experience. Occasionally our neighbour has to explain to us why he is clasping his hands or making queer noises or changing his routine. These are exceptions. Usually the behaviour of those around us is sufficiently obvious, so obvious in fact that it does not occur to them that they might have to explain it. Their intentions and wishes are made clear to us or are betrayed to us by conscious and unconscious signs and expressions. This is not to deny that there are degrees in understanding or that there are levels which are hidden from us. Men do not wear their heart upon their sleeve, and they may have reasons why what they do should not be plain to all. We know also that men very often do not understand themselves. But the point is that our uncertainty is a variant within a surplus of certainty, and this certainty is founded both on our own familiar relations with others and on our judgments of past human actions in our knowledge of human nature which we all share. This common human nature is the presupposition of our knowledge of others living and dead. We are aware that individuals differ and that freedom makes human action unpredictable; nevertheless we presuppose without any hesitation that certain instincts remain constant, that there is a broad way and a narrow way, that the struggle between mind and heart, selfishness and generosity is unabating, that communities form naturally and exhibit common characteristics, and that these and other traits of men can be discerned. Such traits are the stock in trade of novelists and dramatists, and, what it is important to notice, we judge their success by their closeness to the reality we feel we know.

If this be true, then the kind of knowledge to be sought in history and the amount of certainty we can expect is appropriate to the subject matter and has its own standards. But if the outline is there for all to see, the question nevertheless remains how to manage to reduce the tossing ocean of lives lived to some order and intelligibility. As already pointed out, scientific history is a late-comer. Stories and ballads, the chronicles of great men and great deeds, were delight enough at first. Age brought a winnowing fan, replacing credulity with criticism, and the desire increased to have explanations as well as facts, explanations which would lie within history and not depend on myth. Facts had to be multiplied, and moreover facts about peasant and labourer as well as kings, small transactions as well as great. Early writers had comparatively few facts; today we have, on many periods of history, such a superabundance that we are bound to select. How then is certainty of the kind demanded by the historian and acceptable to the philosophic critic to be reached?

To show how this is done it may be well to give an instance, and there is one to hand in a recently-published work by the Phaidon Press on *The Bayeux Tapestry*. This tapestry, which is so well-known by reproductions of parts of it, is really a piece of embroidery worked upon linen in wool, and it has suffered many restorations. It gives a series of scenes, which, as the lettering on them shows, are meant to depict the meeting and struggle between William of Normandy and Harold II, King of England. This Phaidon book provides a model of historical evaluation and of the methods used to arrive at truth. There are essays by experts on the historical background, on the history of the tapestry, on its style, design, technique and production, and on the armour and customs portrayed. Two main questions are discussed, one, its authenticity, the other, its value as historical evidence. These two questions overlap, in that if the tapestry is shown to be accurate in its description of the arms and customs of the time of the Norman Conquest, it is reasonable to assume that its historical evidence, also, will be of value. Now, if the Norman Conquest were thoroughly well documented, a work of art would be of secondary importance as evidence. But, in fact, contemporary authorities are very inadequate. There is nothing written from the English side, at the time, which dwells at length on the defeat of the English. There are Norman accounts, but historians have regarded them as one-sided. Hence for a long while this tapestry was treated as

a first-hand authority. Then came a period when it was sub-
mitted to severe criticism. Here, once more, in this present
monumental work, its evidence is weighed, and found not
wanting.

The first documentary evidence for its existence is in the year
1476 when an inventory was made of the treasures of the Church
of Notre-Dame of Bayeux. The next is in 1724, and after that
there is constant mention of it, of the haphazard care shown
for its preservation, and the dangers it survived, for instance of
being used after the French Revolution as sacking for wagons
or of being cut to pieces to decorate a float during a public
holiday. A tradition, which does not go back clearly before the
eighteenth century attributes the work to Matilda, the wife of
William the Conqueror, who died in 1083. We know that
queens and noble ladies were skilled in the use of the distaff
and the needle, especially at this period, and Matilda left a
chasuble embroidered for her to Winchester. The evidence,
however, from the tapestry itself points rather to the influence
of the half-brother of William, Odo Bishop of Bayeux. Apart
from the association of the work with the place, there are
interesting indications from the scenes depicted. Odo appears
several times, and two names are mentioned, Vital and Wad-
ard, who were feudal subjects of Odo. There is another scene,
too, otherwise obscure, in which the Bishop is seen cheering on
young boys. Moreover he dedicated his cathedral at Bayeux
in 1077, and we know that later the tapestry was hung out on
the feast of the relics of the cathedral and during the octave.
This does more than suggest that the tapestry was made expressly for the dedication. Here there is strong probability.
That the tapestry dates from the second half of the eleventh
century seems certain. In this Phaidon volume it is shown by
comparison with embroideries of this period that the Bayeux
Tapestry belongs to the same kind of work. Likenesses are too
remarkable to be chance. Confirmation is provided by a comparison with illuminated manuscripts, with what is known of
the costumes of that time, the mail worn, the lances and spears,
the kite-shaped shields and the swords. The Normans are
shown as clean-shaven and with short hair at the back, while
the English wear moustaches and let their hair grow longer.
Many details in the design of the tapestry provide clues. One,
well worth pointing out, is the composition of its border. In

common with other borders of the same period, a girdle, for instance, found in the tomb of Pope Clement II (died 1047) and a chasuble belonging to Bamberg Cathedral, birds and beasts alternate with leaf-work. Stories, too, from fables appear which seem to have been greatly in vogue in the twelfth century. According to the poetess, Marie de France, who also used these fables, they were derived from an English collection ascribed to one Alfred.

The gathering together of all this evidence leaves us in little or no doubt about the authenticity of the Bayeux Tapestry. What then of its reliability as history? The chronicles of the time are not trustworthy because they show both credulity and partisanship. The attitude, therefore, taken up by the patron and makers of the tapestry bears upon this question of reliability. Scholars are undecided as to whether the work is English or Norman. If it was made for Odo of Bayeux the work would naturally favour the Normans, and it has been suggested with some plausibility that the scenes form a dramatic whole. What has been included and what left out make up an intelligible dramatic story, if we suppose that all turns on the oath taken over sacred relics by Harold at Bayeux, an oath which makes him the liege-man of William. The story, then, would take on the character of an Homeric epic or Greek tragedy and cease to be primarily historical. In accordance with this view Harold is drawn sympathetically as nearly a hero. He is noble in look, with the makings of a great king. All turns upon the oath he swears in a scene which is the climax of the first part of the tapestry. The second part depicts his being false to his oath, and consequent destruction. Now that the creator of the tapestry in the interests of his art gives a dramatic turn to his story is surely true—and this is all to his credit as an artist. But it is still quite possible that in the main he keeps to what actually happened. Sir Frank Stenton in the first essay of this Phaidon book considers that the straight sequence of events portrayed in the tapestry is a dramatic simplification of a complicated and still obscure story. As he says: 'The history of the Norman Conquest became embellished with fiction at so early a date that it is dangerous to accept any facts, or assertions of motive, which are not supported by contemporary authorities.' The English writers are silent about what was to their discredit, whereas the Normans exaggerated incidents in their favour.

But may it not be said that the very terseness and insistence in the scenes of the tapestry do give us an insight into the minds of the people of the time, and despite error in details, contribute to our understanding of what happened? This is all the more likely, if the story as depicted is a Norman version worked by an Englishman.

The evidence as marshalled by the scholars contributing to this book does point to the work being the product of English artists. Not only are there many English parallels to be found, but various details in the scenes are English in tone and spirit. An English worker might well counterbalance the Norman prejudice, and so help to give a relatively faithful picture of the course of events. In the second part of the tapestry, in the account of William's preparations, the crossing of the Channel, the landing, and the events leading up to the battle and including the battle, many of the facts seem to be fairly given, and so here drama does not diminish history. It is clear, for instance, that the Normans burnt the houses of inhabitants, that they were at first repulsed in the battle and suffered much loss of life. The turning-point of the battle is seen to come when Harold's brothers are killed, and all is lost with the death of Harold.[1]

In this volume of the Bayeux Tapestry we have then a good illustration of the methods used by historians to arrive at historical truth. We see the weighing of evidence, the comparison with various other sources, the appeal to relevant facts known about habits, dress, armour and topography, and finally an interpretation of the meaning of the facts gathered. The result is a mixture of certainty, probability and opinion. Erudition is

---

[1] Sir Frank Stenton and those of the contributors who deal with the point depart from a tradition and old interpretation of the death of Harold by refusing to see in the figure of a warrior struck in the eye by an arrow Harold himself. A figure struck by a sword and tumbling down in death is said to be Harold. Sir Frank Stenton in another place remarks on 'the magnanimity with which Harold is always treated'. Many of those who are slain are shown as tumbling over with their legs in the air, and this common form of dying hardly fits in with the exceptional and 'magnanimous' treatment of Harold. Their faces are often hidden, whereas the face of the figure hit with the arrow is deliberately drawn and resembles in its nobility the other portraits of Harold, and above his head the name 'Harold' is written. Here is a case of interpretation in which it seems justifiable to accept the old tradition.

so brought to bear that the tapestry is made to reveal far more than the untrained spectator can discern. It helps to narrow down the area of uncertainty about the Norman invasion. It confirms certain facts, such as Harold's visit to William, the favour shown to Harold by King Edward when dying, and a promise made on oath in some place in Normandy. Moreover it gives us a vivid picture of the times and throws light upon the lives, not only of the chief characters, but of the people. In this respect historical evidence is different from the scientific. The scientific approximates to the mathematical; real objects shed all their characteristics save the quantitative and numerable. Misled by this, mathematically inclined philosophers tend to think of all propositions as either verifiable or as truisms. But in history, as in life, what to the mathematicians are platitudes turn out to be truths which can constantly grow in meaning. We are now certain of much concerning the chief persons and events of the Norman Conquest, but that does not prevent us from understanding them better and appreciating them more. That is why there will always be historians as well as poets to write with freshness on well-worn themes.

The conclusions which can be drawn from an examination of a historical piece of work, such as *The Bayeux Tapestry*, make explicit the nature of history and the kind of knowledge attained in it. What no historian bothers to defend or explain is the circumambient knowledge which is necessary for him to begin to work with any hope of success. The lettering, for instance, in the inscriptions on the tapestry are for the most part square capitals in the Latin tongue. To interpret them requires a knowledge of Latin letters and the meaning of Latin words and sentences. The knowledge of them did not come from some native or God-given intuition; somehow or other men come to have no doubt that a curious shape stands for a letter of the alphabet, and that there is a Latin language with features which are peculiar to the age in which it was written. (The widespread certainty of this and similar forms of interpretation is seldom discussed.) We all of us read different types of books and usually distinguish between them. Within one type, again, we distinguish one author from another, and often we are not in doubt. Forgery is indeed possible, and literary and art critics have at times been deceived. But for the most part without having recourse to established tests we can sense what is false and what is true. Authors have their signature tune; they betray their virtues and their weaknesses. After a time we may be prepared to swear by the honesty of one, and to distrust another. So it is that the text may help to guarantee the author's authority, and the author in turn will confirm the text. When we have discovered, for example, that some of the scenes depicted in the Bayeux Tapestry are corroborated by other authorities, we are more prepared to accept those scenes where no corroborative exists. In history, too, there is always the personal and the unexpected touch, which strike us as true and so indirectly help to our interpretation. After the scene in the tapestry where Harold comes to William's palace in Normandy, there is an incident which still puzzles the historian. It is the picture of a clerk grasping a woman by her head-covering, and beneath are the words, *Ubi: unus: clericus: et: Aelfgyva;* 'Where a clerk and Aelfgyva.' Nothing is known of Aelfgyva, except that the name is Anglo-Saxon, but clearly the story was so well known at the time that the artist was confident that all who saw the scene would recognize it. As the incident was connected with the Norman Conquest, known at the time and then forgotten, the fact that the artist assumes that all will know it is strong evidence that the picture is contemporary with the incident depicted. The Anglo-Saxon name, too, is a clue of a kind.

The clue, however, is not sufficiently supported by other clues to enable us to make a guess at the meaning of the incident. The skill of the historian partly consists in seeing evidence as interconnected, as clues which begin to point in one direction. They so join together that the unity cannot be regarded as haphazard; it takes on the consistency of truth.

In all historical work there comes into play an activity which 'puts two and two together', which brings order into a chaotic mass of data, recognizes unity, and like a hound sniffs the quarry and follows the right trail. It is present in the interpretation of letters of a foreign alphabet, in solving puzzles, in making out the sense of a sentence or obscure passage, in reconstructing a whole out of fragments, in separating the relevant from the irrelevant evidence, in divining the purpose of an action or a policy from apparently unconnected data. This activity is to be found in most forms of knowing and understanding, but it is at home especially in interpreting the acts and products of man. Man, as Vico saw, has made history just as man, too, has composed poetry and prose and created works of art. The historian and the critic of art meet what is already familiar to them in their own experience. Like Crusoe they know what a shape on the sand signifies, and, far better than the husbandman looking at the sky, they can read the signs of a dead man's thoughts and passions. They can go even half-way along the line suggested by Collingwood and identify themselves in spirit with an ancient author or the life of the times he is describing.

This knack or gift of interpreting others' thoughts and actions, of fastening on to what is important, and seeing connections which the majority miss, is most marked in the interpretation of great poetry and works of art. We have only to think of the emendation, 'babbled o' green fields', Richard Bentley's *Phalaris*, and the remarkable reconstructions of broken works of sculpture, faded paintings and frescoes, Stephen MacKenna's version of Plotinus or Scott-Moncrieff's translation of Proust, to see what an asset this gift has proved to be. Dr. Austin Farrer in his Bampton Lectures on *The Glass of Vision*, gives from another angle an interesting explanation of this power as exercised in what he calls wit and inspiration. 'The excellence of the mind', he writes, 'consists of conscious intelligence, but of a conscious intelligence based always upon acute sense and riding upon a vigorous imagination.' By the recourse of the intelligence to imagination wit and inspiration arise. 'But what springs up through wit and inspiration is not the gratuitous gift of the imagination to the intelligence: the previous labour of the intelligence is thrown down into the imagination as into a cauldron, from which it emerges again fused into new figures and, it may be, enriched with materials from the unconscious sphere, which were never in distinct consciousness at all.' 'In what we call the ordinary operations of the mind the working of wit is mysterious enough, but it does not perplex us because we are accustomed to it. It is mysterious enough how wit proceeds when from signs of personal behaviour it divines and pictures another man's mind, or imagines upon indirect evidence the thought of a character in history. But we accept such inspirations without amazement, content with being able to identify the stimulus to which our wit has responded. Never mind how wit has worked, that is her own secret: but anyhow she was working upon the sense-perceptions we had of our neighbour's behaviour, or upon the written words which have descended to us from ancient authors.'

There is an obvious danger in an over-sophistication or ingenuity in the use of what Farrer calls 'wit and inspiration', and of this danger he is aware. In the concluding lecture of his book he offers an example of his own use of interpretation to solve a New Testament problem, upon which no agreement so far has been reached. The problem concerns the ending to St. Mark's Gospel. Most modern scholars assume that the last twelve verses do not belong to the original Gospel. They then are faced with the difficulty that without these verses the ending is so abrupt and inconclusive as to give the impression that some verses must have been lost. Dr. Farrer takes this problem and offers a most ingenious solution by showing parallels, analogies and interconnections in most unexpected ways, and by this concatenation of evidence he stretches interpretation so as to bewitch the reader. He maintains that it 'is the proper sort of argument for the purpose, and that it belongs to the genre of literary criticism'. As, however, it is a 'genre of literary criticism' which he uses, I prefer to take an example from the Gospels which illustrates historical interpretation, and not from St. Mark but from St. Luke. In the twenty-fourth chapter of his Gospel St. Luke tells us that two of the disciples of Christ went on the day of the Resurrection from Jerusalem to a town about seven miles away called Emmaus. The distance is given in most texts as sixty stadia or furlongs. On the way they met a stranger who talked with them. When they drew near to Emmaus the stranger made 'as though he would go on further. But they constrained him, saying: "Stay with us because it is towards evening, and the day is far spent." ' He accepted their invitation and during the meal which followed he revealed himself as Christ in the breaking of bread. They, 'rising up the same hour, went back to Jerusalem, and they found the eleven gathered together, and those that were with them'. While they were talking together Christ appeared once more and in the midst of them. In the fourth Gospel there is a reference to this apparition in the twentieth chapter, and we are told that 'it was late the same day'. Before this story can be treated as history the manuscripts in which it is recorded have to be tested to see whether they are genuine, their author has to be

established and his reliability examined. Only after a favourable answer has been given to all these preliminary questions
can the particular problem of Emmaus be pursued. Several
places claim to be the Emmaus of the Gospels and each has had
its advocates. But there are only two which are worth considering. Josephus mentions one of these; he calls it Emmaus
and tells us that Vespasian settled eight hundred veterans there.
It is only thirty, or according to other readings, sixty stadia
from Jerusalem. Those who favour this site say that the reading
'sixty' is the correct one; that it must have been destroyed
during the revolt of the Jewish people in the second century,
and that in order to preserve the title of Nicopolis which had
been given to it by Vespasian, this title was transferred to a
much larger city, an Emmaus farther down from Jerusalem on
the way to Jaffa. There is no doubt that in A.D. 386 St. Paula
and St. Jerome had this larger town pointed out to them as the
Emmaus of the Gospels. But the fact that it is 160 stadia from
Jerusalem created such a difficulty that later ecclesiastical
writers reverted to the place which was only sixty or thirty
stadia away. The Crusaders endorsed this latter place, not out
of any antiquarian knowledge, but they found a spring and the
ruins of an ancient sanctuary and they were told by the inhabitants there that this was where Christ had broken bread
for the two disciples. From this time on this place became the
official Emmaus, and the tradition was greatly strengthened by
the discovery in 1872 of the ruins of an ancient church, attributed to pre-Norman times. Further excavations in 1901 confirmed this and made more conspicuous the presence of a house
enclosed by the church. This house resembles the house which
by tradition is the house of the Last Supper and has also been
enclosed within a Byzantine church.

Such is the evidence for the Emmaus which lies near to
Jerusalem. There have, however, always been partisans of the
place in the plains, and when I was in Palestine and was taken
to see it by an archaeologist I learnt that there was new evidence for it. Unquestionably it was known as Emmaus in the
fourth century and St. Paula and St. Jerome regarded it as the
place of the Gospel story. In time the town disappeared and
there were no remains to be seen of the early cult of the shrine.
Some years before my visit, so the archaeologist told me, a
Carmelite mystic of Arab nationality was walking over the

ground and stopped and said that this was the place where the Lord broke bread and that the ground should be excavated. No attention was paid to her for a while, but finally the ground was dug up and the plan of a large church was revealed with here too the marks of a house enclosed within the church. The church was certainly Byzantine of the fourth or fifth century. This discovery, and the remarkable manner in which it was made, revived the claims of Emmaus Nicopolis, especially as there was the best historic evidence for the name of the place, and in the early days of Christianity it had been believed to be the authentic site. The one great difficulty remained; it was too far from Jerusalem. St. Luke had mentioned 'sixty stadia'; this place was situated, according to the Pilgrim of Bordeaux in A.D. 333, at the twenty-second Roman mile from Jerusalem, a distance of 176 stadia or eighteen English miles. At first sight this difficulty seems insuperable; the distance differs from that mentioned by St. Luke, and it seems impossible for the two disciples to have walked all that distance and then when 'the day was far spent' to have walked back again in time to have met the Apostles and seen the late evening vision of Christ. The historian, however, does not abandon a quest easily and with all the resources of modern scholarship at his disposal he can sometimes discover a way through formidable difficulties. And here is a case in point. Several manuscripts instead of sixty read one hundred and sixty, and this would roughly suit the distance of Emmaus Nicopolis from Jerusalem. They are not the oldest manuscripts, and for that reason those who favoured the nearer site argued that the number was changed to fit the place which went by the name of Emmaus after the destruction of the smaller Emmaus. But this argument tells both ways, for it proves that in the time of Origen and Eusebius tradition favoured the Nicopolis site, and it would be easy to argue that the excessive length of the walk and the difficulty of fitting in the times led to 'sixty' being introduced. Now a walk of eighteen miles was not too much for men and women in ancient days. The road was a good one, and the conversation described by St. Luke proves that the two disciples must have started out very early. All they knew was that certain women had been to the sepulchre, had come back with startling news, 'and some of our people went to the sepulchre and found it so as the women had said'. Now St. John tells us that the women had started for the tomb before sunrise, and St. Mark that they reached it at sunrise. The two disciples, therefore, set out not very long after sunrise. While they walked their 'hearts burnt within them' as they listened to the words of a stranger whom they met on the way, and so it is likely that they walked briskly. By the time they reached Emmaus it was afternoon, but there is no reason for assuming that it was late afternoon. The words, 'it is towards evening, and the day is now far spent' convey a different idea to us than they would have done in Palestine at the time. All they meant in the native Aramaic, was that mid-day had passed, and that therefore, so far as the words are concerned, the time might have been twelve-thirty or two or four o'clock. If then we suppose that the two disciples began their journey at seven-thirty and arrived at Emmaus at some time between one and two o'clock and started back after two, they would have arrived home by about eight o'clock, and this would fit in quite well with the Gospel narratives.

The events here narrated by St. Luke are correct substantially in their local colour and in their historical setting. One has the feeling as with the scene of the clerk with Aelfgyva in the Bayeux Tapestry that the author is telling a story well known to his readers and that the two disciples were familiar to many still alive in the primitive Church. The restoration of the details of a story which should be taken as true remains conjectural, though some may get that feeling that they are on the right lines as they follow up the evidence for the more distant Emmaus. This feeling, however, requisite as it is for the tracker-down of relevant evidence can be deceitful, and this is borne out by an expression used by St. Luke. He says that the two disciples 'knew' Christ, when 'he took bread and blessed and brake and gave to them'. It is almost impossible for those who know the eucharistic significance of these words in the early Church and down the centuries not to leap to the conclusion that the two disciples recognized the gestures and symbol of the Eucharist. In the Acts of the Apostles and in the First Letter to the Corinthians 'the breaking of the bread' is a paraphrase for the Eucharist, and so it is not surprising that quick-minded men, like St. Augustine, should have so interpreted this passage. Modern scholars, however, for various reasons, think otherwise. They think that it must have been Christ's custom to bless and break bread at the beginning of a meal. Moreover, these two disciples were clearly not apostles, and therefore had not been present at the Last Supper and did not know of the rite. Against this latter point, however, it could be argued that the Apostles during the time after the Crucifixion must have told over and over again, as stricken and bewildered men do, the story of that saddest of nights, and so these disciples would have known every detail of the Last Supper. There is a pattern in the scenes recorded by the evangelists after the resurrection. They note that Christ is not at first recognized. His appearances seem directed to leading His disciples to accept Him under a new form and through a symbol, such as 'the breaking of the bread', in preparation for the new, mystical Body of which, as St. Paul says, He was to be the Head. Such an interpretation takes us away from history as the historian treats it, and my purpose in mentioning it is that it links up with what will be said later on a Christian view of history.

On the historical plane the proper conclusion to be drawn from this story of Emmaus is that even the most brilliant guesses or intuitions fall short of the ideal of historical interpretation. The same activity, however, is at work. There is more room, and at times greater need, for intuition in art interpretation, though even here, wherever possible, the judgment should be underpinned by extrinsic evidence. The art-expert may be called in to adjudicate on a so-called Giorgione or a 'new' Dürer or some painting found in a cellar and without a name. Sometimes the style may be such as almost to cry out the name of the artist; at other times the school or period may be obvious. Nowadays fakes can as a rule be exposed by X-rays and the age of the paint computed, but in giving a name to the work the expert may still have to rely at times on his experience and judgment. Fortunate is he if he can come across identical drawings of sketches or be able to trace back the history of the painting and establish its pedigree. History and modern scientific methods make him doubly sure. Artistic and literary judgments, therefore have, where possible, to be backed by historical evidence, as historical evidence has to be supplemented by something akin to artistic judgment and appreciation.

We are now nearer to an understanding of the nature of historical certainty. We all believe that we can have some knowledge of the past. There is first of all memory and secondly first-hand evidence. Both of these plant us firmly in the world of past events, though we may be too dizzy or hazy to be minutely accurate. This world is not one of fiction or fantasy; we have a kind of knowledge, but it is of a kind which can be corrected or perfected. It is as though we were in a large house in which some rooms were better lighted than others; the shapes are real, though some are dim and others unfamiliar. We are constantly learning, correcting our first impressions, distinguishing what at first looked the same and with growing experience we come to form a moderately clear idea of the designs of the various rooms and of the mind and habits of the owners. In history there are periods for which we have records based on memories and first-hand evidence; there are others of which we know only the bare outline, and even of that we may be mistaken. Evidence keeps on accumulating; it may change the aspect of the age or it may turn a well-founded opinion into probability and finally into certainty. With the growth of knowledge methods of criticism and interpretation have also developed, so much so that the historian is now equipped with techniques whereby he can test evidence to find if it rings true. Trained in the art of weighing evidence a historian can know how to avoid exaggeration and jumping to conclusions; he can apportion the degree of certainty belonging to each statement he and his fellows make. He is, however, seldom interested in giving a philosophical justification of historical knowledge; it is sufficient for him that other historians, critics and intelligent readers should be in agreement on what is the subject matter of history and what are the standards of judgment. Like the answer to a famous puzzle, *solvitur ambulando.*

Nevertheless history does satisfy the requirements laid down for true knowledge though it is not easy to present the case in a conveniently simple formula. It falls under 'moral certainty' if by that we mean a certainty which is neither that of logic nor science. Human beings in their intercourse with one another are not living in a world of universal deception or make-believe. They depend on one another and they come to some sure knowledge about each other, about society and about the present and the past. All day long we are learning by listening, talking and reading. Far and away the greatest part of our knowledge comes in this way and it is unsupported by personal experience. Even the scientist is throughout his work relying on the word of others. It is quite impossible for him to test by his own observation and experiment all the observations and all the experiments of all those who have helped to build up the body of scientific knowledge. It is true that he feels that if needs be he can verify what he accepts or takes for granted, and that anything he says is in principle verifiable. The fact remains that he does not and cannot verify every statement in every scientific book he reads. What is more he is seldom aware that he is assuming the past and many of the problems of the past, in particular the power of interpreting the thoughts and language of human beings who may once have lived. In other words the scientist is almost as dependent as the historian on there being some kind of historical truth, and he, like everyone else, takes it for granted. He, therefore, should be grateful to the historian who helps him and to the philosopher who tries to show that the assumptions made are solidly founded. What we learn from others rests on their testimony, and human testimony can be a source of true information. This, as philosopher and theologian implicitly admit, rests on universal assent; it is requisite for advance in any branch of learning and it relies on memory and first-hand experience.

From here we have to go on to examine the specific nature of this kind of knowledge. From Vico's principle we see that we are dealing with what is most familiar to us, namely human action and human expression. It separates the subject-matter from that of science and suggests how it should be treated. There are some, for instance, who think that the answer to all historical problems lies in the simple word 'facts'. Facts are stubborn and facts do not lie, the task of the historian is to look for facts. Now it is true that in any historical discussion facts are the all-important counters, and many a brilliant theory has been wrecked by the discovery of a new fact. These facts may be a date or a tomb or a statement by an author. But whatever they be they are not the same as the facts we meet in our own experience. If a friend says that it is a fact that there is a fire burning in the next room I can go into the room and see for myself. If again I read that such and such a medicine immediately takes away a cold I can experiment upon myself and see whether the claim be true. I may know again that my brother was sitting at table at breakfast at eight o'clock and so he could not have been in a car accident at the same time. But the facts of history are not like these; they are not open to the test of personal experience or inspection. They belong to the past and they come to me though the information of others; they are therefore more like statements about facts than facts themselves. They are not the brute things or events outside the mind, for they have been filtered through minds before I have word of them. They are what others have told me either by first-hand experience or by memory or by hearsay and their tale is recorded for me in manuscripts or print or inscription or tradition. They are therefore facts of a different order from those I experience through my senses. What is more: they are facts whose essence it is to be significant. Even dates are an invention by man, a means to aid memory, an artifice to stem and surmount the unending flux of time. Numbers, too, which seem so simple have in past ages been chosen because of an esoteric or symbolical value. Jung and his school have developed what we knew before, that numbers like three and four and seven have an irresistible attraction to the unconscious mind; and this must make us more careful in our acceptance of them when they are set down by an ancient author. Now if even dates and numbers show the impact of the human mind much more so do human actions. They have to be understood, and as we all know sometimes they are immediately intelligible and at other times they remain dark and mysterious. When the little daughter of Marcelino de Sautuola rushed up to her father crying out 'Toros, toros', she had seen the bison frieze in the Altamira cave. She had immediately recognized the shapes of the bulls; they were different from the rock formation; so she had the beginning of an understanding of the difference between a human action and a thing. It belonged however to more mature minds to appreciate this difference fully, to inter-pret the formations on the walls as not merely of the shape of of bull but as a drawing, the work of the human mind and having a meaning.

The fact that historians are not all agreed on what purpose lay behind these drawings in the Altamira cave only brings out the more the difficulties historians have to face and the way they can be overcome. These drawings are the work of human beings like ourselves in their power to represent in lines and colours the objects of nature which interest them, thereby expressing their inner feelings and desires. They may have had a love of beauty in itself—it is hard to conceive that they could have created such beautiful objects without such a love—and perhaps religion may have stirred them or at least magic. Whatever may have been the inspiration we are confident that it belonged to the gambit of human emotions and motives, and that is why these art-figures, which have, so to speak, risen from the grave, are intelligible to us and can be interpreted. This is true not only of all past works of art but of all human actions. The life story of past generations lies before us, and we can piece together the evidence and according to the measure of it enter into the thoughts and intentions of our ancestors. There is the chessboard, the time and space element, which fix the occasion of an action; there are the conditions and the movements and stresses of the people whose life is determined by the 'powers that be', and there are the actions of the knights and lords and bishops and kings and their queens or viziers. Chess is a game which is a microcosm of human behaviour, symbolizing in its rules of procedure the way the chief powers in a State are wont to behave. All of us feel that we know the general moves of human nature, and, to take another example, advertising, that highly developed art, relies entirely on its power of gauging the tastes and ambitions of the average man and woman. Without some such knowledge of human nature history would be a venture in the dark; with it history is a laborious but fascinating attempt to listen in to the past of Everyman, to learn what really happened to those once alive as we are now, and perhaps even to discern a divinity shaping human ends in the ebb and flow of civilizations. This last belongs to the philosophy of history rather than to historical study proper, even though every historian would be grateful for light upon the general pattern of history. He is content, however, to cultivate his own small or large patch, and use all the most efficient techniques for finding and testing evidence about it. With these techniques he is able to control the evidence and select what is trustworthy and to the point. But even in doing this he is making an act of trust. He has, as just stated, to trust in the relative uniformity of human nature, to see in certain actions the expression of anger and hope and ambition and generosity. The actions are signs of these emotions and desires. But he has also to select out of a vast array of evidence. If he were to treat it on the principle of modern democracies that all are equal he would be lost. Some of it he can dismiss as obviously irrelevant, but with the rest he has to use his judgment. In doing this he lays himself open to mistakes of bias; he also gives himself the opportunity of seeing the wood instead of the trees, of hitting upon the truth to which he then will find all the neglected evidence will conform.

If a future historian were to set himself to write the story of the Nazi movement he would have to establish the facts, then ask how these events came to pass, and, finally, why the story worked out as it did. In this last task he would have to try to give an explanation of the movement and of the characters and purposes of the chief persons engaged in it. This future historian will have one advantage and one apparent disadvantage. The apparent disadvantage would be that he was not an eye-witness, that he is dealing with the past. We have already discussed the seriousness of this handicap. The advantage in most people's eyes would more than compensate for this. The contemporary cannot see the wood for the trees and like a soldier in a battle he can only see what is before him. As time passes not only is it possible to gain a perspective of the whole, but more and more evidence comes to light. Well-tried methods of historical criticism enable the historian to make sure of a vast number of important facts. Though these are not facts in the sense of the immediate evidence of the senses they are supported by so much converging evidence as to be reckoned indisputable. Scattered around and shading off into darkness are the events and actions which make the scene credible and coherent. They fill up, for instance, the picture of Hitler's last days. With enough facts established to make up the general picture, the meaning has then to be extracted. What were the causes responsible for the revolutionary movement and the course it took and how are we to interpret the actions of its leaders, their rise and fall? Those who were living at the time viewed it with very different minds; they differed in their interpretation of the steps taken by Hitler and the programme he had in mind. *Mein Kampf* it might be said gave the clue, but the book that a man writes does not necessarily represent his intentions, especially if a book be written by an obviously immature mind before he has had to take on great responsibilities and been confronted with new and unexpected problems. His traits of character as reported and his speeches baffled many, and at the time it was not so easy as it has become now to relate together a number of his actions and see in them a consistent and implacable purpose. Time serves the historian's purpose; it allows him to bring events into focus, to use his scientific technique and to practise his art.

Technique and art sharpened to a fine edge, these are the weapons of the historian. Once upon a time it was the fashion for the historian to proclaim himself the dry-as-dust recorder of facts, the delver into sources and the diligent reader of manuscripts. His duty was to scrape the pot and serve up the untasty result on a dish. But the readers never accepted this judgment and the most prominent historians never kept to their tenets. Stubbs ransacked charters but out of them reconstructed constitutional history; Maitland devoted himself to legal institutions and turned into one of the most original historians of the century. The great historian cannot help throwing light upon dark places and bringing something fresh to his interpretation of the past. So conspicuous is this creative or re-creative genius in the great historians that with a *volte face* Trevelyan can suggest that history is more surely an art than a science, and there are at the present day not wanting others to agree with him. It would appear that history is a half-way house between science and art. The historian has to use his imagination and his sympathy to reconstruct the lives and works of past fellow-men; he is more than a patient research student for he has to find a meaning and shape in the data he discovers. The chaotic mass of facts have to be interpreted and brought into some kind of unity, and this means that he has to select and give a personal and to some extent original view of the historical scene he is looking at. But this selection and this interpretation cannot be arbitrary or ruled by his taste. He is an artist subject to the laws of evidence and concerned exclusively with truth. The beauty of an idea may tempt him but he must put it aside, for truth must take precedence of all else, and because he is pursuing truth he thinks of himself usually as wedded to science rather than to art. When, for instance, the future historian has to consider the mass of material bearing on Nazism he will see better than its contemporaries the interconnectedness of much of it, and how the moves of Hitler, which led to such different interpretations at the time, manifest his mind and his intentions. What was puzzling may seem so clear as give rise to certainty.

The appeasement policy of the British Government was at the time of Munich welcomed by many and then made a subject of scorn, especially by those who were not faced by the perplexities and responsibilities of the leading Ministers. Now that the Documents of British Foreign Policy are being carefully published we shall soon be in a better position to come to a well-informed judgment about it. Even so there will be room for varying opinions and for a great historian to thread together disconnected pieces and by penetrating still deeper into the causes and motives of the protagonists to give us a version which will strike us as closer to the ultimate truth.

The word 'interpretation' has been continually used in the description of historical thinking and judgment. It is now time to explain it, as it is the key word. Newman was the first to develop a theory of how we make our assents in matters which are outside science and logic. His answer was given in what he called the 'illative sense'. The word 'sense' was, however, misleading, and so too was his statement of converging probabilities which passed into certainty. When the professional philosopher uses the word 'sense' he confines it to what falls within the compass of the senses. It is essential for him to keep clear the distinction of thought and sense. The first covers thinking, believing, comprehending, reasoning and judging, and it has no sense organ, particular or general. Sense, on the other hand, is intimately connected with a bodily organ and is tied to sensible experience. In ordinary language we do not observe this distinction, and we fall into the habit of talking of a man of good sense and of an argument making sense. Newman followed this usage. He followed usage, also, in writing of probabilities as if they could of themselves grow into certainty. To be exact, however, probabilities are not objects or forces or realities which meet together and make something else. So subtle is the relation between my thoughts and the reality I am thinking of that we pass from one to another without noticing. In a strictly philosophical account of history, for example, I should have found it necessary to keep steadily apart the past as a series of events and actions which actually took place and the knowledge of them. But since we take for granted that we have knowledge of the past we identify our knowledge with the actual event, and no harm is done if indeed we do have genuine knowledge of the event. The only time when it is expedient to bring this distinction to the fore is in discussing 'facts' and data. The ordinary man does tend to think of historical 'facts' and data as facts and data he can observe with his eyes or touch. But Samuel Johnson could not stamp on an historical fact to prove its existence, and part of the problem of historical knowledge is to certify an historical fact and give it an assured status. Newman seemed to suggest that a hypothetical fact could become likely, then most probable and finally certain by a gradual process. But though there is an intimate connection between the truth of fact and the changes in my mind from doubting it to the gradual acceptance of it, it is well to remember that probability is not a characteristic of the fact but a description of my mental attitude and that I cannot add together probabilities so as to make up a sum called certainty. Here again we make a natural transposition from what we are thinking of to the real object and, as our probability rests on some evidence, when we have new evidence, which seems to us to decide the matter, we speak as if we had added something not only to the evidence but also to the probability. The evidence at one point convinced us that an event was likely; then comes some more evidence, and we now say: 'there can be no further doubt, the event is certain'. We seem here to have passed from a probable opinion to truth, but that is not so. There is a succession of one state of mind to another and there is a definite relation between the two based on our having one and the same object under consideration and on our pondering over the evidence for it. But the probable cannot generate the quite different kind of knowledge which is truth, nor even can addition of evidence of itself be the cause of such a change. The proof of this is that we at times gather abundant evidence and nevertheless our mind remains unsatisfied. Quantity is not sufficient. One item added and, lo and behold, our doubt has disappeared. That item was the missing link, and when we use the word 'link', we give the clue to the right answer and to the importance of the 'illative sense', or what more safely may be called 'interpretation'. A completely isolated object could have no meaning for us, for either objects are in reality so interrelated that they have to be taken together or our mind is so constituted that we cannot understand anything save in a world or community. Hence we discover what a thing is by studying it together with other things, and we have a sense of dissatisfaction until the pieces fall together into a shape which is significant. We meet an infinite variety of unities, shapes, designs, some artificial, others apparently natural. There are large shapes whose edges are blurred, like the 'world', 'nature', 'western civilization' and 'democracy', and tight smaller shapes like gardens, kitchens, calendars, Roman roads and human faces. We say, 'his face is hardly human', or 'this must be a Roman road'. Hundreds of objects are so bound up with our everyday routine that we seldom or never mention them. They are part of our mental landscape and taken for granted. Then there are all the paraphernalia and stage properties which make up human intercourse, the expressions of the face, the movements of the body, the shake of the head, the eloquent silences, the individual turn of phrase, the signs of friendship and aversion, of hypocrisy and holiness. We do not need a dictionary or a training in logic or scientific method to interpret the expressions of those we live with. This is a knowledge by signs and has its own peculiar rules and prescriptions. The dead cannot join our company and be known to us by this language of signs, but as we read about them we learn not only the character of the writers but also of those about whom they write. The dead come alive and we are able to say of an act attributed to one of them that it is not in character or that it is exactly what he would have done. Socrates is more than a name, more even than a clever invention; his personality was such that it controlled the portraits of him; the truth is mightier than the fiction. Similarly with Thomas More, Wellington and—a crucial case —Samuel Johnson. Boswell may be a puzzling figure and much nearer to a genius than once was thought, but it remains inconceivable that he invented Johnson. We are sure that his *Life* is a speaking likeness of an inimitable man.

Collingwood compared historical inquiry to the work of a detective. The detective starts with an unprejudiced mind; he has to weigh the evidence given to him and look for more. This evidence may be conflicting and point in different directions; then gradually it may begin to coalesce and the detective begins to 'feel warm'. But as the evidence is not complete and 'red herrings' are possible he reserves judgment. In the perfect crime story, however, the one and only solution clicks in the detective's mind, the clues become unmistakable and he is certain of the mind and method of the criminal. So too in reconstructing a play or a damaged and obscure text or the remains of an ancient city the scholar is confident of success when the bits so fit into a significant whole that no other alternative is possible. His confidence in the truth of his solution depends upon the degree the evidence holds together to make a significant whole; or as Newman describes the process: 'It is by the strength, variety, or multiplicity of premises, which are only probable, not by well-connected syllogisms . . . by objections overcome, by adverse theories neutralized, by difficulties gradually clearing up, by exceptions proving the rule, by unlooked-for correlations found for received truths, by suspense and delay in the process issuing in triumphant re-actions—by all these ways, and many others, the practised and experienced mind is able to make a sure divination that a conclusion is inevitable, of which his lines of reasoning do not actually put him in possession.'

In *The Nature of Belief* I set forth a theory which would account for the unshakable certainty we have about a number of facts and events for which we cannot, when asked, supply the adequate reason. This theory was called the 'unity of indirect reference', and in short was as follows. A number of items in our experience are so commonplace and so bound up with all that we think and discover that we seldom advert to them and hardly ever refer to them in our conversations and relations with others. If, for example, I tell another that I am going to Paris I do not mention all the pieces of knowledge which must hold true if my statement is to have any meaning or be possible. He has not to be told that Paris is the capital of France, that it is a city with houses and human beings living in them, that it takes a certain time to get there, that there are various means of travelling and innumerable other facts which form the web of my simple statement. Our worlds of discourse and connected sense vary, but there are some facts made so obvious by the infinity of indirect references which support them that it is inconceivable to us that they could be untrue. We cannot prove these obvious statements, not for want of evidence but because we have too much. Everything would crash if this certainty of mine were to collapse, and we seem to know this by an apperception of unity which is like to a rope made up of a number of strands or a cloud of locusts seen at a distance. We accept these certainties because we must accept the universe.

Next, but of a different order though similar in texture, are the certainties of space and time. We may never have seen the Isle of Man or the Azores; our knowledge, we should have to say, depends upon information given to us in books or by other people. And yet our certainty seems to be much more firmly based than on the occasional reference to these islands by a friend or on the number of times we have looked them out in a map. In truth they have been continually presupposed in statements about other places and events and by indirect reference they have grown in certainty with our general growth in knowledge. What guarantees places guarantees also historical events. We cannot doubt the existence in the past of persons like Napoleon and Queen Victoria. Too many other truths would vanish if their place in history became empty. We do not live on isolated truths. We learn by co-ordinating facts, fitting them into what we already have come to believe. Facts complement each other and take hold of others so that what is chaotic and dim comes into the light in terms of complex wholes and unities.

With this background of certainty the historian proceeds to bring together the evidence he has accumulated and has at his disposal into a significant order which has the mark of truth. There is much which baffles him, much too which he can so interpret that it looks likely. Even about what is certain he can say something new and significant, because human actions have so many implications and aspects. He detects new points which have not been given their proper consideration; he may on the strength of his understanding of a man's character see further into his policy, and he may by drawing on the wealth of his own understanding divine the spiritual outlook and tradition of a family, of rulers, a people and a culture. He is a human being interpreting human beings, their actions, the expressions of themselves, as 'each hung bell's bow swung finds tongue to fling out broad its name'. As his experience with his fellows warns him, he lives in a world of mingled certainty and uncertainty. He can learn much about his neighbour, in fact on some points he knows the man better than he knows himself. But every human being is part mystery and mysterious even to himself. Then each of us has his personal 'equation', and is led astray by prejudice or sentimentality or over-confidence. The same weaknesses follow the historian in his outlook on past human history. *Tout comprendre c'est tout pardonner.* We do not comprehend enough to be able to pass judgments with final truth. In reliving the past and interpreting it after a judicial scrutiny of the evidence with a sympathetic understanding we graze truth. We have flashes of insight when our powers of interpretation are working at their best, and of the acres of the past we can say that patches have been tilled and harvested and others well cultivated. In the present we are often confused by events and at the mercy of our emotions. History can be called the emotions of the present remembered and recorded in tranquillity. The violence is over and order begins to make its appearance. The facts are gathered from every quarter, the clerks and the bookworms and the research-student and the antiquary get busy, and then the great historian comes and finds his way through the piled-up data, forming and re-forming the material and seizing upon the essential. He is the historian *par excellence,* learned in his subject matter, ardent in his pursuit of truth and a genius in interpretation. Nowadays, when the technique of research and criticism has become so formalized and almost mechanical and when the historical sources have been so multiplied, there is a danger lest the gift of the individual to diagnose and interpret may be under-estimated and fall into disrepute; even so the old habit of diagnosis in medicine has been weakened by the use of scientific apparatus for every emergency. In his Webb Memorial Lecture, Professor Hancock informed us that in the Board of Trade there are sixteen miles of shelves containing war-historical material. This seems too much for the industry and energy of any one man even if he were a Hercules, and the vastness of material on other subjects, too, is leading to the idea of team work. Valuable as team work is it can never take the place of the great historian, nor can the most up-to-date scientific methods suffice to bring the past alive. History is concerned with the past experiences and actions of man, and just as in the Chinese story a mechanical nightingale could not vie with a living nightingale, so mechanical aids or modern techniques cannot be adequate substitutes for the interpretative genius who makes the past live again.

As H-J. Marrou, an historian of much experience says: 'The great historian will be the man who will know how to raise the historical problem in the richest and most fertile way; will understand what question it is important to ask of the past. The value of history, and by that I mean its human interest as well as its truth, is thereby closely bound up with the genius of the historian—for, as Pascal says, "á mesure que l'on a plus d'esprit, on trouve qu'il y a plus d'hommes originaux"—there will be more treasures to recover from man's past.'

NOTE I

The quotation with which I have ended this chapter is taken from *De la Connaissance Historique* by H.-J. Marrou, a work published unfortunately too late for me to use fully in the text. Marrou writes as one who knows his profession of historian inside out, and he examines its problems with admirable clarity and with a wealth of illustration. He makes a distinction between the past and history. The historian is not called upon to reanimate the past, to renew its existence in the present. To claim to do this is to play with metaphors and to attempt the impossible. The past in becoming history has to suffer many transformations; it has to be remodelled in terms of our thinking and our categories. In fact it has to be known as past and not as present. A painter of the Renaissance, for instance, treated the early Christians and Romans, as if they were living at his own time. The historian, on the other hand, must have an historic sense and realize that he cannot know a St. Paul as a contemporary, as St. Luke knew him. St. Paul is a figure of the past, not of the present, and this fact of centuries of separation in time has to be recognized by the historian. We have to accept our human condition, the historian's own dependence upon his time and culture, and it is better to side with Kant than with Croce, and admit that the past as lived is a kind of noumenal world, whose existence we must admit, but of which we never can have proper knowledge.

The function and gift of the historian is to ask questions. He starts with a question, and then turns to the documents to learn what kind of an answer they can offer him. What they tell him affects his preliminary view. 'The historian is the man who gains familiarity with documents, thanks to which he finishes by knowing with certainty what is their sense, their import and their value—what is the image of the past that they reveal and bring to him.' In so acting the historian behaves in the same way as he does in ordinary life in coming to know and understand others. He sees others acting and reacting and talking; he learns what others think about their friends, and he reaches his certainties on this kind of evidence. There are, however, various kinds of historical knowledge. At times what we are looking for is contained in the document itself. If we wish to know what the *Laws* of Plato is about, the work itself suffices. Similarly Bernard Berenson examines a painting of the past to tell its quality. Another question is to know what the author intended. What, for instance, was the attitude of Cervantes to his own creation, Don Quixote? Thirdly, we may ask whether a writer gives a correct impression of the times about which he is writing, or again whether the facts he narrates are true. Here one witness does not suffice. There is need of many witnesses, who are independent. Only when their evidence converges, 'does the probability become something greater and in the end reach practical certainty'. Marrou does not stand with those positivist historians, who count their gains by the amount of the evidence they are able to collect. It is not, he says, a question of fact and the multiplication of facts which should interest the historian. Verification is all very well, but what we need is good judgment about the significance of the evidence. Should we take Plato's or Xenophon's evidence, for example, on the life and character of Socrates? When we have finished our digging into documents, we are always still at the mercy of events, and we cannot advance without an act of faith. The positivists have become too beholden to the physical scientists and their methods. There is no historical truth, which is, strictly speaking, incontestably true. R. Whately raised doubts about the existence of Napoleon, and Max Müller accepted the hypothesis that astronomy lay at the origin of the Greek myths. These are ludicrous excesses, but who does not admit that every great historian begins with a theory, and though he modifies it in the face of evidence, he is nevertheless driven by it to select his evidence and marshal his facts? As we look back upon past histories we see that they have been all in part conditioned by the outlook of their time and by the passions and prejudices of the particular authors. If we take the subject of the decline and fall of the Roman Empire, we have Gibbon attributing it to the triumph of religion and barbarism; Seeck attributes it to the destruction of the *élite*, Kaphan to physical degeneration, T. Frank to racial decline, Huntingdon to climatic conditions, such as the drying-up of the soil, M. Weber to the decline of slavery and the return to a natural economy, Rostovtzeff to a

class struggle. Piganiol declares that this noble civilization was
assassinated in the barbarian invasions, while Toynbee sees a
failure of response to a challenge, the disaffection of the masses
at a time of mortal crisis.

History, therefore, according to Marrou, combines truth and
relativity, assurance and uncertainty. If this looks an odd conclusion, he answers that it is what we should expect, granted
our human condition. 'Being the knowledge of man by man,
history is the apprehension of the past by and in human
thought, thought which is living and engaged; it is a complex,
an indissoluble mixture of subject and object. To one who is
irritated by this bondage, I can only repeat: such is our human
condition, such our nature.' 'History is true to the degree in
which the historian has worthy reasons for trusting in what he
has learnt from his documents.' 'History is true, but this truth
is partial; we can learn something about the human past, but
we cannot know the whole of that past (not even everything
about some particular aspect of the past, no matter what it be;
there is nothing more foolish than these efforts to sound the
mystery of the person, than, again, these historians who pass
judgment on their heroes, as if they were the Eternal).' It
follows from this view that Marrou must dismiss all the attempts
to construct a philosophy of history, and he does so explicitly
and emphatically. He tells us, that 'with regard to those
theories of civilization, which have multiplied in the period
between the two wars, the true historian will feel an invincible
repugnance, in so far as they accept this postulate of coherence,
of structural unity; he should reject not only the mad lucubra-
tions of Spengler, for whom the metaphor of the "organism",
once it is applied to great civilizations, becomes the object of a
systematic and paradoxical exploitation, but also the synthesis
so conscientiously and reasonably worked out by that great and
fine spirit, Arnold Toynbee.' The historian 'is allowed, certainly, to reach out to general conclusions, as he seeks to find
out relations between various series of events and various
systems. But however successful he is in establishing large
unifications, he must remember that the reality, which is given,
the reality which alone has existence, is neither the fact of
civilization nor the system nor supersystem, but the human
being, whose reality is alone the object of his experience.'

Marrou, therefore, maintains that history is not the same as the past, where he means by the 'past' the lives lived by those whom we come to know by documents. He emphasizes the part played by the historian, and the inevitable limitations of each and everyone, limitations in time and culture and outlook. His work is essentially human; that is to say, it does not consist in just amassing facts and recording them. He has to ask questions of the past, and try to understand by sympathy what the documents reveal, and his industry must be implemented by a power of 'interpretation'. Interpretation is not borrowed from the sciences; it is rather a transposition from what we do in ordinary life, in judging others, to the acts of others peering out at us from the past. It is a knowledge by signs and indications. This being so, we must not demand greater certainty than this human approach can achieve. The historian does not look for mathematical certainty nor for the experimental verification of the scientist. 'The modality of historical judgments is the possible.' Marrou describes this form of knowledge as 'practical satisfactoriness', and in other places he writes of 'practical certainty'.

In so paring down the kind of certainty which the historian can attain, Marrou may seem to disagree with the view I have defended in the text. I think, however, that the disagreement is more a question of words than of fact. He leans towards a more sceptical view because he has in mind the pseudo-scientific views of many of his predecessors and colleagues in France, and he wishes to make it quite clear that a historian does not reach his conclusions in the same way as a natural scientist. He does, however, make a gap between the past as lived and history, borrowing the language of Kant about the 'noumenal' to make his point. Such a distinction, if pressed, would make a serious gap between reality and the historian's version of it, and rob history of its claim to relate some real knowledge of the past. But the general theme of Marrou's book shows that he does allow for a certainty of a kind, which is gained by 'interpretation'; and he hesitates over the nature of this certainty, because he does not give full value to the power of 'interpretation'. If we use the same process of interpretation in ordinary life as in history, then history should be as true as our knowledge of those around us—and few would deny that we can reach real knowledge in thinking of the existence of our friends and their human characteristics.

Chapter II

HISTORY AND HISTORICISM

History, as we have seen in the last chapter, provides us with knowledge in a manner different from that of science. By the unremitting efforts of scholars, much of the past is now within the grasp of every schoolboy. Historians using the accepted canons of judgment for deciding what is certain, probable and/or still a matter of opinion, have freed us from ignorance and prejudice. But if history can now be taken for granted, what of the so-called philosophy of history or 'historicism', as it has been named? As a branch of knowledge it is comparatively a newcomer. The historicists point to writers in the distant past and in the Middle Ages who can be regarded as forerunners or naïve philosophers; as a separate and autonomous study, however, it is modern, and it is not too easy to discover what precisely is meant by it, what it includes and what it excludes. One answer to this last problem might be to take conspicuous historicists, such as Vico, Hegel, Spengler and Toynbee, and try to find out what they have in common. By the 'philosophy' of history is meant not philosophy in the sense of the philosophy of science, where philosophy and 'nature' have the same meaning. The chief experiences and activities of man fall under certain headings, the theoretical and practical, his moral and religious and political and social activities, and his creation of art forms and love of beauty. An inquiry into the nature of these experiences and activities constitutes philosophy. History, as we have seen deserves a special place amongst these activities, and it is, perhaps, because this story of man as man, the passage from barbarism to culture, the rise and fall of so many civilizations, the movement which, it is to be hoped, will be prolonged into a future, that we are forced to ask what kind of unity can be found in this strange story. Opposites are found in it: necessity and freedom, design and accident, progress and frustration. In subordinate studies, such as economics and sociology, would-be scientific laws can be extracted out of the material conditions and forces, and these play their part in history. Again the efforts of man have clearly some aim above the satisfaction of mere animal cravings and immediate pleasures, but they are so confused and obscure that the word 'progress' tells us very little. Almost always in the past, before the distinction between the secular and the religious became fixed, writers turned for explanations to religion, to the influence of the gods and of fate. Now that the sciences are considered self-sufficient and the supernatural is felt to be an intruder, the question arises what status or function religious ideas should have in a philosophy of history. The writers on the subject fall into three camps; those who turn to physical laws, be they biological or economic, those who see in man's own efforts a meaningful drama with a beginning and an end, and those who look beyond man to destiny or divine Providence. Some of the writers in this last category draw near to those of the first, because fate and, for instance, the materialistic conception of history both rely on laws of necessity to which man is bound. Within the religious view there are again striking differences, not only, for example, between Buddhism and Christianity but, as we shall see, within Christianity itself.

If a philosophy of history is to include theology and the supernatural it cannot easily be fitted into the usual corpus of philosophical subjects, which range from ethics to metaphysics. The old distinction which St. Thomas Aquinas made between knowledge based on reason and knowledge given to us by authority from Revelation will have to be ignored. The excuse is that as religion is supposed to throw light upon the purposes and the destiny of man we should be ready to consider any light which it may throw on a subject which is so directly concerned with the history and progress of man. As combining ethics and religion its subject matter should be closer to moral philosophy than to metaphysics, though, it must be said, such was not the view of Hegel. It is unfortunately typical of the confusions in this subject that those who have pronounced upon it should differ even as to the nature of what they were writing about. To Hegel history is the very tissue of metaphysics. Toynbee undoubtedly set out to combine the empirical methods of historical research with a metaphysical and religious pattern in his mind. Dr. Peter Geyl is more modest. He criticizes Toynbee for being too ambitious, and says that we study history, (1) in order to enrich our own civilization 'by the reanimation of old methods of existence and thought'; (2) to cultivate a certain kind of understanding, which in its way may be as fruitful as the natural historian's understanding of the processes of nature; and (3) to put our own world and its problems into perspective, so that we may regard them with greater patience and wisdom. Hegel and Toynbee have here been brought down to earth, and in fact, apart from one dangerous implication of a possible parallel between the processes of history and those of nature, Geyl confines himself to a commonsense view of the value of knowing the past. As to the parallel with nature, even this is derided by Alexander Herzen. 'Who', he exclaims, 'will find fault with nature because flowers bloom in the morning and die at night, because she has not given the rose or the lily the hardness of flint? And this miserable pedestrian principle *we* wish to transfer to the world of history.' 'History', for him, 'is all improvisation, all will, all enterprise. There are no frontiers, there are no time-tables, no itineraries.'

Nowell-Smith, in the paper already quoted, gives us a hint about the methods of philosophical historians which may be useful. In distinguishing between science and history he refers to Toynbee, and he accuses him of using a 'method recognizably like the scientific method'. It is a wrong method because it is one of generalization, the recourse to laws of which particular cases are exhibited as instances. Historians cannot follow this method because history does not repeat itself; there have been many revolutions in history, and they may be said to have a family likeness, but each has its own individual traits and the actors in each have to be treated as individuals and not as types. Now this may be an adequate account of what the historian has to do, but the philosopher of history would, I suspect, claim that the formal object of his study differs from that of the historian in that he is looking at history as a whole and he is trying to find there certain laws or tendencies, repetitions in the rise and fall of nations, constant aims and conditions of progress and decay. He will be rash, if, like Toynbee, he tries to justify his work by identifying himself with the historian and then claiming that his results are the result of purely empirical methods. The historian retorts by detailed criticism and by picking holes in the too easy generalizations of the philosopher. No one who takes in his sweep twenty or more civilizations can be deadly accurate in all his details. It would seem a mistake, therefore, for the philosopher of history to pretend to be like the historian in all respects. He must, as Nowell-Smith points out, imitate the methods of the scientist and work with generalizations. He has something in common with the sociologist and the economist, for they seem to belong to a mixed genre which is partly historical and partly scientific. They deal with a certain aspect of human activity. In so far as the activity is human it is free and unpredictable, but as tied to human products and human productions there are sequences and uniform regularities which can be formulated. If the worst comes to the worst the research student can turn to statistics. Now the philosopher of history has at times followed in the wake of the sociologist with the result that his results look to be almost scientific, and of course very much mistaken. In fact he has to find out the correct way of working, if indeed there be a correct way and not a blind alley.

If we free ourselves from the cramping empirical theories which have been prejudicing both the historians and many writers about the nature of history, we may be able to place a little more accurately the position of the philosophy of history in the map of philosophy. History, as I have argued, does more than attend to successions of events or to particulars within this succession. It is free to look for causes, for motives and purposes, and relying upon a common human nature it can succeed in making sense out of a flurry of human actions. To do this the historian relies upon a power of the mind to discern a unity and a theme, and he is greeted with applause when out of a series of events or the policies or actions of some leader, king or statesman or soldier he can make an intelligible whole. Now in addressing himself to this task the historian brings into play not only the power to weigh evidence and select the relevant facts; he must also use his imagination, possess sympathy and have something like the talent of the artist. So near, indeed, is the historian to the artist that it has been debated by historians themselves whether they are not nearer to the artist than to the scientist. Let us admit that in the writing of history artistry

66

must be present, but that, nevertheless, it serves as a helpmate and not as the principal agent. The facts must always in the last resort control the views of the historian, and he has no excuse if he neglects them because they are there to be known and made significant. But in a philosophy of history the field is so wide that facts can be a hindrance; the trees are unending. The philosopher here cannot ignore facts; he must use his imagination and delight in the personal and in the particular. At the same time he has to convey these facts on to a loftier site from which he can reassemble them in more general terms and then compare the generalizations to see if they make sense. His story begins to have a Miltonic splendour. Both the nature of the material and the form of selection separate it from history proper, though it still deserves the name of history. History, as we have seen, has its own appropriate way of reaching truth; a way which is different from that of science, and none the worse for that. The philosophy of history has a close connection with history, and the writer of it must, so far as he is able, keep to facts, select what is relevant, use his imagination and look for an explanation which approximates to truth. But he might do well to claim that as with the historian in relation to the scientist, so he in relation to the historian should stake out his separate territory. This will deliver him from much of the criticism directed at him by the historians. His aim is not to deal with the episodes of history, to burrow into a tiny piece of ground; his eye is fixed on the whole visible surface. What he lacks in thoroughness of detail he makes up for by seeing relations and interconnexions which are outside the province of the professional historian.

The historian without knowing it has always envied those who played at being philosophers and held in high repute the work of a Thucydides or on a larger scale the works of a Grote or a Mommsen, a Lecky or Acton. The gift of seeing relations and analogies, of bringing together into one pattern what looked at first sight dissimilar and isolated is one of man's highest gifts, one supremely possessed by the poet. It is the artist and the poet in conjunction with historical insight which makes the philosopher of history and gives him a separate rank and office. Poetry has its own justification as art, but, as has been widely recognized, it can, especially in the form of epic or drama, throw light upon the actions of past men and women.

The proper recognition of this has led to a new assessment of what is called myth, which used to be dismissed as fiction. Now we are told that myth is more like to reality as lived through the imagination than to fiction; it is a manner of describing what lies behind the dry facts as noted by the perceiving mind, and it is the recurrent way in all civilizations for giving expression to the innate hopes and desires of man, and to his sense of the past. Poetry and myth, therefore, are enlisted by the philosopher of history to describe the truth he is seeking. Perhaps even more pertinent to the philosopher of history is the view now widely held that human experience can be presented through types of symbols and images. There is a mysterious analogy which runs through the varying levels of human experience, of which the simplest examples are 'left and right', 'high and low', 'up and down'. Material symbols serve for spiritual realities, and, so the psychologists tell us, there are fundamental symbols which contain a wealth of meaning, so that when they appear in religious or poetic form in other civilizations the historian is initiated into the ideas and into the ritual of behaviour of the people who use them. How valuable this can be is seen in the modern approach to the writings of the Near and Middle East in past history. During one period of biblical criticism, for instance, it was almost taken for granted that the early books contained more fiction than truth. This view, however, has lost currency now that we have become more familiar with the way in which the minds of more primitive peoples worked, and not only of the more primitive but of those also with different traditions from our own. Greek philosophy and the rise of the physical sciences have helped to determine our method of approach to history. We have placed our confidence in the clear and distinct ideas provided by deductive and inductive methods and concepts and hypotheses. We now see that without the use of such methods, other peoples have employed symbols and images, parables and stories, not for the sake of what we would call story-telling, but to bring out the significance of the past. This way of history-telling was to them the more apposite in that the history was inextricably bound up with religion and theology; in other words it was a simple philosophy or theology of history. The Bible begins with the origin of man and rapidly sketches the long stretch of time before the history takes more definite shape in the election of Abraham and the varied fortunes of the chosen people. Besides the use of images and symbols the biblical writers employ what has come to be called an apocalyptic and eschatological form. We still have difficulty in interpreting the meaning of some of this literature, but we now have the advantage of knowing what to seek, namely a pattern of history as definitely intended to narrate truth as the Bayeux Tapestry.

A philosophy of history as it has developed within the last two centuries will not be the same as biblical history or an ancient epic. It will gain by leaning on accredited history and, in so far as is compatible with its aims, by relying on historical methods. But it may claim to have an 'esprit' and a formal object which gives it a status of its own. While in its generalizations it approaches the sciences closer than history, and while it draws nearer to history than to science in its method of studying the past, it is not afraid to use as an ally the poetic imagination as manifested in images, symbols and analogies. For this reason perhaps a better name for it would be epic or gnomic history. By withdrawing from the camps both of the sciences and of history, it frees itself from burdens which would crush it. No philosopher of history can know the data of the whole of the past in the same way in which a historian ought to know the small area of history about which he writes; nor again does he seek for the kind of scientific truth which the chemist or the anatomist requires. If criticized for failing to follow or reach the standards demanded by these sciences, he can answer that the critics have been making a 'category mistake'; they are asking him to do what he never set out to do, to furnish what is not necessary for him. Mythopoeic truth is nearer to what he seeks. He must, like the historian, use interpretation; he must be intent on discovering intelligible wholes or patterns, and he can take over from the historian a group of intelligible wholes about which most historians will be agreed. With these he now looks for a greater unity, for a system which will bring these separate wholes into order. His aim is gained when he can produce a pattern or drama which makes such good sense that the reader of it is persuaded to say, 'There must be some truth in this'.

The growing criticism of Arnold Toynbee's *A Study of History* shows that the tide is flowing against philosophies of history. Sir Isaiah Berlin's lecture on *Historical Inevitability* provides some of the reasons why they are unacceptable to the philosopher and historian alike. It is, however, in Professor Peter Geyl's *Debates with Historians* that the ambiguity of Toynbee's position is abundantly shown as well as the misunderstanding which can arise between historian and historicist. Geyl has included in his book four chapters of attack, and by the time he is reviewing the last volumes of Toynbee his patience is changing into restrained fury. As a result he reveals not only the grounds for his dislike of those who, like Spengler, Sorokin and Toynbee, attempt to make a system out of history, but also the correct attitude which he believes an historian ought to adopt. The impression, however, which he leaves on at least one reader is that both he and Toynbee should revise their claims and a rguments.

Geyl admits that there is 'an ingrained habit of the human mind—and indeed it is a noble ambition—to try to construct a vision of history in which chaos, or apparent chaos, is reduced to order'. This attempt consists in making the historical process conform to a line or rhythm or movement with definable and intelligible laws which enable the observer to predict something of the future. 'It used', he says, 'to be fashionable in the eighteenth and nineteenth centuries to do this in a spirit of optimism.' Nowadays it is the past which is looked upon nostalgically, and the historical process is thought to be composed of recurring cycles. Spengler, for instance, pictured civilizations as 'independent and mutually impenetrable entities'; they were like living organisms which had their periods of youth, middle age and decay. He relied on his imagination, on flashes of intuition and drew conclusions from dogmatic generalizations. Sorokin, on the other hand, divides civilizations into two types, the ideational and the sensate. The first is spiritual and lasting; the second is mainly physical, a process of becoming, which has the usual stages from birth to death. Where he differs from Spengler is in his attention to facts, or rather to statistics. He compiles vast quantities of figures, and from these data he fills in his picture of the civilizations. Toynbee, in his turn, found Spengler 'most unilluminatingly dogmatic and deterministic', and felt that there was room 'for English empiricism'. He, therefore, claims that his work is based on an empirical investigation. It is this claim which rouses Geyl's ire. 'Had he really examined history with an open mind, merely formulating the theses supplied him by the observed facts, phenomena, developments, he could never have printed that imposing announcement of the division into so many parts in the opening pages of his first volume, nor could he in his references, as early as 1934, indicate what he was going to say about various chief problems in part 9 or in part 13, in 1950 or 1960.[1] He has been, in fact, selecting just what suited him. His method is vitiated by subjectivism, and apart from truisms there are a series of laws and parallels which are of no practical value because they are artificial.

The root of Geyl's objections to Toynbee and other historicists is that they do not write history. He points out that Toynbee assumes the reality of his multiple civilizations, that he gets himself into difficulties over freedom and determinism, at one moment insisting on indeterminism in history, and at the next preparing to draw the horoscope of the future; but these are incidental failings compared with the basic error that he sits so loose to historical evidence, that 'he soars above the ground of history where we others plod', and that he expects of 'history what history cannot possibly give—certainty'. The historian must always hold large generalizations in suspicion, and be slow to use parallels and analogies. Toynbee's view is bound to be one-sided and subjective, for 'a large view or interpretation like this one cannot possibly be proved by history, nor do I believe that it is derived from a study of history. . . .' It is true that the historian is not just a recorder of facts. 'The facts are there to be used. Combinations, presentations, theories are indispensable if we want to understand. But the historian should proceed cautiously in using the facts for these purposes. It goes without saying that he should try to ascertain the facts as exactly as possible; but the important thing is that he should remain conscious, even then, of the element of arbitrariness, of subjectivity, that necessarily enters into all combinations of facts, if only because one has to begin by selecting them; while next, one has to order them according to an idea which must, in part at least, be conceived in one's own mind.'

In asserting that large views, such as Toynbee's, can neither be proved from history nor derived from a study of history, Geyl

---

[1] This argument, of course, depends upon the assumption that Toynbee had not gathered his facts and planned the work before announcing what he intended to do.

rules out all philosophies of history. What his criticism proves is that Toynbee should not have claimed to rest his case entirely on empirical methods. That Toynbee has done so is a pity, and, I think, a mistake. It is not because he is as omniscient in every period of his story as the specialist historian is in his particular field that his work has stirred admiration. That admiration is aroused because he satisfied quite a different demand of the mind. What that demand is is seen in the interest shown in books with general themes, such as 'The Spirit of Our Day', 'The Decline of the West', or in talks and discussions on the wireless. A recent discussion on the Home Service of the B.B.C., called 'The Divided Inheritance', produced verdicts on the 'present-day football mentality', 'lack of a common background', 'the breakup of homelife'. A commentator voiced general opinion and interest when he said that 'it is good to air a problem', and to hear experts, even though such discussions never come to a clear and unanimous conclusion. There is a type of subject about which an expert or a wise man can enlighten us without overwhelming us with facts or even proving his point. Such a type of subject appears in great drama, in early epical stories, in the first attempts of historians before they have learnt that history and the philosophy of history are separate pursuits. If, to suggest the impossible, Toynbee's *A Study of History* had been written two thousand or a thousand years ago, it would now be ranked amongst the great works of the past. Critics would talk of its insights into human nature, the genius shown in his illustrations, the sweep of his knowledge and the unity of his theme. He would be compared with Herodotus and Eusebius and St. Augustine. In fact most of those who became famous in the past for their story of human affairs tended to satisfy this universal demand for light upon the baffling record of man's failures and successes. Plutarch's *Lives* have never ceased to appeal, because he made character count so much. Voltaire encouraged the belief in a rise from barbaric habits to humanism, and Gibbon only partially concealed under the name of history a great story or drama of morals. Toynbee finds in 'Challenge and Response' the clue to history, and Geyl dismisses it as a truism and shows how variously and with what care it must be applied to any particular historical phase. But those who have been taught to find in the trilogy of Aeschylus on the legendary story of the house of Atreus that sin brings suffering and suffering wisdom do not feel that this apophthegm is just a truism. It is a form of knowledge, a step forward in wisdom, the kind of wisdom which belongs to a study of man in relation to his destiny.

Aristotle made this point when he insisted that we must cut our coat of knowledge according to the cloth, that our knowledge of human actions must differ from that of physical reality. Hence in morals we advance in wisdom when we see that virtue is a mean between two extremes, but the knowledge is not like a physical measuring rod. Similarly in the philosophy of history the kind of knowledge we can obtain is different from the scientific or strictly historical; it answers an undying desire to have some intimation about how human life proceeds. Deep down there is a fixed conviction that there is a meaning and a pattern, and any insight into it is felt to be valuable. This is why the sage figures so often in ancient literature and why the great legends and sagas were welcomed as throwing a dark light upon the human condition. Hence it is that Geyl, while legitimately rejecting Toynbee's own claims for his work, is not on that account justified in his scepticism about the possibility of any philosophy of history. His scepticism recoils upon himself as an historian, for he admits that the historian has to be selective, subjective, and that the idea according to which he orders his facts, 'must, in part at least, be conceived in one's own mind'. I do not see why being 'conceived in one's own mind' should be an obstacle to truth, seeing that every truth, even the most obvious, must be conceived in one's own mind. Nor again does selection necessarily make a view 'subjective' in a bad sense or bar the way to true knowledge. As we have seen, history can be defended, and, as a form of interpretation the knowledge of it can, in a way different from scientific knowledge, be sufficiently certain. The philosopher of history, too, uses interpretation and uses his own norms. He is not bound to accept the rules laid down by Geyl; he looks at history and relies upon history, but he also has something of the art of the poet and the dramatist, or, perhaps, a special kind of poetic art, like that described for us by David Jones in the Introduction to his *Anathemata*. 'The particular quarry that the mind of the poet seeks to capture is a very elusive beast indeed. Perhaps we can say that the country to be hunted, the habitat of that quarry, where the "forms" lurk that he's after, will be found

73

to be part of vast, densely wooded, inherited and entailed domains. It is in that "sacred wood" that the spoor of these "forms" is to be tracked.' The poet, however, is both less and more free than the historian-hunter; for the poet 'may feel something with regard to Penda the Mercian and nothing with regard to Darius the Mede. In itself that is a limitation; it might be regarded as a disproportion; no matter, there is no help—he must work within the limits of his love. There must be no mugging up, no "ought to know" or "try to feel"; for only what is actually loved and known can be seen *sub specie aeternitatis*.' By his love the poet is tied, but he is free to ignore what he does not love. Not so with the philosopher of history. He must hunt in the 'vast densely wooded . . . domains', and it is his duty to 'mug up' facts in the hope that they may stir in him some love or appreciation. He must keep nearer to the earth than the poet in the expectation that he may become familiar with the alphabet of history and in the end discover some of the sentences which compose it. Whether he can succeed or not the quest is an alluring one and it continues to excite hunters, even though the bystanders may warn them that the quarry is as mythical as the Holy Grail.

In Volume VII of *Chambers's Encyclopaedia* Mr. Raymond Aron, after giving a history of Historiography, ends by saying that 'with the progress of knowledge and power, history inevitably dissolves into an infinite number of human societies, each different in its habits of thought and life, each with a different conception of the universe'. This he calls Pluralism, 'a mere juxtaposition of more or less accidental facts more or less causally connected. There is no coherent historical whole, no possibility of conceiving man or of seeing a single idea in the historical process'. . . . 'History, ineluctable and purposeless, without universal unity but unified in each of its parts—such is the dogmatic philosophy of pluralism which today oppresses our historical thinking, teaching that there is no unity, no meaning in the whole.' I do not know whether Geyl would agree with this somewhat melancholy reflection. In a work entitled *The Destiny of Mind*, Mr. William S. Haas offers a new and interesting way back to a philosophy of history in terms of the structures of societies. His chief contribution lies in a sharp distinction between the outlook and structure of Eastern and Western societies. In the West we have now taken the idea of mankind as one race to be almost an innate idea. This he considers to be a development of religion and philosophy. Early man had no such idea, and often identified himself with animals or superhuman beings. But in one geographical area Judaic, Zoroastrian and Greek ideas prevailed. From the Jews came the idea of man as the image of God, an idea which led to the further vision of peace upon earth. This has the makings of a philosophy of history because it presents a goal. Christianity consolidated this idea and promoted it, but at the same time tore history asunder by distinguishing between two kingdoms. The Greek genius opened out the view of a secular history, but was unable to give it a shape. In the Middle Ages these two, the Christian and the Greek conceptions were held together in a tension, but in time the secular conquered, and the old distinction turned into one between mysticism and science, mind and matter, soul and body. The goal of endeavour becomes civiltà instead of salvation, political rather than religious life. Vico represents the change. Civilization is for him one and indivisible with the three strands of law, language and myth. The modern philosophy of history was now well under way. All races were supposed to be developing in an identical manner; all are entitled to progress. The human race could be thought of as an organism, and all the branches of man are homogeneous as parts of the one organism, and help to realize the whole. Time is part of this evolution. 'In the Hegelian philosophy of history this abstract time has no place and meaning. Just as every living organism has its own time, which is not measurable by standard time, but depends upon its own law of growth, so in Hegel's system the evolution of the dialectical, historical process is the reality which is its own measure. And its time is concrete time.' Similarly space is concrete, and history is teleological and not causal. Later, however, Hegel fell into disrepute, and in place of his one organism philosophers fell back upon the idea of a series of civilizations, each independent, and each following the stages of birth, maturity and decay; or else they gave up all attempts to go beyond the findings of empirical and positivist science.

In this record of the history of the West, Haas finds a kind of structure which differentiates it from the East. All its successes, he believes, are due to the habit of setting over against each other subject and object, the inner and the outer world. This opposition remains unchanged throughout the history of the West, and is never overcome, and, as Haas thinks, can never be overcome. 'Were it not for the fact that through the objectifying process the subject hopes to arrive at the final knowledge of itself, one might say that in trying to objectify itself the subject is trapped in its own net.' The instrument it uses is the concept. By means of the concept it brings the object into relation to the subject, linking both together and at the same time keeping them separate. The subject grasps the object through the mediation of the concept. The aim is to possess and understand. This leads to the hypostatizing of the concept or idea, its quasi-independence, which is a condition of the 'scientific mind and, indeed, of the evolution and revolution of social and political forms'. Hence, too, people and nations and humanity are made the agents of history and become the subject of historiography. After two thousand years the West is no nearer to that self-comprehension, which comes in the union of subject and object.

In the East, on the other hand, there has never been this worship of the concept and of nature as something quite alien to the subject which has to be mastered. Man is one with nature, but at the same time free consciousness is all in all to him and tending to pure consciousness. Techniques are invented, such as those of breathing, to rid the self of empirical consciousness, until the consciousness becomes pure and absolute. By these exercises and other means the East by-passes the Western position; the body is gradually broken down, and the subject loses interest in it as in a smoothly-running machine. There is no object left over; there is only freedom. To the Eastern mind nature is a living entity, deeply akin to man. He does not live by his ideas of it, but by entering into its fullness. This means that he does not rely upon the ideas of causality or organism in the same way as Western man; nor does he think of a concrete soul fighting against the body. To him consciousness is all important, a consciousness which, as the instincts are dismantled, emerges into a pure and absolute condition. All the trouble to which the West goes to unify the data presented to the mind seems to the Eastern man waste of time. Pairs of opposites are polarities, and not ultimates; time is not an absolute; it belongs to phenomena like extension and colour, and as our experience grows and we are liberated from such experience; they drop away, leaving us clean and undivided.

In the light of what he has written, Haas concludes that 'any theory, before starting off on its constructive work, will have to determine explicitly what it considers its subjects to be. In Hegel statehood is the predominant criterion, but it only indicates where an authentic civilization may be found, and it is very fallible even then. If neither factors extraneous to civilization such as race, nor empirical elements isolated from the whole, such a statehood, reveal the basic differences between civilizations, then we must look for where the ground floor or structure of a civilization must be found. There are great civilizations which emerge out of inferior ones—and such types, if their distinctive marks can be found, are true subjects for a philosophy of history. The criterion for judging must be of a formal character, and so reside in the structure of the civilization, not its content. So we should proceed from description to typification, and from there to the cognition of the architectural structure.'

The contrast, which Haas has drawn, between East and West is meant, I think, to give a sketch of different structures. If so I fear that it is a case of *lucus a non lucendo*. The distinctions he makes do not seem to be history at all. One is drawn from Hindu and Buddhist philosophy, the other from the Cartesian thought, which no doubt has influenced the modern scientific attitude. Both Plato and Aristotle taught a higher form of knowledge and union than that of the concept, and the Christian ideal is one of a mode of union higher than that of reason. Greek and Christian thought have played a great part in the structure of Western civilization, and if we turn to the East we cannot leave out the part played by Confucianism. Haas seems to favour the Eastern outlook, but he does not tell us how it helps to provide any philosophy of history; nor does he seem to be sufficiently aware of the many difficulties which surround the idea of a 'pure consciousness'.

Chapter III

THE GROWTH OF A PHILOSOPHY
OF HISTORY

Charles Beard, the historian, being asked if he could give a summary of his views on history, replied at first that it would take him a long time. On second thoughts, however, he said that four sentences would suffice, and they were: When darkness comes the stars begin to shine; the bees that rob the flowers provide the honey; whom God wishes to destroy he first makes mad; the mills of God grind slowly, but they grind exceeding small. Few of us deny ourselves some such reflections or gnomic sayings on man and his history. If proof were needed we have only to turn to the collection of wise sayings handed down and our enjoyment of them and frequent quotation from them. The writer who can without triteness or shallowness give us a sense of larger issues and far-reaching truths is much sought after and admired. The old man who has had a life of many experiences, the writer who has read deeply in the pages of the past, the retired statesman and white-bearded philosopher, they are expected to have learnt some lessons which are worth handing on. We are all of us in our unbuttoned moods philosophers of history. It is almost instinctive with us. We cannot live with our minds in chaos. When we learn something which upsets our mental framework we set about making a new framework into which we can fit experience. Egotists, too, that we are, we cannot when we are young help thinking that history is being taught for our benefit and that somehow or other all the past is preaching to the present and prompting it. It is a shock to read Valéry's comment that 'history is the science of what never happens twice'. We hope that history is more like love, of which Lacordaire wrote: 'Love has but one word and it never repeats itself.' As we grow older and our affection for others takes deeper root, our concern for their lives and for the nation and for the human race is quickened, and there presses on us the problem of the mingled insignificance and grandeur of man, his uncertain steps and chequered progress. As T. S. Eliot and others have reminded us, the beauty and pathos of Vergil spring from his sense that Aeneas and his companions, despite the burning of their beloved Troy, the shipwrecks and disasters of their wanderings, are nevertheless marked men of destiny and moving towards it. *Tendimus in Latium.* We become philosophers of history, therefore, all too readily because we cannot help looking for light upon our own lives, those of our friends and contemporaries, and then of all our fellow-men.

During most of the centuries of which we have any knowledge thoughts about man and his history were intimately bound up with religion. Men lived in fear and reverence of the gods or what lay behind the gods, namely fate. Much that happened to man was so obviously outside his control, and so irresistible in their sweep did nature and life appear that most felt that they were entirely in the hands of fate. Clearly man was not master of the world around him. Immense forces seemed to play with him, and at one moment benevolent and at another dark, malignant powers decided his future by destroying his grain, sinking his ship, bringing the plague or rescuing him from peril of death and bringing him prizes and good fortune. He knew little of the processes of nature and was drawn to attribute the unknown to the direct action of a god. It was easy, therefore, for him to formulate a naïve philosophy according to which the gods were propitious to man if he placated them and obeyed their commandments however arbitrary, and hostile if he failed in his proper observances. It would appear also that there was a more profound reason for a philosophy of history based on reward and punishment. That the punishment should fit the crime and that the good should be rewarded is not a passing and naïve superstition. It belongs to the very notion of good and evil and is one of the immovable pillars of all morality. The principle may be crudely stated and applied and the notion of justice may be confused with vindictiveness; but no one can perceive grievous wrong happening without the desire and the hope that the wrong will be righted. Even those who in the lecture-room favoured an amoral world, or one in which no fixed moral principles could stand, were filled with indignation at the Nazi persecution of the Jews and demanded 'justice', that is to say, the restoration of right order and the trial of those responsible. Religious peoples have almost invariably, as might be expected, turned to God in the belief that He is the guardian of justice, who will not allow the wicked to triumph and the good to perish without redress. Even where religion is not in evidence the historian, such as Thucydides, will tend to underline the fatal results of wrongdoing, the rotting of a state through licence and avarice and the fall of pride. The great dramatists can hardly avoid playing upon this theme. Sin brings suffering and suffering brings wisdom is the strophe and antistrophe of the plays of Aeschylus, and in the Shakespearian tragedies we can feel the note of doom from the moment Richard II or Macbeth, for example, display the flaw in their characters.

A very simple but almost fully fledged philosophy of history makes its appearance as soon as man believes that God's justice will work itself out in the mortal life of man. God will see to it that the good flourish and the wicked perish. This is, as all know, the theme of the book of Job. Job, the simple and upright man, who fears God and avoids evil, has his prosperity taken from him and has to meet every kind of misfortune and calamity. His three friends, Eliphaz, Baldad and Sophar come to comfort him, and so overcome are they at his misery that they sit with him for seven days and seven nights without saying a word—a long time. When they do speak, their words of comfort are to the effect that Job must be a sinner, and, if he will only acknowledge his faults and repent, God will have mercy on him. Again and again they come back to the point that his calamities must be the result of his doing evil. That is the law of life and the only theology of life which makes sense. 'If thou wilt put away from thee the iniquity that is in thy hand, and let not injustice remain in thy tabernacle; then mayest thou lift up thy face without spot; and thou shalt be steadfast and shalt not fear. Thou shalt also forget misery, and remember it only as waters that are passed away. And brightness, like that of the noonday, shall arise in thee at evening.' But Job protests his innocence and will not have this unconvincing comfort.

Too often the wicked prosper and the innocent suffer and are brought down. True, therefore, as the principle of justice, of redress and punishment must be, the application of it cannot be seen in this mortal life by the measure of human success and failure. God's ways are mysterious. Man cannot justify himself in His Presence; nevertheless God cannot countenance injustice nor leave the innocent unrequited. 'Behold the fear of the Lord, that is wisdom. And to depart from evil is understanding.'

It is not in man, however, to leave all in mystery, and again and again the history of man is examined and measured in terms of moral justice and injustice. The prophets of Israel warn the people of the chastisements of God for their backsliding and disobedience. It is because the Israelites have neglected the divine commands that they will be defeated and handed over to their enemies. They did not, however, as a rule, apply the same principle of Providence to the world in general, for they believed that Israel was under a special dispensation and charged with a unique destiny. In all likelihood, however, they took for granted that in some way individuals and nations progressed, if virtuous, and perished, on the other hand, if they did evil, as that belief was so widespread. Nevertheless we can see in Job and in other writings of the Old Testament a gradual dissociation of reward from temporal prosperity. In the book of Tobias, for example, we read that the trial of his blinding 'the Lord permitted to happen to him that an example might be given to posterity of his patience, as also of holy Job'. In both Job and Tobias the story ends with the restoration to them of their temporal prosperity and their happiness. The happy ending is what as children we always hoped for—'and they lived happily ever after'—and when the world was young that seemed as it should be despite apparent exceptions to the rule.

When an age of reflection set in the simple answer ceased to have any plausibility in the eyes of the wise. Socrates made a jest of temporal reward; his judges might choose for him a lodging in the prytaneum, but he was thinking of immortality. No longer should man look for the reward of virtue in temporal happiness whether for the individual or the nation or mankind. History was neutral, and either virtue was its own reward, or the reward was to be sought in an after-life. To some, however, an altogether different answer looked true. An inscrutable fate ruled human lives and the most one could do was to observe a certain rhythm in the way it worked. This view has been closely associated by many with paganism. It is even claimed that without the true conception of a living God the philosophy of determinism is an overwhelming temptation. Human endeavour seems to add up to so small a total when the antecedent causes of any event, human or natural, are considered that it can be ignored. Nature, used in the sense of all that is, ourselves included, is, if not blind, at any rate indifferent to human aims and ideals. 'Sceptre and crown must tumble down and in the dust be equal made with the poor crooked scythe and spade.' 'The universe is closed and man cannot escape or change his fate.' That such a belief was prevalent in the East and among the Greeks and Romans cannot be denied, and its shadow is always with us. It was, however, to be ousted in the West by a religion which laid an almost fearful emphasis on human responsibility and independence.

Christianity took over from the Jews the belief in a personal God who exercised His providence over the human race and especially over a new 'chosen people'. It turned upside down, however, the idea of virtue and human reward. So far from attaching any value to success or eminence in this world, by the violence of its denunciation of riches and worldly honour it seemed to spurn them utterly. 'The kings of the Gentiles lord it over them, and those who bear rule over them win the name of benefactors. With you it is not to be so. . . .' The disciples of this new faith are to rejoice when they are ill-treated and suffer ignominy. They are to shun the world and lose their lives to find life. They are to give up all things to follow and imitate a leader, whom the world has hated and crucified. Such a doctrine seems to reverse all human judgments and to make the values of history worthless when weighed by ultimate and absolute standards. Historical progress and culture become unsubstantial, 'shadows and images' which are superseded by ultimate truth. There can be no philosophy of history for there is nothing in human action which is not in part illusion. As if to drive in this lesson the disciples were warned of a second coming, and at first many of them interpreted this second coming as a rapidly approaching end of the world. Already in the advent of the Son of God history had reached its fulfilment. He had come in the fullness of time and after him nothing more perfect could conceivably arrive. There was no point in building up treasures for the future or looking to a long stretch of development.

It would seem, then, that Christianity and a philosophy of history are ideas alien to one another and cannot meet. But this is an over-simplification. In the first centuries when the Christian had to live a catacombal life and be a pariah in Roman society he paid little attention to the world around him. His art when he had to make use of it was adopted from the Roman forms around him, and he straightway made it into a language of symbols of the sacramental and invisible or as a simple method of teaching the Gospel story. Nevertheless there is evidence that from very early times the Christian outlook was ambivalent, that while it preached, 'seek ye first the Kingdom of God', it did not repudiate the world as sheer vanity of vanities. Irenaeus and Origen are aware of a problem which involves human history. The history of the Jews as told in the Old Testament was the work of Providence, a time of preparation for the coming of Christ. It could not, therefore, be dismissed as worthless. Moreover though the advent of Christ brought the world to its climax and completion, life had to go on and Christians had to find meaning in the time-process. P. Daniélou quotes the answer of Origen to this problem. 'The Apostle says that the Law is the shadow of good things to come. Thus those who were under the Law were under its shadow. But we are no longer under the Law, but under Divine Grace. But, although we are no longer under the shadow of the Law, we are, however, under a better shadow. Truly we live in the shadow of Christ among the nations.' This is the beginning of an answer, but it looks only to one facet of the problem involved in the rich teaching of the Christian faith. There is first the fact that the world itself came from the Creator's hands, and as such it cannot be reputed evil or despised. Then there is the world of paganism, given over, as some of the early Fathers of the Church held, to wickedness, with its virtues nothing better, as Augustine said, than splendid vices. Time and experience were bound to modify these views. Next came the Christian himself, committed to time and spending most of his days performing temporal tasks and engaged in secular pursuits. As the centuries passed he became an accepted member of society, and had after the irruptions and barbarian invasions to mend a broken society and re-create human values. What was the relation of all this work of his to the Second Coming, to the everlasting city for which 'his eyes their vigil keep', to the Kingdom of God which was not of this world? A medieval mystic might pray for a *Cloud of Unknowing* and a Francis of Assisi divest himself of everything, but family life, the work of the fields and city, the building of secular cities had to be carried on, and the artist and scientist and philosopher were carried away by the wonders of truth and beauty God allowed them to discover.

History, therefore, could not be treated as a waste land, however unimportant the city of man might seem compared with the city of God. Time has served only to amplify the problem as the genius of man has found more and more scope and new horizons have opened. Nor can it be said that a fully-satisfying answer has so far been given to what is, in fact a concentric series of problems, the relation of natural to supernatural values, of human, or shall we say, humanistic perfection to the ascetic ideal of unworldliness, of human progress to the Advent of Christ, the emergence of so much that is new with the fulfilment of all things in Christ, the connection of time's shadows and images with ultimate truth, of the relation of secular history with Christian history and the relation of both with the mysterious kingdom of God, ever real and ever secret which is to be revealed according to Christian belief at the end of time. The coat of Christian doctrine was one of many colours, so rich in variety indeed that one colour will absorb most of the attention at a time of stress. Thus in the first centuries the other-worldly aspect was naturally prominent and fitted in with the mood steadily growing in the Roman Empire of impending calamity. The Christian art of the time, in so far as it broke away from the Roman forms, so marked for instance in the remains at Pompeii and Herculaneum, inclined towards the hieratical, to stiff, bloodless shapes, what has been described by Arnold Hauser as a 'code language of salvationist doctrine'. That Christianity was not totally averse to the natural and committed utterly to a hatred of what made up our human dignity is shown by the rapid adaptation of Platonism and kindred ideas to its own theology and to the baptizing of pagan feasts and customs.

By the fifth century a hundred years after the Church and the Empire had been brought into alliance by Constantine, the leading minds of Christendom looked out on a different situation from that of the first Christians. They were now saddled with duties towards Rome and the Empire and at the same time they were being libelled as the causes of Rome's misfortunes. The nature of this latter attack dictated the lines on which Augustine made his famous answer in *The City of God*. He was not so much concerned to show the compatibility of the Christian faith with human prosperity and human values as to prove the debility of pagan ideals and the grandeur of the Christian revelation. This led him into an excursus on history in which he argued against the pagan philosophy of the eternity of the world and the doctrine of cyclic recurrence and its further claim that the splendours of human achievement had been ruined by Christian meekness and other-worldliness. He does not, however, try to maintain that the faith is the salt of human nature, that human life can be preserved and exalted by grace and that with such help the earthly city can be an anticipation and even the groundwork of the heavenly city. There appears to be a complete break. What man does with the world into which he has been born has no relevance to eternal life. The ages pass, a culture may be built up, but the Christian is a pilgrim preparing himself for a life which is beyond compare. He does not, therefore, lay down any principles for a philosophy of history as we understand it now. There is no transposition of human values to a different and supernatural key, no equating in any way of human progress with the progress of the kingdom of God. It is only in the eleventh book that he introduces the famous theme of the two cities, and not until the fifteenth book does he develop the theme. What history there is is drawn from the Bible and the story of Rome, and he is hampered by his Platonic bias. So great, however, was his genius and so influential his name that he dictated for centuries the manner of looking at history. Behind, too, the Christian presuppositions there is to be detected a kind of thinking about history which corresponds with a level of reflection to be found in every generation. Cities and nations, at this level of reflection, do seem to rise to power and then decline or collapse through sin or exhaustion, and the process takes place in a movement from east to west. History is thus given a shape. We start with the Assyrians and pass on to the Persians and then to Greece. Athens sums up the greatness of

Greece, is all golden, like the statue of Athene, for a short while and overreaches itself in pride. The sceptre passes to Rome, and, to cut the story short, to Spain and France and England, and is now held by the United States. Even there the western states tend to look down upon the eastern as decadent; but their own superiority would be due to virile energy rather than to the practice of virtue. Such reflections, issuing in rapid generalizations, will not pass muster with the careful historian, though they are persistent and attractive.

Although Augustine admits no fraternization between the Civitas Dei and the Civitas Terrena, between the two loves which made two cities, he had to spend part of his great work commenting on human history. To him it was a sad spectacle. Man at variance with God and with himself chasing false hopes and dreams. Peoples and civilizations rise and fall, and their distresses are due to sin. To Augustine the self-inflicted wounds of men are far more noticeable than his growing welfare, and by emphasizing, perhaps over-emphasizing this fact, he prevents any false optimism and underlines a truth which must be taken account of in any philosophy of history. Orosius, his disciple, is in accord with his main ideas, and fills up the picture of history sketched by Augustine. In the *Seven Books of History against the Pagans* he takes as examples of his thesis some of the great Empires of the past. They are all marked by the sin of Adam, and, therefore, as we must expect, their story is one of violence and calamities. Rome, too, no matter what its pagan defenders say, has a record of oppression, strife and injustice, but God has been more merciful to Rome because of the part it has to play in the coming of Christ. Man being what he is there is no reason for looking for better things in the future. The world will always be a place of suffering and sin, and the Christian alone is blessed because he knows, that after the suffering comes the reward, and that in the after-life true peace and happiness can alone be found. No more than in Augustine, therefore, is there a philosophy of human history. There is, however, a moral or theological view of history running through the thought of Augustine and Orosius and it is this theology of history which became the conventional Christian view until the eighteenth century, and even now it remains the uncritical, spontaneous reaction to history of many religious men and women. It has an echo of Job and of the Greek dramatists. In short it is this, that God who made man exercises a continual providence over mankind, and this is shown in his justice which punishes sin and in suffering which disciplines man to repent and correct himself. Orosius thus states the theory: 'We are taught that sin and its punishment began with the very first man. Furthermore, even our opponents, who begin with the middle period and make no mention of the ages preceding, have described nothing but wars and calamities. What else are these wars but evils which befall one side or the other? Those evils which existed then, as to a certain extent they exist now, were doubtless either palpable sins or the hidden punishments for sin.' Past ages seem to have been far more conscious of evils than people now. It would have been inconceivable for the contemporaries of Augustine to harbour an optimistic and liberal idea of a progress which would emancipate man from life's hardships, robbery, cruelty and selfishness and avarice. They lived in the midst of perils which seemed as natural as the seasons and they were afraid of divine retribution for sin. Orosius has a thought on evil to which we shall have to return, so impressively true is it. He says that people invariably think that the present moment of trial and crisis is worse than conditions in the past or what may happen in the future. By contrast with the present woe all else looks rosy and we inevitably romanticize it. In truth, however, we pass from one crisis to another, and the serenely peaceful day imagined and expected belongs to Utopia, not to this world.

When the barbarian invasions slackened and Christianity was able to send out a dove to find dry land, the old cultured paganism no longer stood out as the rival of the Christian religion. It was left to the latter to rebuild the city of man and more in accordance with the principles of the faith. But this meant that the hitherto unworldly religion had to come to terms with the world and history. The Middle Ages were the result, a culture resting on the Christian philosophy and successful in many directions in adding beauty and wisdom to human life. The answer, however, was worked out more in practice than in theory. The monks continued to live apart from the world and the preachers continued to fulminate against preoccupation with the things of time. The result was a state of happy or unhappy tension. The book which the monk was illuminating might be about vanity of vanities, but into the illustration and its colours and lines gaiety and enjoyment would keep breaking in. Even in Carolingian times among the supposedly so austere Irish monks, love of nature can be found: 'the little bird has let a whistling note resound from the tip of its shining yellow beak; the blackbird sends out a cry over Loch Laig from the yellow bushy tree.' In the cold cells of the monasteries of Tours, Cologne, Ratisbon, Corbie and Winchester, a lovely new art developed which resembled snowdrops before the coming of spring. Later in the twelfth and thirteenth centuries writers and artists like William of Conches and John of Salisbury and Masaccio felt free to show an unabashed love of man and nature. 'Man', as André Malraux has written, 'had climbed up from hell to paradise through Christ, in Christ, and the sense of helpless solitude which had hitherto infused the hieratic arts vanished altogether with his fear. From Chartres to Rheims, in every land where under the Redeemer's hands a world of seed-time and harvest, figured in the bas-reliefs of the seasons, was permeating human lives (where until now there had been room for God alone)—in every land, from Chartres to Rheims, from Rheims to Assisi, artists were seeking after the forms of a world absolved from fear.'

There were, however, setbacks. Living at a time when in Rome, Arnold of Brescia was stirring up the populace, when Pope and Emperor were locked in strife, with war in France and England, and with the Seljukian Turks threatening the borders of Christendom, Otto of Freising wrote a work, a pessimistic outlook on the world similar to that of St. Augustine. The name of the work was *The Two Cities* or *The Chronicon*; the time he called *miseria rerum mutabilium*. He gave it when completed to his nephew, Frederick Barbarossa, in 1157. It is a universal history from Adam to the year 1146, in seven books, with an eighth dealing with the end of the world. It has a very limited outlook, but within that outlook it has received a gentle commendation from Ranke. The theme is the same as that of St. Augustine and Orosius, but it is nearer to our modern conception of history, because it is not written as an apologia for the Church, and he has both a feeling for the sweep of history and a care for facts. He tells us that his intention was 'to set forth, not after the manner of a disputant, but in the fashion of one telling a story, a history, in which, on the one hand, the varying experiences, on the other hand, the progress and achievements of the citizens of Babylon, shall be inter-woven'. The spectacle, however, of the earth and the doings on it fill him with sadness; the times are so bad that the wise man will seek to depart from this Babylon 'to that city which stays at rest and abides for all eternity'. 'For in as much as there are two cities—the one of time, the other of eternity . . . the one of the devil, the other of Christ, Catholic writers have declared that the former is Babylon, the other Jerusalem.'

Europe did not, however, continue all the while to have a calamitous look. Both thought and art developed the affection for nature. In the thirteenth century the unworldly Platonic philosophy was succeeded by the Aristotelian, and though St. Thomas Aquinas, the chief engineer of this change, has left us little or nothing positive on the philosophy of history, his dis-ciples can claim that he prepared the way for such a study. Neither Platonism nor Asian thought gives a basis for history. Events are either only half-real or in the end illusory. Even such a mighty Christian thinker as St. Augustine, in thinking on history, was led to put the stress on divine Providence rather than on man's nature and activities, and sought to justify God's ways to man. Christian Aristotelianism offered a metaphysics in which man's nature and activities are allowed full expression and scope. Man is a free, rational and moral agent, master of his destiny and responsible for the course of human events. In St. Thomas this Aristotelian metaphysic is reinforced, so Gilson maintains—by the Christian belief in a unique humanity, made up of the living and the dead, in progress towards its end and perfection. In the same line of argument M. Chevalier declares that 'neither sociology, nor economics, nor even psycho-logy can provide history with its principles; it is in metaphysics alone, and in a metaphysics based on facts, that history can find it'. Such claims have to meet the objection that neither history itself nor a philosophy of history seem to have been inspired by the Thomist metaphysics. Centuries had to pass before they received their due and qualified as serious and scientific studies. Good reasons no doubt may be given for this delay, and no one can deny that the philosophy of St. Thomas does turn the mind to the goodness of nature and to the value inherent in human activities.

Helped by the blessing of a down-to-earth philosophy the men of the Middle Ages underwent a change of mind with regard to the world. This is shown in the growing tension between the claims of God and other-worldliness and the claims of the world and of history. In the pure and elongated forms of the sculptures at Chartres and the serene colours of Fra Angelico a new kind of earthly beauty had come into being, and it is seen in its most paradoxical aspect in Francis of Assisi. He who with the gesture of throwing off his clothes in the presence of the bishop and his father gave up the world utterly, nevertheless, as the *Golden Legend* tells us, 'went honourably upon the stones for the love of Him that so called stone'. He gathered the small worms out of the ways, so they should not be trodden by the feet of them that passed by. He commanded in winter to give honey unto bees that they should not perish for hunger. He called all beasts his brethren. He was replenished of marvellous joy for the love of his Creator. He beheld the sun, the moon and the stars and summoned them to the love of their maker.

But so far as a philosophy of history was concerned medieval man fell back on the old moral or theological view. God filled the heavens and Christ was the centre point of the world's history. God controlled nature and exercised his providence over man, so that those who were caught in a thunderstorm feared it as the judgment of God and those who saw a man fall sick asked, like the Apostles of the man born blind, 'was this man guilty of sin or was it his parents?' The common attitude is well expressed in Pico della Mirandola's comment on Savonarola: 'It seemed to him that the majesty of divine justice required that terrible penalties should fall on wicked men, and especially on those who being placed in authority, corrupt the people by their bad example at a time when the human race, sunk in wickedness, had for so many ages abused the patience of God, and when the peoples of Asia and Africa were involved in many errors and in the darkness of ignorance. He thought too, that the order of divine providence indisputably demanded the same chastisements, seeing that from the beginning of history we have the record of a series of wonderful and mysterious judgments, whereby the lovable clemency and the terrible justice of God are alike made manifest.' The religious believer takes to this view as a bird or fish to its natural element. His conscience makes him fear retribution, and even when he is not aware of grave guilt he feels fear before One who is omnipotent as well as just, a searcher of hearts and inflexible judge. Only dimly aware of the processes of nature he transfers to the direct action of God all that is outside his own control and unknown. The Christian Revelation brought a new conception of the Fatherhood of God and of God as Love, but the fear of judgment is almost ineradicable from the human mind, because the human conscience starts with the moral idea of justice. The Christian with his vivid sense of the divine providence and presence had also the story of God's dealings with the Jews to confirm him in this moral or theological view of history. How great was the influence of the Old Testament can be seen later in the readiness of Cromwell and the Puritans to ascribe all the misfortunes of their enemies to God's wrath and to assume that they themselves were God's instruments in allotting the punishment. Few religious men and women even to this day can boast that they are entirely free from this moral philosophy of history. Even among non-religious persons, though they might be unwilling to admit it, it is true that a guilty conscience does make cowards of us all.

When the notion of an all-active Providence began to fade away from people's minds in the new light cast by science on the unchanging processes of nature, the over-simple moral and theological view as preached, for instance, by a Savonarola, had to be modified. A thunderstorm could be explained as a necessary natural phenomenon and the lightning might as likely strike the innocent as the guilty. God's ways became more hidden and were forgotten by increasing numbers of people. They learnt to take a pride in science and in being able to give scientific explanations. As science developed its various branches, and even within one field began to divide and multiply, the scientist tended to decry general explanations. It was his job to stick to his last. A more modern historian, Burckhardt, sums up this tendency. He frowned at all attempts to generalize or moralize about history. Religious explanations are outside the scope of the historian and do not matter, and he was equally opposed to attempted explanations by philosophic scientists, materialists or idealists. He had need to issue a warning to thinkers other than religious who were sure that they had the key to all history. Despite the general movement of scientists to confine themselves to their own patch of land, controversy produced a number of theorists. The advocates of the new empirical methods could not resist having a smack at the old, out-of-date, as they thought, ways of philosophizing and generalizing. They were especially hard on Aristotelians and churchmen, and it is not given to churchmen to remain silent when their intellectual qualifications are questioned.

Christian philosophers, as already explained, had not adopted any definite view of history. Their interests had lain elsewhere in metaphysics, logic and morals. Neither of these first two subjects involved the problem of time in their treatment, and morals, though, as we now see, they have varied in time and place, were viewed in the light of natural and divine law, which, all Christian thinkers agreed, were unchanging. Nevertheless a resolute bishop like Bossuet could not allow the Christian view of history to go by default. He is the last of the old school who allied learning to the traditional outlook. He brings out the stock tenets of Augustine and Orosius on providence and justice and retribution, and with the current ideas of past history at his beck he builds up a massive defence of Christianity. The *Discours* was written for the Dauphin and was meant to be edifying in the best sense of the word. The future king of France is to see how the world and kingdoms are governed by God, and how best a king can carry out the work of divine providence. In the first part Bossuet gives a *coup d'œil* over all secular history from Adam to Charlemagne. In the second part he sketches the history of religion, with special treatment of the Jews and their mission in preparing the way for the coming of the Son of God. Christ and the Christian religion are shown to be the culmination of history, the united masterpiece which gives meaning to all creation. In the third part he gives a brief account of the great Empires known then to the educated European and relates their story to that of Christ and His Church. The theology of the *Discours* is unobjectionable, if the first premise be granted, but unfortunately the history is much of it out-of-date and never treated in the critical manner of the modern historian. All is grist to the mills of God which grind slowly and surely according to the ancient formulae of retribution and grace. In his *Avant-Propos* Bossuet tells his pupil to concentrate on the succession of Empires and religions on a great map and fix them in his memory; and 'as religion and political government are the two points on which human events turn, to see what concerns them confined in a résumé and thence to discover the whole order and train of events, is to comprehend in one's mind all that is great in human affairs and have the key to the history of the universe'. A few passages will serve to show Bossuet's conception of history. In the seventh chapter of the Second Part he contrasts God's dealings with Jerusalem and Babylon: 'Who will not here admire the divine Providence, so clearly marked towards the Jews and the Chaldeans, towards Jerusalem and Babylon? God wills to punish both; and in order that all should know that it is He who is responsible, He makes it His good pleasure to declare it by a hundred prophecies. Jerusalem and Babylon, both threatened at the same time and by the same prophets, fall one after the other at the designated time. But God here reveals the great secret and meaning of the two chastisements which He uses; a chastisement of severity towards the Chaldeans and a fatherly one towards the Jews, who are His children. The pride of the Chaldeans (such was the character of the nation and the spirit of the whole empire) is crushed without recovery. The proud one shall fall, and there shall be none to lift him up, said Jeremias, and before him Isaias, and that Babylon, glorious among kingdoms, the famous pride of the Chaldeans, shall be even as the Lord destroyed Sodom and Gomorrha, to whom God gave not any succour. It is not so with the Jews: God has smitten them as disobedient children whom He brings back to their duty; and then touched by their tears, He forgets their faults.'

The same thought is still more marked when Bossuet deals expressly with the history of the ancient Empires. In the very first chapter of the third part, he says: 'Thus it is that the empires of the world have ministered to religion, and to the preservation of the people of God; wherefore that same God, who caused the different states of His people to be foretold by His prophets, caused the succession of the empires to be also predicted by them. You have seen the places where Nebuchadnezzar was pointed out as the person that was to come and punish the haughty nations, and especially the Jewish people for their ingratitude to their Maker. You have heard Cyrus named two hundred years before his birth, as him who was to restore God's people, and to punish Babylon's pride. The destruction of Nineveh hath been no less clearly foretold. Daniel, in his admirable visions, hath made the Empire of Babylon, that of the Medes and Persians, that of Alexander and the Grecians, pass away in a moment before you. The blasphemies and cruelties of Antiochus the Great have been there prophesied as well as the miraculous victories of God's people over that violent persecutor. We there see those famous empires fall one after another, and the new empire which Jesus Christ was to establish, is there described so expressly by its proper characters, that it is impossible to mistake it. It is the empire of the Son of Man, the empire that is to stand amidst the ruins of all others, and to which alone eternity is promised. . . . Thus it is that all the great empires which we have seen upon this earth, have contributed in diverse ways to the good of religion and to the glory of God, as God indeed has declared through His prophets.' In his concluding pages he sums up his views on divine Providence. After having laid down that all depends upon the secret orders of Providence, and that God promotes and thwarts in His secret dispositions conquerors and statesmen and the wise, he goes on: 'In this way God works out His fearsome judgments, according to the rules of His ever infallible justice. It is He who prepares effects in their far-distant causes, who strikes those great blows whose repercussions stretch just so far. When He wills to weaken the last in power and change empires, all becomes feeble and confused in their counsels. Egypt, once so wise, moves with a drunken, stupefied and uncertain gait, because the Lord hath imparted into their deliberations a spirit of confusion; she knows no longer what she does, she is lost. But let not men deceive themselves; God, when it so pleases Him, can restore the wandering senses; and he who would take advantage of the blindness of others, falls himself into an even deeper darkness, though there be no other cause for his madness than long-continued prosperity. Thus it is that God holds sway over all peoples. Let us not then talk of chance or fortune and use the unjust as words to cover our ignorance. For what seems to our uncertain judgments to be chance is a design contrived by a higher wisdom, that is to say, in the everlasting mind who has all the world's causes and all the effects contained in one single order. And so it is that all works together to the same end; and it is through lack of understanding the whole that we hit upon chance or irregularity in our individual experience.'

From these quotations the line taken by Bossuet in explaining the history of the world is clear. No Christian thinker could take exception to the general thesis. If God be really God and if Christianity be the unique Revelation of the Son of God, all falls under Providence, and Providence centres round the words and work of Christ. But just as the Christian doctrine of grace leaves the problem of human wills and human history untouched, so this general and theological explanation is too unembodied to satisfy the historian and the philosopher of history. We have only to compare the work of a Toynbee, defective though it be, with that of Bossuet to see what is lacking in the latter's vast enterprise. Moreover Providence does not let us into the divine secrets to the extent demanded by Bossuet. It is quite a different matter to say that all works to the glory of God, to the well-being of the chosen people and the Christian faith, and to maintain that the evidence for this is shiningly clear in the unfinished record of mankind. The Christian knows it by faith rather than by sight, and the more he studies history the more is he struck by the different fortunes of different peoples and individuals quite independent of their goodness or reliance on God. The historian must keep to the evidence and stand free of any predetermining view of events. When he does this he is able to assign natural causes to catastrophes which by Bossuet would be called the wrath of God and he will observe also that God's sun shines indifferently upon the wicked and the good and that in the catastrophe, the good suffer equally with the bad. Bossuet tries to prove too much, and his method, despite the high regard with which his *Discours* was received when it was published, has long since been abandoned. He may be called the last of the old school of prelates who looked over the field of history and explained it all in terms of divine providence. Bossuet and those whom he followed forgot perhaps how strongly their own faith influenced their outlook and charged natural events with a significance unseen by others. To them the sight of suffering and disaster excited the thought of sin, justice and mercy; to the modern mind this very problem of evil is the most serious difficulty against a providential direction of the world.

Voltaire is supposed to have given the *coup de grâce* to this old moral and theological view of history.[1] Undoubtedly he

[1] The sudden transition from Bossuet to Voltaire is well brought out by Paul Hazard in *The European Mind* (1680–1715), London, 1953.

contributed to the change of mind, but other cases were at work. The eighteenth century ends with the apotheosis of reason, with a woman symbolizing reason adored in the streets of Paris. Human reason, so it was believed, had the key to progress and to an explanation of history. Instead of sin and divine punishment a new dialectic gradually made its appearance, sometimes in terms of positive and negative thesis and antithesis, and amongst the less philosophical, of fall and rise, degeneracy and revival, of the clash of opposing principles. Hegel and Marx are not so far away from Augustine and Bossuet, but whereas Augustine thought in terms of two loves and two cities and Bossuet of God working good out of evil, the dialectic of Marx limits itself to the opposing forces of society and their economic needs. In the transition period there is one great thinker who stands on ancient ways and nevertheless invents a modern philosophy of history; this is Vico. There is one outstanding iconoclast, Voltaire, and there are the precursors of modern political thinkers, Montesquieu, Condorcet and Comte.

Vico deserves a chapter to himself and his thought belongs almost as much to the present as to his own day. Voltaire follows directly on Bossuet, and in what he wrote of history he had Bossuet's views in mind. Bossuet had in his grand sweep of history dealt with the writings and nations which every classical humanist knew. The humanist read the Greek and Latin ancient writers and also the Bible. Rome, Greece and Palestine were, therefore, what constituted history for him, and his knowledge of other nations, such as Egypt, Syria and Persia was drawn from his knowledge of the 'classics' and confined to the relation of other races to the Jews and the Greco-Roman world. But in the eighteenth century the East aroused interest and some of its history began to be known. This was grist for Voltaire's mill, and he took pleasure in pointing out that Bossuet's history was defective in range and that his supreme confidence in Providence came from an abuse of evidence, and of evidence which was cooked. M. Pangloss saw all events as providential, and providential to the Jews, on the principle that as 'our legs are clearly intended for shoes and stockings, so we have them'. 'If the kings of Babylon in their conquests fall incidentally upon the Hebrews, it is only to chastise these people for their sins. If a king named Cyrus becomes the master of Babylon, it is in order to allow a few Jews to go home. If Alexander is victorious over Darius, it is in order to establish some Jewish second-hand dealers in Alexandria. When the Romans annex Syria and the small district of Judea to their vast empire, it is again for the instruction of the Jews.' In fact, Voltaire maintains, China shows a civilization which is superior to the vaunted Jewish and even the Christian one, for the Chinese escaped many of the barbarities of Europe and were by comparison wise, pacific and humane. So instead of building these vast castles in the air it would be much better if we were to cultivate our own garden.

The old providential view of history could scarcely survive this deadly satire, and besides the climate was becoming more and more unfavourable to theological explanations. The weather-vane was veering to man and the progress of man, and the Christian hope in the after-life was changing to a hope of secular progress. Christian values and the indirect fruits of Christian teaching did not die, but the framework of the old theology was ignored. Montesquieu, for instance, owes much to Bossuet, but his interest is in the actual and observable causes of the rise and fall of nations. He compares England with France and inquires into the nature of tradition, and on such evidence he draws conclusions and asserts principles. But like Bossuet he is too inclined to rely indiscriminately on the ancient authors. As a reviewer in *The Times Literary Supplement* remarks: 'But Montesquieu . . . cites Livy or Dionysius or Plutarch or Cicero as if they were authorities of equal weight, as if Numa Pompilius and Ulpian were equally historical figures and as if we knew as much of the Kings of Rome as of the Caesars.' In the last resort, too, he falls back upon the moral criterion, for he attributes the fall of governments and peoples to corruption in high places and the abandonment of justice. Condorcet, on the other hand, keeps only the faith and optimism once imparted by the Christian Revelation and transfers it to a creed of liberated man. With astonishing fervour he proclaims the glorious possibilities which are opening out now that the people have thrown off the yoke of political tyranny and religious superstition. Knowledge can be the guide to an earthly paradise. Just as knowledge by the development of the physical sciences has enabled man to master the earth and predict the course of natural events, so knowledge of the mind of man and his moral constitution should serve to destroy evil, the fruit of ignorance, and achieve perfect contentment. There is no reason why a science of thought and morals should not rival the physical sciences in predicting and bringing about a new world of prosperity. History can be made like to science, and the future can be made as open as the past. By these means the perfectibility of the human race can pass from a dream to a reality, the goods of this world can be multiplied, the resources of the earth infinitely extended, and even the length of human life vastly extended. When the already advanced nations have extended the benefits of their knowledge and civilization to the backward peoples of the East, the whole world will be ready to be organized into a peaceful and happy humanity. Condorcet here anticipates many of the attempted solutions which were to follow, the belief in progress and in universal democracy, the reliance on economic forces and biological evolution and in a kind of Internationale. Enthusiasm and hope ran high at the beginning of the French Revolution. Karl Lowith has described in his *Meaning in History* the deep disappointment felt when it became clear that neither social revolutions nor the advance of science proved to be the gateways to a promised land. 'In the midst of frantic progress by means of scientific inventions in the middle of the nineteenth century, a mood of aimlessness and despair cast its first shadow upon Europe's most advanced minds; for the very progress seemed to proceed toward nothingness.' He quotes Flaubert and Baudelaire, Burckhardt and Tolstoy. He could, too, have found representative writers in England sharing the same disbelief in the new radicalism's claims and fighting against a sense of despair.

The followers of Voltaire and the rationalists took over from the old theological historians. The Christian thinkers had been debarred from attempting a too determinate philosophy of history by their two-mindedness on the subject of human progress. As life was but a pilgrimage to a better world whose relations with this life were never clearly defined, it was natural that they should leave many loose ends in discussing this world and its history. The rationalists had no such hesitations. This world was all in all, and now that human reason was emancipated, it ought to find no difficulty in thinking out a true philosophy of nature, life and mankind. What the sciences had done for nature, they hoped that the new Enlightenment would enable them to do for history. It was the age *par excellence* of reason, and even those who professed a form of Christian belief like Hegel, exploited heaven and earth in terms of Mind. God became the Absolute, the unconditioned reality, from whom all proceeded and to whom all returned. Not only was the war-drum to throb no longer and the battle-flag to be furled in the Parliament of Man, the Federation of the World, but man was to come 'on that which is', and catch 'the deep pulsations of the world, Aeolian music measuring out the steps of time, the shocks of chance, the blows of death'. God, as Browning wrote, was to be the 'tame confederate' and lose His mystery. The aim was to make history truly scientific and so to control events that the future would be predictable. The ambition was never fulfilled, but what is perhaps more surprising is that the ration-alist did not realize that with success history would have ceased to be. Human life is what it is because we have a certain responsibility at each moment for ourselves and others. The future is what we will make it no matter what the momentum of the past and present may be. This is what helps to make life worth while and gives an edge to what we are doing each moment of time. That the future should be in part the creative act of man, that it should lie darkly before us waiting to come into shape by means of effort and artistry, this it is that provides scope for ideals and the essential incentive for achieving them. We seldom pause to think what life would be like if we were certain of what is to be and what is to happen to us. Imagine the child watching as it were on a screen his successes and failures at school, perhaps then illness and death or a war in which he will straightway be killed or an unhappy love affair or marriage. Even if we keep to the general picture, and accept the philosophy of determinism and view all as predetermined and carried along by the wheels of destiny, our lot becomes subhuman. The Universe is in such conditions a closed one, and there is no escape by imagination or by heroic striving to what transcends the dusty now and hereafter. It is too late to seek a better world.

Voltaire in his tale *Le Micromegas* tells how a visitor from a star to the planet Saturn comes across some small animals. These animals call themselves men and one of them, a Thomist, informs the visitor that the whole creation was made for man's benefit. The visitor is mightily amused. The convenient scheme of history taught in the classical school and handed on by Christian scholars and humanists fell apart with the discovery of the new continents and of the remote beginnings of man. The Universe seemed to have become quite different and to show the slow ascent of man from an animal condition. This was a good stick with which to beat the over-confident and silly theologians, but it did not prevent the rationalists from preening themselves on the magnitude and perfection of reason. Human progress could take the place of Providence and reason could dispense with mystery. It was no doubt very tempting to bring order into all the new knowledge acquired and to build a new ark into which all the new species could enter and be catalogued. From the time of Voltaire to the present day there have not been wanting philosophers of history, and a succession of failures has only served, as in other sciences, to inspire new hypotheses. So different is this new philosophy of history that it has only an analogy with the work of an Augustine or a Bossuet. It begins with a series of most ambitious theories; then it falls under the aegis of science and works hand in hand with the biological hypothesis of evolution; so close indeed is its connection that it is often impossible to tell whether an evolutionist is writing as a philosopher or strictly as a scientist. Then once more it becomes a separate department of philosophy or history.

The giants of the first phase belong to the period of the German Enlightenment, and the chief characteristic of their work is the speculative boldness. Kant, interested as he was in moral problems, had scrutinized the possibility of a philosophy of history. He was troubled by the apparent lawlessness of history. Its lack of apparent purpose scandalized him. It was his pupil, however, Herder who, ignoring the caution of Kant, embarked on *Ideas for a Philosophical History of Mankind*. A gigantic enterprise of twenty-five books, of which twenty were completed. Herder intended to keep his nose to the earth and with this good intention in mind gives an enormous amount of miscellaneous information about the physical universe and animal life. He belonged, however, to the spirit of his time and a chiefly remarkable for his speculations. There was, he thought, is vital force running throughout creation from inorganic matter to man and the purpose of this force was to liberate the spirit of man and bring him into his kingdom. As all contributed to this great event we have to take notice in history of the various influences, climatic, agricultural and economic, which help or thwart man's development. This idea, when followed out, serves to distinguish civilization from civilization, nation from nation, even as analogously a species of tree or flower will vary according to soil and climate. The development of man is on all fours with that of the tree and flower in that he grows naturally and inevitably; and so it is that in the vast movement of history there is true growth; there is, too, a purpose which can be detected.

A complete humanity lies at the end of the upward movement of the Universe, and this is the explanation and the law of history. Hegel is animated by the same passion as Herder, but instead of a brilliant romanticist, a philosopher of most unusual breadth of vision, speculative power and moral purpose is at work. Whatever we think of the results of his philosophizing no one can deny his genius nor the effect on future historical and philosophical thought. His influence can be traced in Marx and Engels, T. H. Green and Collingwood in England, and Croce and Gentile in Italy. Hegel incorporates into his system all previous and, as he thought, mere fragmentary ideas on the nature of history. He adopts the prevalent idea of human progress with its insistence on liberty; he is the protagonist of mind and yet at the same time would justify the Christian conception of Providence and purpose. Furthermore he tries to avoid the cursory and airy explanations of the old theologians, and this by attending to the facts of history and marshalling them into an order. Critics of Hegel have been too ready to assume that he invented a dialectic and fitted his facts into it in an arbitrary manner. But the mistakes of his predecessors warned him against this and he seems to have had a genuine interest in historical studies. In studying the course of history one cannot but be struck by the rhythm of rise and decline, success and failure of nations and cultures, and also by the prevalence of evil and the way in which it seems to bring to naught the best efforts of the good. But this very impression is bound to give rise to the question how can progress be compatible with such defeats and 'to what final aim these enormous sacrifices have been offered'? He finds the clue in the law which the West has discovered and Christianity consecrated, the law that change is not a barren repetition of life and death. Change goes on never endingly, and the pagan world and Eastern philosophy interpreted this in a static way.

What comes to be dies away and all begins over again without any advance, like the monotonous repetition of a bird's song. Christianity, however, above all saw in death the beginning of a new life. The old is never repeated in identical fashion; life begets death and death life. 'Change, while it imports dissolution, involves at the same time the rise of new life, so that while death is the issue of life, life is also the issue of death.' Now life and death are opposites, though they do not cancel each other out; they constitute the law and rhythm of progress; they are what Hegel calls the dialectic. This dialectic is first and foremost, however, the property of Logic, of the concepts and categories of pure reason. By this Hegel means that knowledge grows by saying something which we see to be true, then recognizing that despite its truth it is not the whole truth and has to be corrected. To take an example which is not so much Hegel's as Christian and scholastic; if I say that God is immutable, the truth of it is óbvious; and yet I have made a very misleading statement if the statement is left by itself. God is alive and loving and full of wisdom, and not an immutable force or unchanging solid. Hence in one sense of the word it would be truer to say that God is not unchanging, not an inert mass. It is only by combining the first idea with the second that we can have the beginning of an adequate idea of what God is like. What is true of predicates of God is true also in its own way of each of our categories. We start with the simplest category 'to be' rather than 'not to be'. An angel takes us by the hair of the head and pointing at the vast universe says: 'Behold what is!' We are duly impressed until the next moment the angel whispers to us: 'It is an unsubstantial pageant, a shadow of what really is, and what looks so permanent is, even as I speak, passing away.' On this basis Hegel proceeds dialectically from the very simplest notion of reality up to the highest Pure Spirit. We are familiar with Marx's application of the dialectic to the class struggle. He omits the movement of ideas which is essential to Hegelian thought. Hegel regarded the real as the rational; that is to say, the object world we meet is potentially spirit. What is opaque at first, just a thing, becomes steadily more and more transparent. Nature is nothing but concealed thought and as science and philosophy bring it into order and implement its meaning it returns to Spirit as the prodigal son returns to his father. The world issued forth from

Mind and returns as Concrete Spirit. History is a part of this great return, and therefore the philosopher of history has to trace the process. He bases himself on evidence and on the records provided by the empirical historian and by reflecting on the fragmentary character of the evidence marks out the various stages of the advance of Spirit. The clue to this development lies in the growing consciousness of freedom and the spread of it in states and in society, for Spirit may be defined as 'that which has its centre in itself'. It has not a unity outside itself, but has already found it; it exists in and with itself. Matter has its essence outside itself. Spirit is self-contained existence. Now this is freedom exactly. It is in this perspective that he views the march of mankind as treated in detail in the history books, the despotic oriental empires, the great blow for freedom in the victory of the Athenians over Persia, the development in the West out of slavery and feudalism to the independence of nations and culminating in the Enlightenment in the splendid liberty of the Germanic peoples.

Hegel's *Philosophy of History* stands like a gigantic pyramid dwarfing all rivals. Colossal as the achievement is it nevertheless manifests just those weaknesses which seem to cling to all attempts to make sense out of history. It takes progress for granted and regulates that progress under the sanction and in the light of an ideal being made concrete. It assumes a notion of freedom which belongs to the idealist philosophy and at the same time makes the stages of the progress so inevitable that it is hard to see where freedom is exercised. It identifies the dialectic with the designs of Providence and sets out to be a defence of God's ways to man, and in doing so it takes the heart out of the Christian religion. There is an ambiguity in the use of the word Spirit such that to this day critics are unsure whether Hegel is not committed to pantheism. Reason is given such honour that in its enlightenment the nature of divine providence is fully revealed, and what is more the Kingdom of God, which to a St. Paul and a St. Augustine is beyond the dreams of man and to be reached in its perfection in an after-life, is identified with the progress of mankind upon earth. These and many other inconveniences can be found in this ambitious system. All such philosophies run the danger either of dogmatizing about what man has done and will do and forcing events into the pattern of their ideas or generalizing too rapidly from the evidence before them. Hegel did not neglect the evidence of the historians of his day, but the trouble is that those historians are now out of date and much of the evidence has been corrected or has changed its significance. Then again if the divine intention is brought down to earth and identified with an actual historical situation there is grave danger lest that state of affairs be made the excuse for what in no sense can be called righteous. Rulers and revolutionaries, can boast that they are the agents of the divine will, and what is becomes what should be. Hegel tries to escape this by arguing that the heroes and villains of history follow their desires and have an inferior kind of freedom which is praiseworthy or culpable, but that Providence works in and through them bringing about what must be. They are the dust raised by the chariot wheels of destiny. This is not an easy position to take up, nor is it made more easy by Hegel's declaration that all the heroisms and sins and, in short, the 'sacrifices that have ever and anon been laid on the altar of the earth are justified for the sake of this ultimate purpose'. This is too close to the ancient doctrine of fatalism to be comfortable, and almost indistinguishable from 'everything for the best in the best of all possible worlds'—only that for the actors it might seem more like the worst. This form of spiritual determinism is worlds apart from the Christian doctrine of freedom and responsibility of choice, and shows that Hegel was swayed more by the ideas of his time, which were coming into fashion, than by the old Christian ideas. Scientific determinism, evolution and Marxian ideas of economic necessity were to dominate the future, and as a professedly Christian philosophy Hegelianism ran with these ideas rather than against them. But where Hegel showed himself most markedly as a child of his age is in his identifying the City of Man with the city of God. Whatever association the Kingdom of God may have with human progress—and this must be examined later—there can be no doubt that one essential of Christianity is its other-worldliness. Human thought can never claim an equality with God's, and the supernatural end of man which is to consist in a union with God himself can never be found in this world, be man never so happy in classless societies or peaceful federations. The degree of self-sufficiency, that is, freedom in Hegel's definition, attainable by man, is very uncertain. Neither experience nor theory is very informative; but whatever height

it reach it remains precarious in this life and can have no relation to that enjoyed by Absolute Spirit. It is, moreover, a dis-
heartening thought that only at some future date will there be a
race of self-sufficient people, the concrete manifestation of
Spirit. The countless millions who have lived and died in the
centuries of slow progression towards this ultimate state are, it
seems, left out. They have not even seen the promised land
from Pisgah. No theory of religion or philosophy which has to
liquidate nine-tenths of the human race for the benefit of a
select few can be called Christian or human.

With Hegel the great idealist and absolute systems came to
an end to be succeeded by the pessimism of Schopenhauer and
Nietzsche and the empiricism of Comte and Marx. The philosopher began to lose caste, and the scientist to take his place.
The desire to make sense of history and life remained, but it
was felt by most that the scientific, and if possible, encyclo-
paedic, genius was more likely to be successful than the abstract
thinker. The Universe was providing more and more surprises.
Hypotheses could not keep up with the rate of physical discoveries. Both the telescope and the magnifying-glass revealed
new worlds; the origins of life and of man were pushed back
thousands of years, and new critical methods were devised for
controlling evidence. This new advance in knowledge made
many of the older generalizations look fustian. On the other
hand so diverse and startling was part of this new information
that it made for confusion, and this confusion was felt to be a
scandal. Some attempt must be made to give sense to the larger
problem of the Universe and to the new vast evidence for races
and peoples and for early man. Comte set the tone in his *Cours
de Philosophie Positive*. He rejects religion and metaphysics and
every kind of *Deus ex machina*. The historian like the scientist
must study the phenomena and give a provisional explanation
which the evidence justifies. There is no denying that we have
grown in knowledge, and this has come about by doing our
best with the evidence we have at the time and discarding the
provisional generalization and law as our knowledge improves.
The secret of advance lies in this acceptance and use of relative
truth. Every age is conditioned and those who live in it cannot
step outside it. The error in the past was to aim at absolute
knowledge and to step outside the positive, though relative,
knowledge gained and to seek false aid from religion or meta-

106

physics. Gradually we purify our knowledge and succeed in grouping more and more of the infinitely varied data under law. The ideal is to have all phenomena explained by one single law. Comte believed that there were three stages in every civilization. In the first the savage attributes unknown causes to spirits and gods; in the second he substitutes an abstract metaphysical principle for the gods, and in the third he forsakes these false scents and turns to nature itself and follows the true path of empirical science.

It will be noticed that he has no doubt of progress, human as well as scientific, and this assumption governs most of the nineteenth-century thought. Marx's Dialectical Materialism is not intended to be a philosophy; it is action, and ideas separated from action are repudiated; all the same there is implicit throughout the dialectic the assumption of a perfection, the classless society gradually coming into being. Other adventures in Philosophy, the Life Force, the Élan Vital, the cumbersome categories of Herbert Spencer are likewise the offshoot of a general belief in progress. Evolution proved a most convenient handbag for every kind of theory. With truth Professor E. H. Carr has written: 'In the nineteenth century, belief became general in a principle of progress, whose laws were exemplified in the events of history; the study of history was the key to an understanding of these laws. The laws of history were thus strictly analogous to the laws of science. After Darwin it was even thought that they were substantially the same laws; Darwin had proved that evolution proceeded through the struggle for existence, the elimination of the unfit and the survival of the fittest. It suddenly became obvious that these forces were also at work in the advance of mankind through history. Progress in history and progress in the natural world were different facets of the same process. As late as 1920 J. B. Bury, in the preface to his book *The Idea of History*, called progress "the animating and controlling idea of western civilization".'

Carr goes on to describe the change which has come about since Bury's confident statement. Theories of progress, he says, have vanished as rapidly as last year's snows. Pessimism has taken its place and writers have dilated on the decline of the West. This was the title of Spengler's celebrated work published in Germany in 1918. Carr mentions also Toynbee and Butterfield amongst the Cassandras. He himself is not interested in these emotional attitudes. He seems to deny any objective truth or value, as he argues that it is a fallacy to appeal to 'historical data' and futile to try to construct some perennial philosophy of history out of them. There is no inherent pattern in the events of history, but the historian must select those which seem to him relevant in the passing situation in which he is, the point, that is, of intersection between the past and the future. By 'relevant' he means relevant to planning for the future. 'The function of the historian is not to reshape or reform the past, but to accept it and to analyse what he finds significant in it, to isolate and illuminate the fundamental changes at work in the society in which we live. . . .' By this means the historian will be able to understand the problems which his own generation has to face and have some kind of guide for the future. Carr, therefore, declines the assistance of philosophy and delimits his task to that of the positivist; he will bury the ancient Caesars without praising them, and as a tribune of the people give good advice on how to conduct future affairs. History is sufficiently like science to allow him to do this, and the main contention of evolution that life is a struggle for existence ánd only the fittest survive will do as a hypothesis in history as well; with the one important exception that science is repetitive whereas history is continuous and never repeats itself. The assumption of evolution is made transparent in his declaration of faith, without, however, the trimmings of optimism or pessimism. Since the turn of the century there may have been a gradual decline in the belief in progress; that does not mean that the laws which govern the changes of life and of species are to be abandoned. Man is subject to them in the same manner as the animal; but whereas in the nineteenth century it was confidently believed that our period was one of advance, now it looks as if we were passing through a phase of decline. This was the verdict of Spengler, and it corresponds with the mood of recent times.

Carr refers to Spengler and Toynbee as representative historicists of the last thirty years. Their works are certainly well known, and Toynbee at least has offered a key to history which all have to consider. But in truth there are at the present moment no schools of thought so large as to have representatives. At most Spengler may be said to represent a recurrent mood of pessimism among German romantics, and Toynbee's work is recognizable as the product of a well-known type of English scholarship. He has been attacked from all quarters. Carr complains, for instance, that he has so defined civilizations —as bundles of phenomena conveniently lumped together—that he has no right to make historical generalizations about them. Furthermore he has swallowed science too completely and made history one long repetition of groups of events. Other critics hold it against Toynbee that he does not define his terms, that the societies of which he writes have no common characteristic, that his method of differentiating these societies is artificial, that what he says comes almost to nothing, or, on the other hand, that he is far too speculative and ambitious.

Most of these criticisms and other possible ones are so well known to Toynbee that he forestalls them in his volumes. Carr, for instance, is surely mistaken in thinking that Toynbee has not carefully explained what he means by 'civilization'. What falls within a civilization can in scientific language be called a bundle of phenomena, but that does not exclude its also having characteristics which historians can recognize. These bundles have their specific properties, specific because they are human events, and treated as such by historical students. By carefully comparing the features which are common to societies, and the relation of societies to larger groupings, Toynbee is able to construct a working theory of the constituents of a civilization, and by working with it to test its truth. As this theory is given in an abridged form in one volume by D. C. Somervell and at the end of the volume there is a still shorter résumé of it, there is no need to do more than mention one or two of its chief characteristics. Toynbee, first of all, from an empirical study of the past distinguishes primitive societies from civilizations and reckons the former to number about 650 and the latter to amount to no more than twenty-one. He then explains his intended method of procedure. He accepts with qualifications the Aristotelian distinction between the techniques of history, science and fiction. The distinctions are not water-tight. History, for instance, is supposed to be the ascertainment and recording of facts, but, as we know, it selects facts, has recourse to fictions and makes use of laws. 'England', 'the Conservative Party', 'public opinion' are fictitious personifications, and popular opinion is right in its insistence that no historian can be 'great' if he is not also a great artist; that the Gibbons and

Macaulays are greater historians than the 'Dryasdusts'. . . . History furthermore is only too ready to take into its service a number of ancillary sciences, such as economics and political science, which formulate general laws. None the less the distinction first made by Aristotle is valid in a general way. Where the data are few all that we can do is to ascertain and record them; where the data are too numerous to tabulate we have to survey them, and formulate some laws; where finally the data are innumerable we have to use the technique of fictions. Now there are innumerable data for the study of personal relations, and therefore that is the province of fiction. But when we come to the study of primitive societies and civilizations we are not concerned with the personal relations between every man, woman and child. We confine ourselves to social relations, and to those social relations which are a constant in every group of human beings. These social relations can be called institutions in so far as they are the means and the mechanism whereby human relations are maintained. The continuance of societies depends upon these institutions, and they can be treated as a special subject of study. As such they do not involve the innumerable data of personal relations. Primitive societies are just large enough to allow us 'to make a beginning with the formulation of laws'; civilizations, on the other hand are so few that most historians are 'discouraged from attempting more than a tabulation of facts'. The intelligible and comparable units of history are indeed few. Nevertheless Toynbee declares his intention to risk the elucidation and formulation of laws and to apply to the field of 'civilization' a scientific technique.

The summary of Toynbee's expressed intention in writing his immense history disposes of a number of the objections raised against him, and makes clear what he is after. His next step is to ask what is the explanation of the genesis and growth of a civilization. This may be called the primary question of a philosophy of history, for we are clearly asking for the clue to history, to the story of successive peoples and nations and civilizations and to what has been assumed to be the progress of humanity from a primitive state to the present day. Toynbee first of all discusses hypotheses, that of race and that of environment, and he argues that neither is satisfactory. He begins his own answer with a recourse to myth and gives a very good reason for doing so. Ruskin warned his readers against the pathetic fallacy, that is to say, reading our own emotions into the inanimate world. Toynbee suggests that historians and philosophers should avoid the opposite tendency, the apathetic fallacy; that is to say, we can overdo the application to human beings of methods which are suitable to the non-human. In other words if we are to find an explanation of human events, we are more likely to find it in one or more human characterists than in physical or biological ways of behaviour. Myths are said to speak the language of the heart and the hidden mind. Now in the myths of many different peoples there is a common and recurring theme, an encounter between two superhuman personalities, often between what is good and what is evil, and the consequences of this encounter are a change from peace to strife, happiness to suffering, a new strength and glory, and in all cases the victory of the good. Toynbee analyses the complications in these myths and has perhaps some dubious comments on the theology contained in them. The lesson, however, contained in them for history is sufficiently simple and important, and it is this, that life is a continual challenge to man, and, especially at certain junctures, man's responses spell advance or decay. Life is a tension, what von Hügel called 'friction', and 'in the productions of civilizations, the same race or the same environment appears to be fruitful in one instance and sterile in another'. This refutes in itself the attempted explanation by those factors, and it also leaves the free will of man as the determining and at the same time the uncertain factor. Never can we with absolute certainty predict what will happen, for there is always the unknown quantity, the 'reaction of the actors to the ordeal when it comes'. At the end of the Abridgement, Toynbee sums up the results of his application of this hypothesis of his. He says that we can hear the beat of an elemental rhythm 'whose variations we have learnt to know as challenge and response, withdrawal and return, rout and rally, apparentation and affiliation, schism and palingenesis'. This rhythm is not to be regarded as an indefinite repetition nor as a cycle or a treadmill. It is not the wheel of Ixion, for the two notes do not make a discord but a harmony.

This statement of Toynbee shows that the criticism of Carr lacks foundation; it differentiates his view, also, from that of the old pagan idea of the wheel of fate, from that of Nietzsche and Spengler, and it introduces us to the neglected idea of providence. So disastrous have been the last thirty years that, as already shown, the belief in progress has been profoundly shaken. Toynbee asks the question, whither are we going? and is there a 'living garment that the Earth Spirit weaves? The past is strewn with failures, with a deposit of universal states and universal church and barbarian war-bands'. Are they mere waste products, or will these debris prove, if we pick them up, to be fresh masterpieces of the weaver's art which he has woven, by an unnoticed sleight of hand, on some more ethereal instrument than the roaring loom that has been apparently occupying all his attention? Toynbee answers that these debris are both an end and a beginning, or at any rate they do relate one civilization with another. We are too inclined to take the units of civilization separately and forget their continuity. But having said this Toynbee lapses for the time into silence, leaving the tremendous question unanswered. In relating one civilization with another Toynbee separates himself off sharply from Spengler, and moreover he gives an explanation which is human and not drawn from the example of organic growth. Spengler had in mind the processes of plant life; Toynbee argues, as he thinks from historical evidence, that the successful response to a challenge is made by one or a few. (His appeal here is rather to the history of a race or nation than to a civilization.) An internal energy is generated by the successful response, and the minority, who are responsible for it, have their way for a time. The multitude, which is not fully conscious of what is happening, follows this minority and obeys them. But since this mime is preconscious more than conscious, the relations between the two give rise in time to new troubles, and these may lead to disintegration. In the end various possibilities lie open. One is a new form of tyranny; others are a master state or the rule of the proletariat. One other alternative, however, comes more and more to the fore, and it is one which is in accord with what is highest in human nature. This is the Universal Church. It alone seems to be the ultimately successful response to the problem of civilization and the world. It alone is forward-looking and independent of those forces which make for decay. To refuse this answer is to stay in the past and invite rout and collapse.

The immediate and obvious merits of Toynbee's theory are that he seeks an answer to the meaning of history in what is peculiarly human. That we live by meeting challenges and advance or deteriorate according to the quality of our response is, if we think of it, a platitude, which is so obvious as to miss recognition. It corresponds on the human level with the struggle for existence in nature, and is, therefore, a universal truth. By drawing this truth out of the ancient mythologies Toynbee wiped the dust off it and gave it a new look. Being an answer in human terms it has, too, the merit of allowing both for a degree of determinism, the constant in human nature, and also for a degree of free choice, which makes prediction good guess work. For his evidence, also, Toynbee scours all the quarters of the universe, and so avoids the charge made against many of the old historians of being at best European in their outlook. In such a vast field he claims to be an empirical investigator and to draw his conclusions out of the evidence. It is here that the historians cry out in indignation. They contend against him that his divisions of civilizations are arbitrary, both in number and in their composition and that out of the vast material before him he selects what will suit as evidence for his purpose. Not only does he choose incidents which favour his view, but in the incident itself he pays no attention to what would modify or correct his interpretation. To quote again the example of the Norman Conquest, there is no simple right response to a challenge. For all we know William may have tricked Harold into a promise, and he owed his success to a variety of factors, such as the attack of the Norwegian King, the treachery of Earl Tostig, the wind in the Channel being favourable at the right time, the rushed preparations of Harold, all these and others in addition to the vigour of William and his ability to follow up his victory. If in such a miniature scene of history there are so many factors, what a multitude must be taken into account in the vast canvas of a civilization! Toynbee, let it be said, is fully conscious of the variety and uncertainty of human responses in crises, and he examines which should prevail as well as those which are likely to prevail in the long run. For this he has been called by some a pessimist, though it would appear that he is really an optimist. His argument is supposed to proceed empirically and with a minimum of value judgments, but as it develops it becomes more gnomic and epical; pride moves to a fall, and the importance of the saints grows larger. The Creative Minority, who promise true pro-

gress, are inspired by religion, and even amongst them pre-
ferences become noticeable. 'The stone which Zeno and
Gautama have so obstinately rejected has become the head of
the corner of the temple of the New Testament'; and in a
passage at the end of the chapter on 'disintegrating societies
and individuals' he writes: 'When we set out on this quest we
found ourselves moving in the midst of a mighty host, but, as
we have pressed forward, the marchers, company by company,
have fallen out of the race. The first to fall were the swordsmen,
the next the archaeists and the futurists, the next the philosophers, until only the gods were left in the running. At the
final ordeal of death, few, even of these would-be saviour gods,
have dared to put their title to the test by plunging into the icy
river. And now, as we stand and gaze with our eyes fixed upon
the farther shore, a single figure rises from the flood and straightway fills the whole horizon. There is the Saviour; "and the
pleasure of the Lord shall prosper in his hand; he shall see
of the travail of his soul and shall be satisfied."'

From such statements it seemed evident that Toynbee's
answer to the question of the meaning of history would lie in
religion, and in particular in the Christian religion. The first six
volumes pointed in that direction. The last four volumes were
published in 1954 after a delay of fifteen years, and they do not
fulfil the expectation. No one could quarrel with Toynbee for
modifying his views during such catastrophic years, but it is
regrettable that there should be a break in the very form of his
thinking. The first volumes claimed to be the work of an historian
using empirical methods and drawing philosophical conclusions
out of them. Even his gentlest critics fail to recognize the same
genre of writing in these last volumes.[1] He has adopted part of the
Jung psychology, and whereas before the challenges in history
were substantiated by reference to historical events, they are
now made to depend upon a struggle between unconscious and
conscious forces. The subconscious forces are seen in a monotonous uniformity, and the conscious forces express themselves in
freedom. What interests Toynbee is the meeting of God and
man in history, God challenging man in order to bring him to
Himself in a universal and spiritual kingdom, and man's varying
responses. Civilizations, therefore, are now of a different worth

[1] V. 'Toynbee's Vision of History', by Albert Hourani in the *Dublin
Review*, No. 470, 1955.

according as they bring man nearer to a true religion. Christianity is no longer the exemplar and sovereign religion, as was hinted at the end of the first volumes; it shares priority with Islam, Hinduism and Mahayana Buddhism. The tone of the writing is that of a prophet rather than that of an historian, and Toynbee makes claims for a gift of mystical intuition into the past. Six times, he tells us, a vision has been vouchsafed to him which set him in communion, not with some particular person or events of the past, but 'with all that has been and was and was to come'.

In any estimate of the worth of Toynbee's contribution to a philosophy of history it is more fruitful, then, to concentrate on the methods and the views expressed in the first six volumes. There is an additional reason for doing this because of an essay he published in a series of Studies by Members of the Anglican Communion, called *Christian Faith and Communist Faith*. This book was published in 1953, so that the essay is contemporary with or possibly subsequent to the last volumes of *A Study of History*. In this essay he distinguishes within the higher religions and philosophies two groups, the mythical and the historical. Both have played their part in history, but of the mythical group only one has survived, the Mahayana. The others, dependent as they were on man's attitude to physical nature before the rise of science, have faded away with the knowledge of nature acquired by science. Six of the ten in the historical group are still alive today. The reason why the Mahayana religion has survived, he suggests, is that it is concerned with the problems of the spiritual side of man, which science has not touched, and 'another reason why the Mahayana is still a great spiritual force in the world today is that the path along which it has diverged from the older Hinayanian Buddhist philosophy points in a Christian direction'.

Among the historical religions Christianity has the mark along with Judaism and Islam, of seeing existence in terms of the encounters between a personal God and human beings, and these encounters 'take the form of historical acts and events in this world'. Christianity, however, by its attitude to suffering and in its central belief, Christ's incarnation and crucifixion, can claim to be 'the historical religion *par excellence* (however vigorously Confucianism may dispute this claim)'.

From this central belief Toynbee argues that the value of this world is guaranteed—'the tragedy of human life on Earth has a value for the human actors in it. . . .' Secondly, not only has history a meaning but a 'direction and a purpose'. Thirdly, Christ's passion 'assures us that this tragedy (of life upon-earth) is neither the meaningless and pointless evil that it has been declared to be by the Buddha and Epicurus, nor the inexorable punishment for inveterate sin', as taught by certain 'schools of Judaic theology'. Now that the field of history has been extended by thousands of years we can see that the early religions made their appearance and provided an answer to 'the harrowing experience of living through the breakdown and disintegration of a mundane civilization'. These occasions provided the opportunities for men to grow in an appreciation of the spiritual world. Mankind has had to grow in time and by degrees in religion and morals, and the successive failures, with their accompanying suffering, have been the means of making an advance in the form of the response to a challenge. Sometimes the response has, however, been 'Dead Sea fruit', in the shape of a philosophy which taught a total abnegation of life, but usually it has been a kind of preparation for a Kingdom of God that is to come on Earth as well as in Heaven. In the light of this Christianity ceases to appear the chance episode and tiny event in the vast panorama of the years, and as science now promises a future of indefinite duration the late coming of Christianity will appear less of a mystery as the Kingdom of God continues to offer a fulfilment of time and time's offshoots.

These views seem to flow from the earlier volumes of *A Study of History* and make its themes clear and consecutive. It has echoes of Vico in the part he gives to providence, but whereas Vico uses the idea of original Sin to explain the falls after each successive rise in civilization, Toynbee uses the formula of challenge and response, and brings to bear an immense body of evidence picked from the stores of universal history. Vico wished his work to be treated as a science, a science comparable with that of the fashionable physical sciences, but more within the compass of the human mind precisely because history is, unlike nature, a human achievement. Toynbee, also, claims that his work is properly scientific. Nevertheless in his last volume, where he permits himself to be autobiographic, he tells us that he was inspired to write his history by the feelings he experienced one long summer's day as he sat 'musing on the summit of the citadel of Mistra', near Sparta in the Peloponnese. He felt 'the cruel riddle of Mankind's crimes and follies', and had 'a horrifying sense of the sin manifest in the conduct of human affairs'. His fellow-historians and others dislike the use of the capital in 'Mankind', and pounce upon such a word as 'sin' as out of place in a work of history and as revealing a religious or romantic intention behind the composition of his work. This criticism rests on the sober belief that the historian must not try to be a poet and moralist and religious advocate as well. The different roles are bound to clash. In the one he ought to look coldly and judicially at the past and from its data make generalizations which may or may not serve to define laws of progress, if we mean by progress an indefinite movement in the future along the same lines as the past. This is a world of cause and effect and of an horizontal advance; and there is no room for higher purposes or ideals which do not belong to the horizontal plane.

Now the positivist historian cannot ignore the motives of men and women nor the part which saints, like St. Leo the Great or St. Bernard, or religious faith have played in determining the course of events. But it is one thing to allow for such determinants, it is another to seek for an answer to historical questions in terms of religion or the supernatural. Much that happens in the spiritual order is nebulous and may be spurious, and it cannot be dealt with by the accepted criteria of an empirical scientist. Hence one school of historians would banish moral judgements from history, and many more fight shy of the mystical element. Toynbee, on the other hand, tries to justify his transition from science to morals and religion by arguing that a given series of successful responses to challenges indicates growth. In growth the action 'tends to shift from the field of external environment, physical or human, to the *for intérieur* of the growing personality or civilization. In so far as this grows and continues to grow, it has to reckon less and less with challenges delivered by external forces and demanding response on an outer battlefield, and more and more with challenges that are presented by itself to itself in an inner arena'. In the higher stages, therefore, at least, the moral and the spiritual cannot be disregarded by even the most polemical scientific historian. His critics, however, point to the errors and weaknesses which follow such a method of writing history. The gravamen of their charge is, I think, not so much the views he dares to express as his pretension to be writing as an empirical historian. The latter has his techniques and limited field of operations, but that does not preclude another way of writing about history which would embrace a larger field and have other aims. The philosopher of history may be permitted to break away from the prescriptions of the historians and to look to dialectical materialism or evolution or religion or even a specific religion for help. The positivist methods of the historians have led to a reaction within recent times comparable to the protests of the existentialist philosophers against rationalism. As Kierkegaard turned his back upon the excessive systematization of a Hegel, so later on a reaction began against what Péguy called the 'secular, atheist, positivist, democratic, political, parliamentarian world of modern science' and the 'importation of the modern scientific method *en bloc* into the realm of history and humanity'. Péguy, like many others, felt that the individual was being suffocated by scientific planning and programmes. His personal tragedy was buried under technical apparatus and files of statistics. As Mr. Alick Dru puts it: 'What Kierkegaard called the principle of association, and what Péguy called *la politique*, get command and swallow up every other principle and every other order' and lead to 'the annihilation of that which was to benefit from the programme—the individual. The system of levelling produces equality, but the equality it produces is an abstraction (like all that the intellectuals produce). The problem is not to produce "equality", as though it were a boot, but to produce the individual, to produce the thing which always is equal; and the touchstone is the hero and the saint, the criterion of individuality, and of equality.' The same discontent and reaction against the wholesale method of treating individuals and the binding together of lives into stooks for the harvest can be found in writers of very different temperament and outlook. In his essays R. L. Stevenson cried out against the teaching of his time: 'In the joy of the actors lies the sense of any action. In (so many) books we miss the personal poetry, the enchanted atmosphere, that rainbow work of fancy that clothes what is naked and seems to ennoble what is base; . . . for no man lives among salts and acids, but in the phantasmagoric chamber of his brain with the painted windows and the storied walls!' So antipathetic is G. M. Trevelyan to much contemporary historic writing that he has protested that 'the appeal of history to us all is in the last resort poetic. . . . It is the fact about the past that is poetic; just because it really happened, it gathers round it all the inscrutable mystery of life and death and time.' The inscrutable mystery of man which escaped all indexing was also the theme of the Russians Solovieff and Berdiaeff and the German Theodor Haecker. Haecker felt that history as it is ordinarily understood only skirted round the central and mysterious figure, man himself. 'The person is the supreme being, the supreme good in this created world, but at the same time a hidden being. No wonder that the real history, in which the ultimate meaning of all history is implied—the history of persons—is such a hidden history.' These are not lone voices crying in the wilderness; they are the spokesmen of a widely felt dismay at the encroachment of the machine into what is human.

The theologians, too, have not been silently acquiescent. Haecker, who was theologically minded, tore up the smooth lines of history when he wrote that 'the history of the Salvation of persons is indifferent to all that we call culture, civilization or barbarism of men. No doubt man is designed to possess culture and civilization; this belongs to his progressive character, without which he could not be man at all. But his history must have had its beginning, and man at the beginning of his history is just as much man as at the end.' So far does he take this thought that he declares that the final order of history as the history of Salvation excels as perfectly sovereign and absolute every other order of history. He then adds that this truth does not take all meaning out of the growth of man in civilization, for the reason that the history of civilizations and the history of man as a person and of his Salvation are interrelated. By this strong affirmation Haecker brings us back to the problem mentioned already, one which shadows all attempts to write a philosophy of history. It is this in short; man is himself at every stage of history; he does not wait on the last scene to reach his fulfilment, and therefore any theory of history, such as the Marxist, which makes the lives of successive generations but steps to an ultimate achievement of life, must be fatally wrong. Human beings cannot be the mere means to produce a perfect society in the future; they are ends, not means, and each human being in the long history of humanity has his acceptable time and is the heir of all the ages. But if each man is a miniature cosmos how can this fact be inserted into the moving stream of history, as it is usually understood? Haecker tells us that there is a connection, but he does not explain how each man with his head in the clouds and his eyes peering through to the heavens can be at the same time the map reader moving steadily onward to an earthly city. Once again we are confronted with the vexing question of the relation of the spiritual to the temporal, the city of God to the city of man. During the nineteenth century this problem passed out of sight. So bright seemed the prospect before men that it dazzled their eyes. Even many professed Christians hitched their wagons to this new star which the Magi had never seen. A form of Christianity called liberal brought theology down to earth, its most conspicuous tenet was a belief in reason and in man. But the new covenant did not last long, and within the last thirty years a violent reaction has set in. This reaction is indelibly associated with the name of Karl Barth in theology. He, however, is only one among many who have called men back to the pure gospel of faith. They have an apocalyptic tone and their shibboleth is the word, eschatological. Between human history and the saving word of God there is an abyss which cannot be crossed. Whatever value may belong to civilization, to art, science and philosophy, it has nothing to do with the kingdom of God. Religion must regain its autonomy and make its sovereign demands, and forswear all covenants with secular history.

This then is the present position. In the light of it Toynbee's early work seems to belong to neither camp. He has used all the devices of scientific industry to make sense of history. To that extent he belongs to the secular historians. But he does not rest satisfied with a positivist account of the past. He takes a principle which is derived from the evolutionary hypothesis, the struggle for existence and the survival of the fittest, and converts it into human terms, challenge and response. This means that human life too is a struggle and that those who meet the challenge will survive. There is not much difference so far between the animal kingdom and man. But as Toynbee's book goes on the principle grows more and more peculiar to man until at length it becomes applicable to the conduct of a saint and hero and in only a limited sense to the conqueror and politician. In the end, therefore, Toynbee is approaching the camp of the new theologians. The Barthian, however, and the Eschatologist will have nothing to do with him. Nevertheless let us not despise the principle of which he has made so much use. It is a possible instrument for opening the casket of history, and it does provide a link between the positivist and the moral and spiritual approaches.

Chapter IV

THE NEW SCIENCE OF VICO

As we have seen Bossuet took the accepted views of his time about Providence, and wrote about it for the instruction of the Dauphin. He was a survivor of the medieval attitude to history. The past illustrated the works of God, and past men and women were looked upon and judged by the moral and cultural standards of the time of the writer. History, like the moral law, was static. By the modern historian the past is seen in terms of change and growth. The man, who carried on the religious traditions of the Middle Ages, and also wrote the title-page of modern history and historicism, is Gianbattista Vico (1668–1744). The name he gave to his great work declares this: *Teleologia Civile Ragionata della Provedenza Divina*, or, in short, *Scienza Nuova*. He meant to give a new view of history, new philosophically or theologically, and new in its empirical methods. He spent twenty-five years working upon it, and then another twenty exhausting years revising it in new editions. The work, unfortunately for him, fell on rocky soil, for it was a time when theories of knowledge and theories of science were all the vogue. His criticism of these current views were disdained, and his originality was taken for *naïveté*. The literati of the time were too much under the sway of Cartesian ideas, and to be thought up-to-date the study of the methods of the physical sciences was prescribed reading. The eighteenth century, too, was a political age. The leading governments and courts of Europe had learnt their lesson from Machiavelli; they were not interested in Providence. Vico was out of tune both with Bossuet, who had written his *Discours* in 1681, and died in 1701, when Vico was a student, and with the worldly humanism, which was current. Its politics were shallow, and he must have felt that he had given in his book the answer to the problems of his time. He contended that the past showed a constant disregard of justice, and, nevertheless, the world had advanced in humanitá because the pressure of Providence in and through the very desires and actions of man himself had corrected the abuses of justice. Again, thinkers should turn their attention to the work of man himself instead of tiring the eyes of the mind with far-off metaphysics, playing with the idea of an eternal law set up in the sky for all men to see, or experimenting with nature to discover its truth. In the *Scienza Nuova* Vico had maintained that nature was made by God, and not by man, and, therefore, its truth must escape his powers; whereas politics and the arts and law, history in short, were made by man, and as such they fell within his comprehension. Cold truth may be found in mathematics and metaphysics, but in the growth of societies man, living by the light of authoritative law amid his own works, has certainty, the 'certum'; and this 'certum', as civilization develops and external authority passes into a law of reason, can become in time 'verum'; knowledge, based on fact and authority, leads on to knowledge of the causes of the belief.

What gave Vico the clue to this New Science was probably a light which came to him in his study of law. In the classical tradition, which was taught in his day, natural law was considered to be a fixed, unchanging norm, which served as an exemplar and directed from on high the framing of the civil law. Vico became convinced that such a conception was due to a false Platonic influence, and that it was more correct to think of the eternal law as the vitalizing principle, which brings in time, in and through human institutions, a better understanding of moral law. Before the age of Reason, so Vico thinks, barbarian man swung from one side of a precipice to another. (He had no romantic illusions about primitive man.) What he calls *la barberie dei sensi* expressed itself in intemperate savagery, dark hates and polytheistic cults. It was countered and then paralleled by *la barbarie della riflessione*, a melancholy and decadent gloom, which is a foretaste of the more refined scepticism that goes with disbelief in man. Both forms bar the way to true life, and, therefore, there must have been an innate tendency to civil progress, helped by the good and conditioned by external necessity, which lead man into the age of reason and universal law.

Vico was proud of the fact that his 'science' was based on a right method and grew out of historical fact. His predecessors, so he held, had applied a standard to law and art and civilizations which was external to history itself. This standard was either the Supernatural or the moral law or reason. Using his knowledge of law and philology he gathered the evidence for his theory from language, literature, custom, law and religion, and depicted history as the long story of how man becomes human in the high sense of the word. He distinguishes three stages; in terms of literature, the periods of the god, the heroes and men; in terms of man's faculties, the periods of sense, imagination and reason; in terms of law, chaos and custom, external authority and rational obedience. The changes come about, partly through the free will of man, and partly through the force of choices and circumstances outside man's will. 'Humanity is man's own work, with tragic overtones of failure. In the interplay of human events is the eternal idea. Man wends his way, weaving the loom of Providence.' We pass from the obscure times to the fabulous and the historical; the cave dwellers live in primitive misery, and the strong lord it over the weak. Heroes, however, arise and rescue the situation, and they in turn make others serve them as serfs. From the beginning, however, the ideal is stirring, in rituals and in burial services, in phantoms of the gods. Necessity, too, plays its part, because man and woman make up a family, and inevitably from family life and from the groupings of families laws are made. As he pondered over the growth of law and language and read history Vico felt that he had in his hands the principles of man's development.

There could, in other words, be a science of history. Such a science would have to be as empirical as the physical sciences, but at the same time its scope would reach far beyond that of the science of nature. As already stated, a science of nature explored ground the laws of which had been made not by man but by God. History on the other hand was man's own work; the action of the individual writ large. But just because it was the story of man it involved not only ethics and politics and the kindred arts but also theology. Vico was a heart-and-soul theist; he believed that he could prove the existence of God, the Maker of the world and of himself. He was also a professed Christian and believed in Original Sin and in the Redemption of man. From introspection he held that man was aware of the law of conscience, which directed him to what was higher, ever pressing him on towards perfection. The danger of introducing these theological ideas into his science of history was that it would cease to be an empirical science. The solution to this difficulty lay along the path marked out by his discovery of the immanence of the 'natural law'. He need not rely on an abstract metaphysic or on a pure theology. He had not to seek the *verum* but the *certum*; he could avoid the abstract by keeping always in touch with man in action, that is to say, with man as 'engaged' in thinking morally and socially. The theology had not to be first theoretical and then applied; it could be found in the movement of society as much as in the movement of conscience and personal desire.

In so formulating his ground plan Vico thought that Plato was a better guide than Aristotle. 'The metaphysic of Aristotle leads to a physical principle which is the matter from which particular forms are educed; God then becomes a potter who moulds things outside Himself. But the metaphysic of Plato leads to a metaphysical principle—the Eternal Idea—which educes from itself, i.e., creates matter itself to be a sort of seminal spirit which itself produces the "ovum". In conformity with his metaphysic, he bases an ethic upon one virtue or one justice, which serves as an architectonic idea. As a consequence of this, too, he is able to plan out an ideal republic . . . though through ignorance of the first fall, he is unable to achieve it.' This interpretation of Plato permits him to bring together the doctrines of Christian theology and the positivist methods of science in the new science which he describes summarily as follows: 'Hence this science can, at the same time, give an account of an Ideal Eternal type of History, in accordance with which can be traced in time the histories of each nation in its ascending, its maturity, its decline and fall. We would even go so far as to claim that he who practises this science, expresses, in himself, this eternal ideal history to this extent: that, since this world, with its peoples, is certainly made up of men, and since, therefore, its various modes must be found within the modifications of our own human minds, he finds therein the proof of the "what had to be, what has to be, what will have to be", if he himself makes the search, because there can be no more certain history than the narration of him who performs the deeds. The procedure of this science then is exactly like Geometry, which, whilst it is more than the elements it includes or contemplates, itself precisely constitutes the world they make up in figure and size with so much the greater reality as laws have over the other affairs of man—which have neither points, lines, surfaces or figures. And this is the argument such proofs provide of a divine form, which ought, gentle reader, to give you a divine pleasure; because in God at His good will, knowledge and creation are one and the same thing.

'Hence, in our life of letters, we give expression to a certain demonstration by a metaphysical proof of which we have continual experience in the operations of our own souls: the demonstration proves, at one stroke, four great truths:

(1) That an Eternal Idea is the principle of all things mortal.
(2) That God is the free principle of all that is produced *ad extra*.
(3) That the world has been created in time.
(4) That there is a Divine Providence, which by Its will, keeps all created things in existence.

'Universally, in the "what had to be, what has to be, what will have to be" there is an archetypal and quasi-creative mode which can not be found except in the eternal ideas of God; because the "what had to be" is valid only in terms of "what was made", the "what has to be", in terms of "what is made", the "what will have to be", in terms of "what shall be made". Just so, in a certain sense, the human mind allied to this science continues to produce from itself this world of civilizations, even as the Mind of God is responsible for the production of the world of nature—He, the High Maker who, in His Principle, His Word, His Eternal Idea, utters, in time, the *Fiat et facta sunt*. In like manner, this science with that "value" stressed by Aristotle, comes into being *de aeternis et immutabilibus*.'

In this summary Vico compares and contrasts the science of nature and the science of history. In both an 'eternal idea' is at work, but in nature it is God who is the author and the scientist comes upon the traces of nature's laws. In history, on the other hand, the eternal law is written in the heart of man, and it is in the process of time and by his own action that the law is fulfilled. Time is a necessary function, and man's own shortcomings are the tell-tale. As the primitive steam engine or the first crude motor-car dictate the very lines of further improvement, so that perfection slowly emerges, so in the history of man his civil life marks the stages of his development, the working out of the law of his perfection. By studying the past we see the ideal eternal history in what 'had, has and will have to be'. In our own selves we see how we are composed of sense and imagination and will and intellect; these make up the whole man and they represent stages in our completeness in so far as we pass from sense to the world of imagination up to that of self-reflection and understanding. There in the reason conscience imposes what 'ought to be' on our attention and whips us forward on that chase of perfection which gains in impetus after every stop. In Vico's eyes the inner movement of the self corresponds with man's advance in civilization. The past has an utterly different meaning to us from any discovery in nature of a chemical element. The ancient parchment or code or treaty is as familiar to us as our own thought and action, for they are all of one piece. They express us and are our work. The marks on the papyrus or on the stone are as nothing until we read into the marks and scratches a meaning. They are the marks of man on the move and working away at the city of man. 'Dear city of Cecrops, or shall I not say, dear city of Zeus!'

In accordance with his principles, Vico tries to examine the past as a positivist scientist should. He uses the name 'philology' to cover the study of man in the context he requires; that is to say, man as he appears in history from his earliest beginnings. It is by interpreting his remains, especially his arts and writings and codes, that we learn about him, and that is why Vico finds 'philology' an appropriate description. Family and social life, customs and laws and treaties, myths and traditions and writings, all fall under it. In his day the learned still thought of the ancient world in terms of Greece and Rome and Jewry, and as a consequence the range of Vico's inquiry is very restricted. But within that scope, with the limited knowledge of those peoples at his disposal, he is both a dispassionate and original observer. He looks to find at first an unreflective barbarism, when the senses and the feelings and passions are unrestrained. Then he expects to see the uprush of imagination in myth and poetry and the vigour of memory. Only later will reflection set in and reason take charge. Like some modern scholars, therefore, he lays emphasis on myth as the ground of what later will manifest itself in laws and systems of ideas. Later criticism will not so much undo the past as release what was there already, and poetry and the work of the imagination are to be regarded as both a phase in development and a lasting expression of the spirit of man.

But still more remarkable, perhaps, is the way in which he works the facts in with his view of the eternal law, with its ebb and flow, inundating human life and bringing with its advance civilization and culture. It is as if there were a greater force within man than he was aware of which profits by his very errors and vices to enlarge and unify the human 'city'. Vico describes the first condition of man as the Age of the Gods. There is mass movement, tribal activity, and fear and wonder, mixed superstition and religion. Man belongs to his environment, and is so immersed in it as to act like a sleep-walker. If all were as we should desire the romantic picture of the simple savage, with his sensitive contacts with nature and reverence for God, might be realized, but in truth he is more like to the beasts. Here Vico introduces his Christian belief, which he considers justified by the facts. Owing to sin primitive man lives in fear and superstition and is devil-ridden. The omnipresent sky-God dissolves into a host of terrifying presences and demons. But the very fears, worthy and un-worthy, produce a result beyond that foreseen by the primitive, a result, however, in accordance with the dynamic law of man's being. Fear drove man to seek his good outside himself by union with others, and so it came about that family ties were strengthened and the sense of community was developed. Similarly out of the selfish and savage insolence of the primitive heroes came genuine heroism. The shallow imagery which produced the large-sized bully passed into the valorous and loyal chief, the protector of the clan and of women. The myth which had been at first so crude and blood-stained grew in shape and beauty so as to be an inspiration as well as a reminder of moral ideals. Vico has the wisdom to see that though myths no longer rule men's minds they still can be healthily active, and as Jung would confirm, continue to influence conduct. So important is this point in Vico's view that he has a special name for the proper function of these past 'moments' or crises. He calls them 'ricorsi', 'recurrences', and he insists that for true progress past traditions must not be thrown away. Neither must they be held on to with obscurantist tenacity. To live in the past is to stifle life; to let it run on into the present and be regenerated and increased by the present is the law of progress. In this way he would correct the false romanticism which bids us return to the simple life or the heroism of our ancestors, and at the same time check the inordinate desire for novelty and revolution. In his mind the France he knew was heading for disaster. The French were like the Greeks, and the University of Paris had forgotten its great inheritance, neglecting the ideal course of European history which was shaping towards a world state of justice and peace. When we realize that Newman's *Idea of Development* and the evolutionary theory were not to come for a hundred years the discernment of Vico becomes the more striking.

In demanding the 'recurrence' of the past in the present Vico has always his main object in mind, namely, the historical process which turns out to be the development of civil society and the unfolding of the eternal law in time. In the case of the Age of the Heroes he argues that the age of Reason which succeeded it would become inhuman and sceptical if it were not supported by the generous and loyal traits of the heroes. Regress is possible at any moment instead of progress, and sin is always an obstacle. Nevertheless, however delayed, progress goes on and often by means of the difficulties and checks. Just as the elements of matter inevitably stabilize themselves in bodily forms, so do the forces in human nature tend inevitably, though freely, to bring about a stable form of society. Individuals cannot help but rely more constantly on the ties of family, and groups of families are brought together in common defence and to insure a food supply. By this means families develop into the tribe, and at first a few will dominate in the tribe, treating the rest as a subject population. Then in time patrician and plebs will fight for mastery, and justice will become more widespread, and out of the civil strife the nation will grow. So the process will continue. A nation is a larger civilized unity than the family or tribe, and it brings many benefits to its members, protection against outside foes, the advantage of a common law and the recognition of similar rights; but it takes time for justice to be evenly spread, with full enfranchisement, equality of opportunity, and the extension of justice to other peoples, especially subjugated ones. From the nation emerges the ideal of a federation of nations and of universal peace.

Vico succeeds admirably in showing how justice does not spring full grown from the head of man, but has to wait on time. This is the tide in the affairs of man, and Vico uses it to prove his thesis that the eternal law implanted in the heart of man carries him to the recognition of it despite all the warring circumstances. The lawyer in him noticed how law gradually takes shape, how what begins in force, as Leonardo said, ends in liberty. Naked power is most visible at the beginning, but without the presence of some justice, felt more than understood, chaos would have ensued. Instead, the power assumes a rudimentary justice and reserves it for the few. The few become gradually the many, and so the constitutions of cities are formed as well as institutes of law and terms of treaties with neighbours. On the horizon is the *jus gentium*. Now this could not happen, so Vico maintains, were there not active the philosophical and theological principles he has assumed. The history of man, that is, is not explicable without the science which he has created. History becomes intelligible, the law and form of progress are defined, and we understand the past because human beings like ourselves with the same primitive and rational urges created it.

Vico is careful to point out that the development of the nations and of justice is not the product of deliberation. Despite themselves men are forced to take certain measures which work out far differently than was at first expected. Often the intentions of legislators and rulers are quite opposed to progress, and it takes time for the results to make themselves felt. In the whirligig time brings its revenges and an unsuspected increment; and it is here that Vico inserts the part of Providence. He knows that if he is to keep up the standard of an empirical historian, keeping to his subject matter, and drawing his conclusions out of that alone, he must avoid at all costs a theory of Providence which seems like a *deus ex machina*. That there may be an express divine intervention is to the Christian proved by the history of the Jews. But that must be treated as an exceptional case. The universal history, with which Vico is concerned, must be dealt with as strictly as any other empirical science, and it is his contention that the work of Providence is immanent in the chequered career of man. He has shown that there is real development, that the eternal law emerges in the slow rectification of injustice and the growing possibilities of a universal society given over to the ways of peace and concord. But it is manifest that this process is continually being thwarted by the evil dispositions of human beings, that selfishness is always undoing the gesture of good will, that families and nations destroy themselves by their greed and indulgence. The evil that men do does live after them, and the dread realm of chaos is always close at hand. That there is no linear development is obvious, but that the momentum of good should succeed, and go on succeeding, is the subject for wonder. It is clear that there is a rectificatory influence, which makes what is crooked smooth and levels down the obstacles set up. Like iron filings the various disparate movements of man come together and form a human association which embodies the ideal in humble fashion. The injustice remains, and the evil goes on, but it seems powerless to stop the upward trend. How, asks Vico, can primitive life, which is to all appearances so irrational, nevertheless grow into the rational, and the wild, disconnected outbursts of primitive man set a mark of universality and seeming immortality on their own works? Since, as has been laid down, man must be considered a political animal even more than a rational one, and since politics is man's own affair, his own creation, there must be a force transcending his own instinctive and conscious acts which keeps his movements in accordance with a plan.

In his view that developments in civilization are seldom, if ever, deliberate, Vico anticipated Marx's view of the dialectic in history, which is outside man's free choices. But we can see in most of the leading writers of the *Aufklärung* and the early nineteenth century, the reflections of Vico's ideas, even though, strange to say, there is no evidence that Vico was studied. What he did was to bring to boil prematurely ideas which later were to be hailed as all important. Implicit in the New Science, for instance, is the sharp distinction between scientific thinking or rationalism and romantic sentimental experience. The Romantics rejected the Cartesian ideas; Vico said that they were out of place in history and that there were 'certainties' which could be attained in the study of human achievements which lay outside the scope of the physical sciences. Goethe and Hegel were both concerned with the warring forces of the head and the heart—and both borrowed from Spinoza and Herder—from Spinoza the ideal of a perfect Mind or Wisdom; from Herder the image of life moving from the inorganic to the organic, and up to reason itself. Herder, indeed, gave Hegel the sense of the Absolute implicit in historical processes—a sense which Vico had already discovered in his account of Providence. Perhaps Hegel, who started with theological ideas, would have avoided some of the ambiguities of his Absolute in history if he had availed himself of Vico's Providence. As it is we have the German idealist movement ignoring Vico, yet so closely attached to his main insights that Benedetto Croce was able to offer, as he thought, a more perfect form of Historical Idealism by joining Vico to Hegel.

Whatever we think of Croce's interpretation of Vico, he did justice to the genius of Vico—and it is greatly due to him that we now can see what a decisive place Vico occupies in any true account of the philosophies of history.

Chapter V

PROVIDENCE

From what we know of early man it is clear that he believed in the presence of agencies, spirits or powers outside himself, which were capable of doing him harm or good. In a confused way, too, he believed that the better a man was, the more likely would it be, unless he provoked their jealousy, that the gods might be propitious to him. Individuals and cities and tribes sought for the patronage of one of these deities. Later, at a stage of greater maturity, the question was asked whether the gods or God protected and directed human beings towards some destiny. The affirmative answer to this question gives a meaning to what is called Providence, the belief, that is, that human life is directed to a good and happy end by an all-seeing and all-powerful being. Such a belief is rarely found in a pure state. It depends upon an act of faith in the face of experience which seems to contradict it, and it is usually mixed up with superstition and a sense of doom or fate. The clearest example of a pure belief in Providence is to be found in the Jewish religion, which rose steadily and defiantly above the mists of surrounding beliefs. Yahweh is the one, true God, who created the world and has a purpose for man and a mission for His people. No matter what disasters befell them the Jews returned to this faith and hope at the instance of their prophets. 'The Lord is the everlasting God, who hath created the ends of the earth. He shall not faint nor labour, neither is there any searching out of his wisdom. It is he that giveth strength to the weary, and increased force and might to them that are not. . . . They that hope in the Lord shall renew their strength. They shall take wings as eagles; they shall run and not be weary; they shall walk and not faint.' The Gospels place in

133

the forefront this idea of Providence; the teaching of Christ begins with the declaration of God as the Father who makes life precious by His care for it, and this assurance is more than ratified by the act of the Son of God, who shows His surpassing love for man by dying on his behalf.

In the Christian dispensation Providence is looked upon as both universal and particular. As particular it means that every individual is cared for by God, even to the hairs of his head, or as St. Paul describes it, that all things co-operate for the good of those that love God. As universal, it means that though history is made by the co-operation and clash of human wills, God works in and through it, so that His purposes are fulfilled. This is the idea of Providence which has prevailed in the West and wherever Christianity has penetrated, and it lies behind the attempts of various Christian thinkers in the past to sketch a providential view of history. Christians from time immemorial have their own personal needs. Such prayers pervade the liturgy, of which one example is the collect asking that 'God, by whose never-failing providence the world is ordered', may 'remove from our path all hurtful things, and give us all that will be for our good'. Such prayers are warranted by the Lord's Prayer and by the belief of Christians that the divine and human meet in a personal relationship. The language of friendship and love does not, however, lend itself to theory, especially to a theory of history in which the part of God is to be explained.

The new hope stirred at the begining by the Christian message was not due to any theory of history. *Une grande espérance a traversé la terre; malgré nous vers le ciel il faut lever les yeux.* It was the fact of the existence of Providence which produced a radical change, removing the dark fears that human life signified nothing. Comfort can come when we are sure that all is well, even though we have no idea of how the happy ending is to be brought about. The fact and the explanation need not necessarily go together. Those who unite them and construct a providential theory of history must maintain that within the content of the Christian revelation enough material is provided for a theory; or they can turn to the history of Christianity and argue from that. But here a formidable difficulty has to be met. A man of faith may find in that history much grist for the mill, but, if he claims to be an historian arguing from evidence, he will not find grace among his fellow historians. Evidence needs to be interpreted, but there are rules of interpretation which provide a yardstick for the historian, and the supernatural and the providential are not measurable by this yardstick. If, for instance, a writer says that the victory of Charles Martel in 732 or that of Don John of Austria at Lepanto was an act of God, he must not expect to be treated as an historian. There is the same evidence before the historian and the Christian writer. The one finds an explanation in terms of empirical observation and human nature, the other sees the working of Providence.

Most historians would agree that Europe was enormously benefited by St. Benedict and the coming of monastic life at a period of great crisis. It is not too much to say that the monasteries proved to be the necessary link between the old and perishing civilization and the new, and brought peace and the Christian life to a world in travail. The historian recognizes the work of St. Benedict as in a loose sense providential; the Christian uses the word in its real sense. The two points of view do not, however, usually meet. There are occasions, indeed, when the historian is baffled, when all the evidence favours a non-natural explanation, and he has to argue either that a benefactor to humanity, otherwise sane, must have been an hysteric, or that there were factors present which we do not understand. St. Paul, for example, was utterly convinced of the supernatural character of his vision on the way to Damascus. St. Augustine of Hippo had no doubt that his hearing a child crying *Tolle, lege*, was by the intervention of Providence. Nothing could make St. Joan of Arc disbelieve in the voices which she heard. The fact that many Christians are far too ready to see the hand of God in human affairs predisposes the lay historian to discount all such interpretations, and I think that they make the mistake of supposing a common attitude amongst believers which is credulous and unscientific. But the difference between them and serious believers does not lie there. It lies in a different way of looking at the evidence. Both ways can be valuable, as the evidence of a police-detective and a member of the family can throw light at a post mortem on what happened. The credulity of the believer is balanced by the narrowness of the empirical historian. The Christian, and many a philosopher also, complains that the empiricist has barred the questions which most concern us all. He is measuring a symphony in terms of string and gut, as Dean Inge once remarked. Even the most positivist approach implies a philosophy—and a bad one. But even the more humanistic historians lose their touch when confronted with certain events or series of events in history. Their hypotheses whittle away the substance of the story. They make a virtue of incredulity, and hunt for any explanation which will save them from admitting an unpalatable truth. Many a sceptic, for instance, has invented a theory to explain away the Gospel account of the empty tomb. The inadequacy, however, of these theories, and their very multiplicity, suggest that their authors are of the breed of the unbelieving Thomas. The Christian, on his side, is obliged to use the standards of historical criticism and to offer a reasonable defence of what he believes to be the truth. He may not expect his arguments to win consent from all. Often it is a case of removing prejudices, the *muscae volitantes*, the motes which impede vision. The belief in Providence, and in the special Providence of the Old and New Testaments has its own credentials, which are not inferior to those of the confirmed rationalist. This is not the place to argue for this point of view, and it has to be stated dogmatically in order to justify, what otherwise might seem arbitrary, suggestions, which are to follow later, about the possibility of a Christian philosophy of history.

The biblical story of God's dealing with His chosen people leaves in the mind an image of a living personal God very different from the God of the philosophers. This distinction has been now incorporated in the distinction between existence and essence. The existentialists revolted against reducing life to a conceptual scheme, a process of geometry or emanation or dialectic of ideas. The Christian view of Providence, while it does not throw overboard metaphysical doctrines, emphasizes the providential activity of a God, who has created free living beings. Such a view must not, therefore, be confused with some of the metaphysical philosophies of history, which have irritated both historians and logical analysts. Sir Isaiah Berlin in his Auguste Comte Memorial Trust Lecture, *Historical Inevitability*, refers to these 'metaphysical-theological theories of history, which attract many who have lost their faith in older religious orthodoxies'. He condemns all such theories, because they make abstract norms do service for real agents and end up in a deterministic view of history. They play with capital letters; the Past, Tradition, the Masses, the Race, the Life Force, the Spirit of the Age, 'Race, colour, church, nation, class, climate, irrigation, technology, geo-political situation; civilization, social structure, the Human Spirit, the Collective Unconscious to take some of these concepts at random, have all played their parts in theologico-historical systems as the protagonists upon the stage of history'. Berlin says that they are 'represented as the real forces', which determine historical events. The result is that human responsibility is diminished, and history is reduced to a natural science or a metaphysical or theological scheme. Impersonal entities take the place of free human action, and we can do no more than watch the determined processes of history.

The weaknesses inherent in many philosophies of history are unmasked by Berlin in his lecture. Perhaps, however, owing to the need of compression he does not make clear whether the Christian advocates of Providence are included among the sinners. He does refer to the 'neo-metaphysical romantics' and to 'theologico-historical systems'; he mentions also the Church in the same breath as the Human Spirit and the Collective Unconscious, and he is severe in his judgment upon a teleological view of history. Dr. Karl Popper in his *Open Society* and *The Poverty of Historicism* is at one with Berlin in condemning the personification of abstract or general nouns and predicates, and in seeing in their use a threat to personal responsibility. Both seem to be influenced by the assumption of modern empiricism that realities must not be multiplied without necessity, and therefore as many universal and spiritual realities as possible have fallen under the axe. The story of this pogrom is told very candidly in Mr. J. C. Urmson's *Philosophical Analysis*, and of its cessation when the analysts found themselves unable to get rid of words like 'nation' or 'people'. The scandalous pseudo-realities contained in such a statement as 'England declared war in 1939' refused to be liquidated.

NOTE

The theory was that classes could be treated as logical constructions out of propositional functions. The whole realm of being, to which Meinong had given a status, Pickwicks and dragons, could be explained away, but not such everyday realities as states or governments or churches, which refused to sacrifice their names. The analysts had the ambition of developing an ideal logic on the model of mathematics, a language in which atomic objects would have their proper atomic equivalent in words. This was in violent reaction against a wordy metaphysical language, which, it was claimed, signified nothing. Philosophers have always had to face the problem of the apparent inadequacy of language to describe reality. The successes of mathematical logic suggested a new answer, a desperate one since it meant a desiccated world of discourse, even thinner than Esperanto. They ignored the fact and its implications that poets, novelists and skilled writers had in all civilizations managed to overcome in part the handicap of words. Poets discovered that in some mysterious fashion words belonging to one sense could be used to reinforce the words belonging to another, as when the child described the pins and needles sensation in her foot as a ginger-beer-fizzy feeling. A poet passes with ease from one sense to another and manages, also, to describe non-physical emotions and experiences and thoughts by analogies drawn from the sensible. There is some law of analogy which runs through the various layers of reality, permitting us to make intelligible to others what is most private and what is most sublime.

Moreover there are, where 'distinct and clear ideas' are unobtainable, signposts and approximations to full knowledge, which are too despised by the mathematical thinker. Most persons would say that they had a rough idea of what they meant by the word 'England' in the sentence, 'England declared war in 1939', and they can carry on an intelligent conversation on subjects such as nations, races, capitalism, socialism, business and games, governments and parties, churches and institutions, Byzantine and Baroque art. They are not talking nonsense; so far from that, conversation is one way of correcting mistakes and improving our knowledge. Lord Russell has argued that 'as we cannot directly confront the past, it cannot be certain; we cannot even be sure that the world existed five minutes ago'. On an artificial definition of certainty this may be so, but it would be more fruitful to use the fact that we do know something of the past (we should be idiots if we did not, and not even aware of our own name—not to mention our own family and friends!) to explore the conditions and degree of our knowledge of the world and of ourselves. Besides clear and distinct ideas we can grasp the character of a whole without knowing all its parts or details; we can understand the point or meaning or function of an object or group, knowing thus the outline or shape, though we have still much to learn about its contents. In his *De La Connaissance Historique* Marrou points out how constantly in learning and in investigating we make use of preliminary models or schemes. Sometimes these are based on certainties, such as humanity or language or history itself. Of combined certainty and uncertainty would be schemata such as 'civilization' or 'culture' or 'Zeitgeist'. More in the manner of a model, or what Max Weber called *Idealtypus*, would be Fustel de Coulanges' *La Cité Antique*, or the Baroque period or the Middle Ages. Marrou says of these latter that 'they never attain to the essences of things; they are only sketches, working drawings, mental constructions, whose purpose is to obtain some real knowledge, where the bewildering complexity of the real world defeats our efforts to fix it in a mould'. He goes on to warn his readers against the temptation to take these sketches for real objects. There is no doubt that philosophers and historians have fallen to this temptation, and it is against this habit that the modern empiricists, including, I think, Berlin and Popper are protesting. But protests against an abuse are different from a general denial of the right to use such schemata. I do not see why we should not continue to use both genuine universals and fictitious ones in moderation; we can continue to look for patterns in history as well as for 'natures' and Providence.

Now general and universal terms are part of the language of communication, and common sense, a favourite court of appeal nowadays, finds no difficulty in the use of them. The indignation of many at the inclusion of a dog in the Russian satellite rests on the belief that there is something common to dogs, that there are general characteristics to be found in each and every dog. The modern empiricist, as we have already seen, handicaps himself in his attempts to analyse induction and interpretation without conceding any intelligibility to objects in themselves; he has been overdosed with bad metaphysics. Assuredly we have to call a halt to those who crusade for a dogmatic rationalism, who whistle up essences everywhere and invent spurious entities, with which not only metaphysicians but historians and scientists and demagogues delight to play. We are made to think of civilizations as if they were creeping caterpillars, or of Energy or Evolution or the Unconscious as if it were a substitute for God. Such errors are chronic, and the empiricist does well to reiterate the warnings of bygone thinkers against a constant temptation. But such a discipline in the art of correct thinking is not the preserve of any one school of philosophers; nor are the analysts the first to discover the ambiguity in such terms of reference as Liberalism and Conservatism, the democratic and the republican party, or sovereignty. Hegel and his followers are anathema to them, and the main tenets of Hegelianism are exposed as meaningless nonsense. One need not be an Hegelian to feel that such criticism is more damaging to the critic than to the object of it. Hegel believes in Providence, but it is a peculiar version of his own. The Absolute Mind is said to embody itself in progressive stages in history. The theory cannot be ruled out at the start, for all depends upon whether Hegel can overcome certain very formidable initial difficulties and produce a convincing account. The objections to his view are that he fails to show how the essential attributes of God can be reconciled with a process of becoming, and secondly that he imposes his view on history and can be proved to be wrong. The Christian, on his side, does not claim that in a providential view of history God is to be identified with the processes of history, and, if he turns to history for evidence of divine providence, though he may see constant marks of it, he is not committed to any theory of the way in which it works. As I have said before, a distinction must be made between the certainty of the fact of Providence and the knowledge of any full-blown theory. All that he is prepared to maintain is that God does care for his creation and disposes of all things wisely, and that in the Christian dispensation he has revealed the way and the truth and the life.

Such a view of Providence cannot be separated from teleology, and Berlin in his lecture includes teleology amongst the idols which must be cast down. Does this mean that for him the Jewish and Christian view of Providence is regarded by him as a malevolent idol? I do not think so. Teleology, as he understands it, 'is not a theory or a hypothesis, but a category or framework in terms of which everything is, or should be, conceived or described'. It makes life into a play in which, whatever the actors appear to do, and no matter what the tragedy or comedy be, all is really determined. 'The puppets may be conscious and identify themselves happily with the inevitable process in which they play their parts, but it remains inevitable, and they remain marionettes.' Such a criticism has an echo of Bergson, when, in his earlier writings, he argued that teleology was incompatible with real freedom and freshness. The old objection to Bergson that such a freedom is arbitrary and inexplicable has its force today against those who reject the idea of any purpose or end in human life. When Aristotle began his *Nicomachean Ethics* with the, to him, obvious statement that human actions and human life must have an end, he believed, and rightly, that he was making sense of human freedom and choice. From the context of his remarks Berlin appears to have in mind the Hegelian and Marxist conception of freedom, that is, freedom as the consciousness of necessity, but I wish that he had made this more clear. The image of a drama is applicable to the Christian view of Providence, but the players in it are not puppets, and the good or bad ending to the play, so far as the individual players are concerned, depends upon their free response to divine grace. Freedom and Providence go together, for Providence is not like a script written beforehand, nor, as in Hegel, a process determining events. It works in and through the freedom of individual men and women, and its law is love. The necessity which can be observed in physical nature changes into spontaneity in living beings, and in human societies a new phase is reached where necessity is continually reduced and duty and desire take its place. At the summit all is governed by love. The successes of love have nothing to do with compulsion, for love does not need justification outside itself. It does not determine beforehand nor stand at the end forcing the players to carry out what they alone can do by their own free choice. Whatever the choice made, the perfection of the love given and of the design remains unchallengeable.

The idea of Providence, therefore, by its very nature rejects and rebukes the doctrine of determinism. The annunciation of it at the advent of Christianity was the more welcome in that it freed the mind from the oppression of fate and impersonal law. The believer was convinced that there was both a care for the individual and a general providence. He did not expect to understand its workings; he was content with the fact, and now that we are so much better aware of the immense complexities of human affairs and of the multiple factors present in every single incident of human life, the wise man will feel inclined, even more strongly than St. Paul, to cry out that the ways of God are unsearchable. The Christian revelation lays special emphasis on the importance of the individual, and that very fact increases the difficulty of harmonizing their interlocking histories. It is as if after having decided that the life and actions of a great historical figure had been responsible for revolutionary events, one was told that there were a vast number of others, whose names are unknown, who were in truth equally responsible. The historian can and must ignore such an hypothesis and the Christian will follow suit when studying and writing history. He will be aware, at the same time, that there is a different and more ultimate scale of values which he is leaving on one side. So far as individual providence is concerned he may sense that in his own private experience he is touching at every moment of his temporal existence something eternal, and he may sense, also, that in some mysterious fashion he has a part to play in some invisible and crucial issue, and that, like Atlas, he has to carry the whole world on his shoulders. Such an experience or certainty he cannot, however, translate into what is the accepted pattern of human events called history.

Newman had this sense of mission and of the presence of the invisible to a high degree, and this made him when reading history constantly aware of Providence. This comes out in the Essay he wrote reviewing Dr. Milman's *History of Christianity*. The law of Providence, he says, 'works beneath a veil, and what is visible in its course does but shadow out at most, and sometimes obscures and disguises what is invisible. The world in which we are placed has its own system of laws and principles, which, as far as our knowledge of it goes, is, when once set in motion, sufficient to account for itself—as complete and independent as if there was nothing beyond it.' He then, after developing the truth of the close texture of nature and human life, argues that God, as present to His creation, will act 'by means of its ordinary system, or by quickening, or, as it were, by stimulating its powers, or by superseding or interrupting it'. Miraculous interference will be, by the nature of the case, rare, and, as God is present to nature, he will act 'through, with, and beneath those physical, social, and moral laws of which our experience informs us'. Now it is the firm belief of Christians that God's Providence is not 'general merely, but is, on the contrary, thus particular and personal', and it is for ever concurring and co-operating with the system which meets the eye. This means that the visible world 'is the instrument, yet the veil, of the world invisible—the veil, yet still partially the symbol and index: so that all that exists or happens visibly, conceals and yet suggests and above all subserves, a system of persons, facts and events beyond itself'. What then is called cause and effect, 'is rather an order of sequence, and does not preclude, nay, perhaps implies the presence of unseen spiritual agency as its real author'. The visible and material are not set aside; they are left complete. God uses what is there. 'He does but modify, quicken or direct the powers of nature or the laws of society.' Hence the 'great characteristic of Revelation is addition, substitution. Things look the same as before, though now an invisible power has taken hold upon them. This power does not unclothe the creature, but clothes it. Men dream everywhere; it gives visions. . . . The Israelitish polity had a beginning, a middle, and an end, like other things of time and place; its captivities were the natural consequences, its monarchy was the natural expedient, of a state of political weakness. Its territory was a battle ground, and its power was the alternate ally, of the rival empires of Egypt and Assyria. Heathen travellers may have surveyed the Holy Land, and have thought it but a narrow strip of Syria. So it was; what then? Till the comparative anatomist can be said by his science to disprove the rationality and responsibility of man, the politician or geographer of this world does nothing, by dissertations in his own particular line of thought, towards quenching the secret light of Israel, or dispossessing its angelic guardians of the height of Sion or of the sepulchres of the prophets. Its history is twofold, worldly to the world, and heavenly to the heirs of heaven.'

Newman's Essay is a criticism of Milman's attempt to give a naturalistic explanation of the story of Israel and the rise of

Christianity. In order to set Milman right he expounds a view of Providence and the way it works in the Old and New Testaments. The principles he lays down can be applied to all history, but it is not Newman's aim to give a philosophy of history, nor, indeed, would the principles take us very far. Within recent years the interest shown by scholars in the eschatological texts of the New Testament has provided a new approach to history, and full advantage has been taken of certain key words, such as Kerugma, Parousia, kairos and krisis. The most systematic and impressive interpretation of this eschatological literature in its relation to history is that which has been given, and is still being given, by Professor Paul Tillich. He writes as a philosopher and theologian, a convinced and passionate Protestant and a participant in the tragic German struggles which ushered in Hitler. His view has an immense sweep and is daring in its construction. He tries to keep what he believes to be the biblical conception of God as the Unconditioned and at the same time harmonize with it the Logos of creation. As he says: 'God as being-itself transcends non-being absolutely. On the other hand, God as creative life includes the finite, and with it non-being, although non-being is eternally conquered, and the finite is eternally reunited within the infinity of the divine life. Therefore it is meaningful to speak of a participation of the divine life in the negativities of creaturely life. This is the ultimate answer to the question of theodicy. The certainty of God's directing activity (Providence) is based on the certainty of God as the ground of being and meaning. The confidence of every creature, its courage to be, is rooted in faith in God as its creative ground!' (*Systematic Theology* I, 270.)

I begin with this passage, first, because it introduces us to his conception of Providence, and, secondly, as an example of his philosophical style and lineage. It is a German lineage, and there are traces of Schelling and Hegel and Marx and Husserl and Heidegger in his thought. His metaphysical virtuosity and affection for abstract terms would not commend itself to Sir Isaiah Berlin, nor to G. E. Moore or Quine. Locke and Hume and the present representatives of their school have not touched him, and one reason for this is that he regards their attitude and form of thinking as the mirror of a bourgeois society, by now spent and out-of-date. In answer to their accusation of

144

insobriety of language and confusion of thought he distinguishes between what he calls 'the definitional and the configurational'. This latter consists of notions which resist definition, such as 'ontological concepts'. The philosophical task with respect to them is not to define them, but to illuminate them by showing how they appear in different constellations.

Such a distinction, even as to the language, is typical of Tillich, and while very antipathetic to some, this form of address has greatly impressed others. They recognize a fertility of mind, which, allied to a religious and penetrating insight, appears to open out new aspects of Christian philosophy. This fertility, moreover, is combined with a constructive power and unusual love of system. So dependent, indeed, on each other are the various parts of this system that a summary can hardly do it justice. What helps to the understanding of the shape of his thought is the historical context of it. His thought developed during those years in Germany after the débâcle of the first war. Salvaging had to be done, and salvation sought. Karl Barth saw man as fallen from grace, and acted like 'a flaming sword, turning every way, to keep the way of the tree of life'. In this case the 'tree of life' was God's revealed word, which could only be profaned by any contact with the philosophies of man. The faith, therefore, was not at home in human history. Tillich equally convinced of the saving power of the Christian faith took another line. His thought ran along the metaphysical lines of Schelling and Hegel and the German phenomenologists, but he also had a deep concern with the social and spiritual welfare of the world around him, and he would not, like Barth, forsake man. Besides, he accepted the conviction of Marx that ideas and action are inseparable. He read into the Bible a dialectic of good and evil, the constant struggle between these contrary forces in history, and he noted that the prophets were for ever proclaiming the judgments of God in the crises they faced. The Old Testament tells of a series of crises and judgments; they precede the coming of Christ, when the world came to the supreme crisis. In Christ it had its kairos, its unique opportunity of encountering God. This moment and this new kingdom Tillich called the New being in Christ, when the Unconditional enters time and overcomes the estrangement or alienation of the world. From then on history is beset and determined by this divine event, and its meaning is revealed as a series of crises, in which the unique Kairos is prolonged, thus providing in time subordinate kairoi or opportunities for the return of man to his essential being in God.

The initial insight into the meaning of history and its connection with Revelation has developed in the years into the *Systematic Theology*, on which Tillich is now engaged. The system enables him to find a place and meaning for both his religious and his social beliefs. The supremacy of Christ is assured, for Christ becomes the centre of history, the principle of reconciliation. Whereas older theories, relying on fixed concepts, made Christ too static, He now is the meeting place of the Unconditional and the finite, transforming the temporal and overcoming man's estrangement from God. Again room is left for freedom. The weakness of Hegel and many other philosophers of history lay in their too formal sequence of ideas, which made the work of Spirit inevitably deterministic. A purely doctrinal and propositional statement, as formulated by the scholastics, also divorced Christianity from movement and growth in time. In Tillich's view Christian history is a never-ceasing battlefield of opposites. Man is in the existential order (he here accepts the plea of Kierkegaard and the later existentialists), and in a state of angst. He is, in fact, defined by Tillich as 'finite freedom', a being, who is estranged from essential being, and so placed that he has always to battle to find his essential destiny. There is a deep ambiguity in everything human, due to Original Sin, 'the split', as he calls it, 'between the created goodness of things and their distorted existence'. This contradiction is described by the use of the word 'demonic'. What takes form corrupts in time; and this phenomenon is most manifest in the life of human persons. History is marked by this rise and fall, by crises, which in turn provide the kairos, the moments when the situation is saved by a Gestalt of Grace.

This theory of minor kairoi and the Gestalt or Constellation of Grace is one of Tillich's most original contributions to a philosophy of history. He tells us in *The Interpretation of History* (p. 52) that 'my Christology and Dogmatics were determined by the cross of Christ as the event of history, in which divine judgment over the world became concrete and manifest'. 'The logos becomes history, a visible and touchable individuality in a unique moment of history.' The Unconditional—what is essential being—restores man to his place in the divine life,

Christ is the New Being, and now throughout time this work of redemption continues, and shows itself in and through the exercise of human freedom, in the interplay of failure and success. Human life cannot be the divine life; it has the shadow of imbecility about it, though it has its own true level and autonomy. But it contains this great negative in it, which would reduce all history to ultimate meaninglessness, were it not open to grace. 'If Evil has demonic or structural character limiting individual freedom, its conquest can come only by the opposite, the divine structure, that is, by what we have called a structure or Gestalt of Grace.' (*The Protestant Era*, p. xx.) The Gestalt of Grace makes history sacred history. Its presence at the time of Kairos, is not, however, to be taken to mean a supernatural interference. It is in and through the very historical events and movements that the sacred must be discovered. His catchword for this is 'that culture is the form of the sacred, and the sacred the content of culture'. Excited by the discovery of this 'truth' in earlier days he incautiously leapt to the conclusion that the future hope (that is the Christian hope) of the world lay with the socialist struggle in Germany against the retrograde forces of capitalism, and that the group under Marxist influence, with its sense of reality, were the instruments of Providence. He identified their success with the Gestalt of Grace. He learnt from this mistake, but he has never forsworn his belief in the dialectic of Yes and No, and to him the atheism of Marx is not totally black; it can serve as a corrective of false or worldly, or even too unworldly religion, and be providential, as providing the moment, the kairos, when the unconditional meets the finite. He learnt that he was mistaken in this particular case, because what he prophetically saw as a new order of grace turned into despotism. He introduced, therefore, a new idea into his sytem; he holds that there can be a period of time, a vacuum, which he calls 'the sacred void'. After the first world war, 'like those who interpret the signs of the times, we always were both confirmed and refuted. . . . When, after the second world war, I spoke of a 'void' which we should experience as a "sacred void", by taking it patiently upon ourselves, this also was an interpretation of the present moment in the light of the eternal; it was also a proclamation of a *Kairos*. Only this *Kairos* was not a *Kairos* calling for transforming action but for waiting in a vacuum.'

Throughout his interpretation of history Tillich keeps to the facts of history, and maintains that he is not trying to impose a view upon it. He is constantly writing of a dialectic, but the dialectic is reminiscent of Marx more than of Hegel, in that he is concerned with action and not with an idea. This does not prevent him from making distinctions which serve him as a guide. He says, for instance, that reality can be looked at for its truth or as a matter of concern. From this distinction he goes on to give his own definition of religion, calling it 'ultimate concern'. This rather startling definition is explained as follows. In every situation and predicament man is committed, as the existentialists have shown us; hence he has to make decisions. There is a cleavage between what is here and now before us and what might be, a cleavage between subject and object, which impresses upon us the need of a reconciliation. The ultimate, therefore, makes its presence felt in our concern; we are in the presence, that is, of the transcendent, the unconditional, and in the overcoming of the imminent crises the kingdom of God is being established in time. There is no dichotomy between history and another world, as former theologians have usually taught—to their own loss. The doctrine of the supernatural is gratuitous and harmful, as it has taken us away from the real, and creates a mythical realm, which can excuse us from responsibility in the world we experience here and now. Certain forms of Christianity ignore the element of time and look to Utopia. They are less realistic even than Marx, who did use time, though he too asked vainly for a Utopia. Time itself to Tillich is created in the ground of the divine life, and is therefore essentially connected with eternal life. The finite, indeed, when Christ, the New Being, eventually is 'all in all', brings to an end, in a complete reconciliation and fulfilment, the tensions between opposites, which make up history. The meaning of history, then, in brief, to borrow the words of Mr. James L. Adams, 'is found in the process whereby the divine, through the instrument of human freedom, overcomes estrangement through love'. The divine, which takes the form of Providence, does not control life from outside. 'The unconditioned is never a law or a promoter of a definite plan of the spiritual or social life. The contents of the historical life are tasks and ventures of the creative spirit. . . . What we are confronted with is never and nowhere an abstract command; it is a living history, with its abundance of new problems whose solution occupies and fulfils every epoch.' (*The Protestant Era*, p. 51.) The historian, therefore, can work undisturbed. If he is a genuine historian he is knitting the garment of the spirit.

This outline enables us to see the sources and inspirations of Tillich's system. He had relied in great part on the prophetical and eschatological passages of the Bible and applied them to history as it is now in the making as well as to past history. Now, as St. Paul declared, is the acceptable time, and this language of the New and Old Testaments finds its way into a German metaphysical language, derived from Schelling, Hegel, Marx and Heidegger. Hegel in his first writings had used the theological conception of man's estrangement from God and final reconciliation. This idea had a Pauline matrix, and its truth is revealed in the actual processes of history. Again, in the Fourth Gospel, Christ is the Logos, and this makes Him the centre of history, the meeting place of the Unconditioned and the finite. He is the supreme Kairos, the guarantee that thenceforward all history would provide the moments and the opportunities for the successful reconciliation of this finite world.

The bold, constructive energy of Tillich merits comparison with the great systems of past theologians and is especially welcome at a time when positive contributions to philosophy are rare. It is good, also, to see metaphysics rearing its head, though I wish that it had not taken a form which is both unpopular and very vulnerable. St. Thomas used a metaphysical system, which, while it too has been assailed by the logical analysts, is nevertheless limpid and intelligible. The terms, which Tillich uses tend to create a fog, and this fog envelops the most precious beings and events of the Christian Revelation. God becomes the Unconditional, the Ground of Being, Christ is the New being, religion, we are told, is ultimate concern, and the human individual is human freedom, while sin, of which we are too well aware, turns into something quite strange, namely, 'the disruption of the essential unity between God and man by man's actualized freedom'. Tillich distinguishes between various senses of the word 'essential', but 'essential' has had too long a history and too steady a connotation to be played with, especially when the issues are most serious. In the above passage on the definition of sin, Tillich writes of a disruption of the essential unity between God and man. No one reading these words could help but think that God and man are essentially united, that is, essentially one. Tillich is far from holding this, and he has in mind a variation on the existentialist use of the term. But the existentialist ideas are not fireproof, and Tillich's own description of God as 'being itself', which 'transcends non-being absolutely', and at the same time 'creative life', which includes the finite, only darkens the understanding. In any case sin is not a disruption of any metaphysical unity between God and man; it is an offence against God by a man who has already been created.

These are only choice examples of the many obscurities generated by a certain type of metaphysical thinking. So far as history is concerned Tillich's interpretation promises to be alive and illuminating, for what we have become accustomed to think of as secular history is now brought into the very centre of Christian belief. The Christian revelation is not only not separate from it, the revelation is even to be sought in what was regarded as purely secular. The first effect of this idea is like a flare of light. Has the Christian been mistaken in looking elsewhere for guidance and doctrine? But on reflection I wonder what we have learnt. If we discard the old distinction of the natural and the supernatural, and deny that we have to be born again into a new life, passing from a human life into a participation of the life of one who is truly God and truly man, we are left with nothing but a faith that the dialectic of history contains the whole answer. Events happen, choices are made, and in retrospect we see that some choices were evil and others good, that some evil has worked out in the end to good, and some good, on the contrary, has produced much evil. To a Karl Popper history is summed up in the quest for power; to a Bunyan it is Vanity Fair, and only grace can lead one to the Celestial City. What light, in fact, does Tillich throw on this dark scene? He does not turn to Calvin's doctrine of the elect, nor to the Pauline favourite image of membership with Christ in His mystical Body, nor to the Catholic interpretation of the Body as a visible Church, which confronts the world, mingling with it but never identified with it. It looks as if we must not look beyond history itself; the truth and import of the Christian religion is embedded there. 'Culture is the form of the sacred, and the sacred the content of culture.' History is a series of conflicts, of moments when a decision has to be taken, and never is there a decision such that it can end the struggle. This is a symptom, if not law, of the finite, and the symptom also reveals the presence of the Unconditioned, of a reality, which is free of this imperfection. In other words, God is revealed in the very finite texture of history, and the constantly recurring crises in it are religious as evoking in us 'ultimate concern', and as providing 'kairoi', which are the opportunities for final reconciliation. The existential order, which is that of the finite, is by its very nature distorted; it is under the sign of Original Sin, and of itself it cannot be restored to the condition of its essential destiny in God. It needs a 'constellation of grace' to save it from ultimate meaninglessness. Our Christian faith assures us that this grace is active. The Cross of Christ, The New being, is the proof; for the Cross is the sign of contradiction, the paradox of 'Godmanhood manifesting itself within and under the condition of human existence which contradicts original Godmanhood'. Christ both passes judgment on man in his state of Original Sin, and as bringing the presence of essential New Being into the world of existence, makes of himself the new centre of history and the supreme Kairos, which guarantees final reconciliation.

This, when reduced to less metaphysical language, implies that the historical situation itself gives rise to the belief in God as the super-essential reality. Existence is meaningless without some such Unconditioned Being, for existence is strife, is distorted, and cannot cure itself. God, it should be noted, is not proved. Tillich explicitly denies that God's 'existence' needs proof. God is bound to appear whenever we change over from looking at life to being concerned with it. Ultimate concern is religion, and in that state of 'existential commitment' God as 'the power of being' is revealed, as 'presupposed' in all such encountering. Reason can only take us to the horizon of the relative; to get beyond it, as we do in our existential commitment we have to have a kind of apprehension, which Tillich calls 'ecstatic reason', an experience which is akin to faith, though not wholly the same. This experience of the Unconditioned becomes Christian when Christ is realized to be the bridge between God and man, the passage from essential to existential being, and the Cross is the saving symbol which shows that in the very dialectic of history grace is being poured out and reconciliation made. Tillich, then, has dispensed with the idea of God as truly known by reason or revelation. We can use words about him as symbols; we can speak of God as living, existent, personal and loving, but these symbols do not convey any real knowledge. He has dispensed, also, with the traditional views of Christ and of the Church as a unique society, founded by Christ, and growing in history. Christ is called the Centre of history, so that now we are assured that culture is sacred, that by a dialectic of opposites, the sign of contradiction, the kingdom of God is being advanced and that it will finally triumph.

As I have already remarked, it is difficult to do justice in a summary to the richness and complexity of Tillich's theological ideas. As just stated they emphasize the importance for a proper interpretation of history of the eschatological themes in the Gospels. But it is questionable whether these themes have been rightly understood, and, again, whether the historian has received much guidance from them. Tillich uses philosophical and theological terms in an original and personal way, and this creates difficulties. Hardly a single one of his ground terms is on first reading acceptable. The Christian God and the Unconditional of Tillich look far apart. Unless the God revealed in the New Testament is more than a symbol, Christianity loses its distinctive message; it becomes the appanage of a philosophy, and a more than dubious philosophy. Religion, again, is said to be 'ultimate concern'. Religion is worship, the reaction of a creature before a Being, who is, as the Psalmist cries, most wonderful and adorable. There have been an infinite number of matters of ultimate concern, and not all of them have been religious, nor have some of them had any foundation. Fears, imaginings, false reasonings have too often been responsible for making classless societies or utopias or catastrophic ends or fate or death into matters of ultimate concern. The expression has a downward tilt towards the meaningless. Christ, too, is not the Godman, the Word made Flesh, of traditional theology. We are told that He is the divine Logos, who appears in the shape of a man. We ought not to say that God became man, but rather that 'the Incarnation is the paradox of essential Godmanhood, manifesting itself within and under the conditions of human existence, which contradicts original Godmanhood'. The import of the language here depends upon Tillich's understanding of the meaning and relation to one another of 'existence' and 'essence'.[1] Existence is made a special mark of man, as contrasted with an essential state which would make him one with God. It appears that by the very fact of being created man loses his essential state and is outside himself, in some strange condition of alienation or estrangement. This being outside God and His essential state is identified with Original Sin, and the Christian Redemption is the mode whereby man is brought back to essential being, to being truly himself and divine. There is no advertence to the fact that both Scripture and the traditional meaning of sin imply that man, after creation, by a free act of his own chose to offend God.

Such philosophical and theological objections could be multiplied. What is more to the purpose is to indicate the special view which Tillich has of historical fact and its relation to Christian belief. Just as in his acceptance of God and his dealings with man Tillich seems to occupy a half-way house—if not a no-man's-land between knowledge as the cognition of reason and private non-rational experience, so his faith in the Christian revelation seems to lie between the knowledge of historical fact and faith springing from his participation in the society of believers and participation in Christ. (He calls this latter 'the state of being grasped by the ground and abyss of being and meaning'.) The Revelation of Christ, if I understand him aright, is normative, but it is ill-served by being turned into articles of the Creed, which have to be taken as true statements or propositions unaffected by time and the historical consciousness. It is in history, and not outside it, that Revelation is to be found. Supernaturalism is an error. 'Man and the rest of reality are not only "inside" of the divine life, but also "outside" it. Man has left the ground in order "to stand upon himself", to be actually what he essentially is, in order to be "finite freedom".' The reconciliation of this condition of 'outsider' with the full interior life of Godhead can be brought about only in one way, the normative way. This way is revealed in the unique occasion in history, when the Unconditional assumes finite freedom, and directs all future choices of man in history towards the fulfilment of all things in Christ. Tillich has co-ordinated the great movements of German metaphysics,

[1] Were this a philosophical treatise I should attempt to show that the use made of these words is quite untenable.

its Idealism, Existentialism and Marxian socialism, into one system of theology, in which he believes the Protestant Principle and genuine Christianity can be expressed. Now having established history as 'the outstanding category of interpreting reality', we might expect him to emphasize the supreme importance of historical fact and historical evidence. This he does to the extent of demanding complete independence for historical criticism, but he refuses to draw his certainties and his belief in Christ from so-called historical truth. He makes a distinction between what he describes as events known in a photographic sense and the religious picture; 'the religious picture of the New Being in Jesus is a result of a new being; it represents the victory over existence which has taken place, and thus created the picture'. In another passage, quoted by Mr. A. T. Mollegen from an unpublished manuscript, Tillich tells us that 'historical, for the biblical view of things, is the continuous process of the divine self-revelation in a series of events, combined with the interpretations of these revelatory events. It is in this sense that we must speak of "historical revelation", namely of revelation through historical events. "Historical" for the scientific view of things are those events which are verified within the limits of every historical verification by special methods of research'. This distinction might at first sight seem to correspond with one developed by St. Augustine and other theologians. This is summed up in the saying that one man at the foot of the cross saw a Jew dying, another saw God redeeming. The point here illustrated is that faith gives new eyes to read a deeper meaning and a new truth into evidence, which is objectively there and waiting on an interpretation. The historical fact or evidence is necessary and justifies the interpretation. Tillich, however, while appearing to say something similar, makes this somewhat disturbing distinction between history as known, so to speak, photographically, and history or 'historicity', the interpretation of events by faith. The first gives only probability, the second certainty. This is disturbing because it makes a cleavage between two forms of history, and, secondly, in doing so it removes one of the requisite grounds for certainty. Tillich is prepared to ignore or even jettison some of the historical facts of the Gospels. He would, I think, say that it is the work of the historian to settle their truth or falsehood, and at the best such facts can only be probable. But this is to put the Christian religion at the mercy of the historians' passing judgment. The traditional view is that the Gospel story as a whole is verifiable, that Christ was born, suffered under Pontius Pilate, died on the Cross and rose again. So necessary is this for a reasonable faith that St. Paul tells the Corinthians that 'if Christ has not risen, then our preaching is groundless, and your faith, too, is groundless'. The relation of historical fact to the interpretation of faith is shown in the example given above. There is no doubt that a man is dying on the Cross; it is that fact, which seen by the eyes of faith, tells us that God is redeeming man. If, however, the interpretation by faith is separated from 'photographic' history, it becomes difficult to see on what the certainty of faith is based. The same difficulty presented itself in Tillich's view, already touched on, that we do not encounter God by reason. He introduced a notion which he called 'ecstatic reason'. This ecstatic reason and what he means by faith are suspiciously like the supernatural and the order of sanctifying grace, which he has ruled out. But they cannot be kept out in any genuine assessment of Christian beliefs, and so they have been brought back in a form which touches neither earth nor heaven. The historicity of this biblical interpretation by faith is supported, so it is said, by 'an analogy of pictures'; the revelation contained in the Bible is discerned by those who are receptive to its message; and this reception and interpretation is saved from being subjective in a bad sense, an inner light, because of the recipients' sharing in the 'Church which is the actual continuation of the history of revelation. . . .'

Tillich has not yet completed what he has to say about the Church and the work of the Holy Spirit within it; so it would be premature and unfair to offer criticism of this part of his theological thinking. What he has so far given to us, in so far as the question of Providence and history are concerned, claims to be biblical and Protestant. He himself would admit that his emphasis is more on the prophetic than the sacramental and doctrinal aspect of Christianity. Of this I will say nothing more. His idiosyncrasy is to give a theology of history in an abstract and metaphysical language, which would not win commendation from Berlin or Popper. The historian's reaction to such historico-theological writing can be found in a passage from H.-J. Marrou's *De la Connaissance*

Historique: 'The historian must attempt to grasp all that is real; his knowledge must embrace its intelligible structures and its anomalies, must state as precisely as possible the relations which exist between the diverse constituents, series and systems which he may be able to discover. He must, also, even when after analysis he feels sure that his generalizations are justified, remind himself in time that the fundamental datum of history, what has "really existed", is not the fact of civilization, nor the system, nor the supersystem, but the living human being whose individual life is the one true organism authentically given to us in experience. Even here the idealist temptation besets us; to read some of our contemporary writings, one has the impression that the actors of history are not real men but entities, *la Cité antique*, feudalism, bourgeois capitalism, revolutionary proletariat. This is going too far; even if it would seem after the examination of the documents that such and such an historical phenomenon is explained by one of these socio-cultural abstractions, the historian must keep reminding himself and never forget, that he is dealing only with a construction of the mind. It may be undoubtedly unavoidable (since it is the only means of mastering the complexity of the real facts), and it is legitimate, within the limits of its use; but, nevertheless it remains an abstraction, an artificial product, and is not the real itself, nor, above all, is it, as some people end in believing, the super real.'

Marrou is here pointing to the discrepancy between our human concepts or constructions and human life as experienced individually by the dramatis personae of history. He would not deny, however, that they can give us a true view of the real—though the more concrete they are the better. The paradox in Tillich's *Systematic Theology* is that it is at one and the same time exceedingly metaphysical and abstract in its approach and sceptical of reason in what concerns religion and faith. This is a Kantian legacy. If he were more chary of abstractions, but prepared to defend their applicability, when necessary, to matters of faith and to divine things, all might be well. Conscious of the difficulty of denying the possibility of a natural theology, and, nevertheless, of writing at length about theology, Tillich ventures on a view of his own about the meaning of a 'symbol'. He remains, however, antipathetic to doctrinal propositions, and feels that the Protestant Principle demands of him a return to the prophetical element in the Bible. But has he not ignored the fact that, after the fulfilment of prophecy in Christ, the 'New Being', the Holy Spirit replaces the work of the prophets, and, as Christ declared: 'it will be for him, the truth-giving Spirit, when He comes, to guide you into all truth'? Moreover, if we are to trust St. Paul, it is the Spirit which makes us cry out, Abba, Father, an image-concept, which is both more concrete and revealing than the statement that God is the Unconditional. As an aid to an understanding of Providence and for a theology of history, resort to a dialectic is of less avail than the image of the divine Fatherhood.

Chapter VI

CHRISTIANITY AND HISTORICISM I

Christianity is an historical religion; it began at a certain date and continued in a visible society. Though by its nature uncommitted to any group or nation or race, its historical influence has been most marked in the West; so much so that when St. Augustine took up his pen to write on the City of God he had no knowledge of the Chinese or Indian civilizations; he drew his contrast between the Greco-Roman world and the Christian ideal. Later Christian writers, as we have already seen, followed suit, and the last of the traditional writers, Bossuet, based his view of the providential course of history on his knowledge of the classical writers and the Bible. As new horizons opened up and the scientific outlook superseded that of the Christian, the old way of summarizing history, in terms of providence, lost its appeal. Many of the scientifically minded grew sceptical of philosophical and theological generalizations; they used empirical methods, so far as they were available, to discover the exact sequence of events in some particular field of history. Those on the other hand who could not keep from larger themes attempted a general theory which would be, as Comte claimed, scientifically exact, or they sought for principles within history or human nature such as could serve to co-ordinate the apparently chaotic story of mankind. Some of the leading theories were examined in an earlier chapter. But in the meantime Christian thinkers have not been asleep or silent, and the question returns, though now in a different form, whether Christianity has anything to say of significance about the life of man as it is lived in human societies and in secular pursuits.

In the Christian belief there are at least three cliff-like ideas

158

which are hard to scale and to see in the same perspective. The first is what may be called the eschatological element in the New Testament; the second is the other-worldliness of the Kingdom of God or grace, and the third, which has a deceptive appearance of simplicity, is the doctrine of Providence.[1] Now one popular explanation or interpretation of this doctrine would rule out all possibility of a philosophy of history. God in the teaching of Christ is the Father; not only the creator but the loving parent of man. In His hands is the government of the world, and nothing can happen without His consenting or permissive power. That power is exercised so that even the hairs of a man's head are counted. 'See how the birds of the air never sow or reap or gather grain into barns, and yet your heavenly Father feeds them; have you not an excellency beyond theirs?' The Father looks after human life and directs it to a divine end. Therefore we must say that there is a Providence, and that there is a plan in human life, in the slow development of civilizations as well as in the story of every individual. There is a philosophy, a divine intention at work in history, but— and here is the rub—it is necessarily mysterious and beyond human understanding. No one can hope to understand it until the end of the world, the last day, when all will be unfolded and made plain. If this be so then any attempts to give a philosophy of history seem to be condemned from the start—and it is on such grounds that Mr. C. S. Lewis has attacked what he calls historicism as a pseudo-science. His argument has the advantage of being precise and at the same time comprehensive. There are many legitimate objects an historian can pursue, he says, but if he tries to discover by the use of his natural powers an inner meaning in the historical process, then he becomes an historicist and not an historian. In other words the historicist is one who 'tries to get from historical premises conclusions which are more than historical; conclusions metaphysical or theological or (to coin a word) atheological'. 'When Carlyle spoke of history as a "book of revelations" he was an historicist. When Novalis called history "an evangel" he was an historicist. When Hegel saw in history the progressive self-manifestations of absolute spirit he was an historicist. When a village woman says that her wicked father-in-law's paralytic stroke is "a judgment on him" she is an historicist. Evolution-

[1] For a more detailed examination of theories of Providence, v. ch. v.

ism, when it ceases to be simply a theorem in biology and becomes a principle for interpreting the total historical process, is a form of historicism. Keats's *Hyperion* is the epic of historicism, and the lines of Oceanus,

> *'tis the eternal law*
> *That first in beauty should be first in might,*

are as fine a specimen of historicism as you could wish to find.'

This linking together of village women, Hegel and poets shows how widespread and natural is the habit of interpreting history in an improper way. That it is improper, Lewis continues, becomes clear immediately we consider what we mean by history. It has several senses: the total content of time, past, present and future, or just the whole of the past, or the past in so far as it is discoverable from surviving evidence, or what has actually been discovered, or the part of the past which alone is subject to critical and scientific survey, or lastly that vague picture which is in most men's minds when they talk of 'history'. In this last sense history, just because it is a vague picture, lends itself to imaginary patterns, even as we like to read faces in a fire. But these patterns disappear as soon as we pass from the vague to the particular and study the details. As to the other senses, clearly we cannot make theories of any value out of the unknown, and it is only too true that vast tracts of past time are hidden from us, as hidden as the future is. We are in possession only of a fragment, of a small selection out of the innumerable experiences of millions of individuals in the past. The historian dealing with a specific subject such as economic or military history has the right to make a selection out of the infinite data. The reason is that he has limited his study to a particular field. But the historicist claims to be able to show the significance of all history, and he has no means of knowing what is important and what is not important. The end of the play may show that the one page he knows and has studied may bear quite a different meaning in the light of the end, and furthermore that apparently trivial incidents described on that page were in fact more decisive than the apparently important ones. In short we are in no position to make up theories about history in general; we are part of it and it is 'a waste of time to play the historicist. The philosophy of history is a discipline for which we mortal men lack the necessary data'.

Historicism, therefore, in the eyes of C. S. Lewis stands self-condemned, just as much as the youth who would at the age of seventeen interpret the whole of his life, past, present and future. Nevertheless it seems endemic in man to ponder over life and fate and to try to bring some meaning into history as a whole, and not all the warnings and prohibitions of positivists or Christians, like C. S. Lewis, will prevent men from peering into the mystery. There are, *pace* Mr. Lewis, different kinds of questions which can be asked, and to some of them an answer may be forthcoming. Let us accept the fact that only the author of life, God Himself, can give the final and complete meaning to history. But only those who deny God or reduce Him to a geometrical spider could dream of denying this. A materialist who thinks that all life can be understood in terms of chemistry, an evolutionist who conjures out of some primitive form of life the splendours of Shakespeare or Dante, may indulge in the kind of historicism which Lewis attacks, but their views are always an over-simplification of the data presented by history. What is not so clear is that we can have no inkling of the trends of history and of some of the principal causes at work. If in some patch of history we discover, as we think, an important principle, without which the patch would be unintelligible, we have the right to apply it also to other patches to see if it provides also a clue there. Again, even if no principle proves to be of far-reaching or of universal value, there are other questions of interest. What part does morality play in history, and to what extent do the ideals or specific doctrines taught by a religion, such, for example, as Christianity, affect our verdict on human events? A doctrine might not help us in our search for a general explanation, but be of the utmost importance in showing us where to turn if we wish to know truth about certain characteristics of man and of civilizations. If there be ultimate truth in the Christian religion, we are bound to ask what is its relation to the truths and to all the values discovered in the slow ascension of man from barbarism to civilization.

Mr. C. S. Lewis is so concerned to unmask the errors of historicism that he tells us little of the meaning he attaches to history. The historian must not look for an 'inner meaning' and he must not go beyond the conclusion of his premises. This might be interpreted in a positivist sense and exclude the introduction of moral or religious judgments. If they are excluded then he removes from human action what makes it truly human. If they are not excluded then it is difficult to draw the line between history and historicism. St. Augustine, for instance, is placed amongst the historicists, and yet much of his argument is to the effect that the Roman Empire has suffered the fate it deserves because of its failure in morals. Similarly with regard to religion. Religion and religious movements are part of history, and their tenets have certainly affected human motives. Moreover, if, perhaps on other grounds, we are convinced of the truth of some religious doctrines, for example, the providence of God, are we to deny ourselves this knowledge when we approach history? Vico claimed that by following empirical methods he was able to show how man developed, and that for this development it was necessary to invoke Providence. He argued that human action manifested an ideal operative in the most short-sighted policies of men, in the development of law, in the growth of primitive communities into cities and nations. This ideal was not a law laid up in heaven, nor apparent in its naked majesty; it came to light gradually in the very time-process and in the evolution of man. But that ideal, owing to the selfishness and folly of man, was continually suffering eclipse, and therefore there must be inherent in the very process the operation of a divine Providence rectifying the crooked and retrogressive tendencies in man. Here is a theory which claims not to go beyond the premises and nevertheless is essentially a science and philosophy of history.

Whatever we may think of the success of Vico in establishing his point, there does not seem any reason why he should not be granted permission to make his attempt, unless we confine history to matters of fact. This is what the positivist wishes to do. Dr. Karl Popper and others insist that history must look after itself without the adventitious aid of a philosophy. The systematization which a philosophy brings involves that over-simplification of the data with which the historian should be concerned. Professor Renier, for instance, in his *History: Its Purpose and Method*, describes history as 'the story of the experiences of men living in civilized societies'. There are events for which we seek the traces and conditions and there are questions relevant to the society, in which we exist, and to the future to which answers can be given. But it does not belong to the historian to generalize and appear in the false guise of a philosopher. The most he can do is to provide material for economists and sociologists. But the positivist in his effort to keep the slate of history free from historicism almost wipes it clean. This is the penalty he pays for studying man as he might be were he not moral and religious. Courage and cunning and selfishness and goodwill are to be met with on every page of history, and the acts proceeding from these virtues and vices have had a determining effect on cities and civilizations. Mr. C. S. Lewis is not positivist, but he does not make clear where he draws the line between the historian and the historicist. If human nature has any laws it ought to be possible at least to gather how man will behave and what the effect will be of behaving well and badly, and if he be moral and religious these characteristics might well lend themselves to historical generalizations more or less philosophical. And yet Mr. Lewis seems ill-disposed to any such generalization on the ground that it is not history. He rejects, for instance, a remark made by Père Paul Henri in his Deneke lecture at Oxford, that Judaic and Christian thought was to be distinguished from Pagan and Pantheistic thought by the significance which they attribute to history. He points out that the Norse gods and the Roman epic have close relations with history. This may be accepted, though it seems to ignore the special point of Père Henri that pagan history is ruled by fate, whereas in Judaic history the actions of men count and make history; but what is noticeable is that Lewis in quoting Rome is arguing that Père Henri is wrong in his history, not that his historicism is necessarily abortive.

Once we allow moral judgment to enter into the historian's account of the past, we open the way to historicism. Thucydides and Gibbon and Lord Acton are historicists, and so far from blaming them most would say that their interpretations are enlightening as well as human. The dictum that 'all power corrupts and absolute power always', is a far-reaching principle and essentially moral. What the historian may not do is to take a set of moral or religious ideas and principles and foist them on the human scene. If he does this he may show himself a good moralist or a worthy propagandist of a faith, but he is exploiting history. The judgment must arise naturally and almost inevitably out of the facts, a conclusion which is seen to be contained in the premises. Our judgments on Cleon and the Athenian demos must be generated by their story; we must not condemn the early tyrants of Sicily just because the word tyrant tends now to prejudice us from the start. The violence and cruelties of the French and Russian revolutions, of Nazism and Fascism may well shock us; we have not to put aside all our moral sentiments in order to pass a correct historical judgment, but what is essential is that we should not judge with prejudice or without weighing all the relevant circumstances. We can go even further than this and generalize in the manner of Acton, praise or damn the 'revolts of the masses', side with Grote in favour of democracy or with Mommsen in favour of Caesarism, or draw out of the evidence of history, like Toynbee, a spiritual and far-reaching principle of 'challenge and response'.

Historians of the present day, partly owing to the constant accumulation of evidence for even the slightest episodes and partly because of the positivist influence, are not as a rule willing to play the part of the philosophic historian. Professor Butterfield in his series of broadcasts and in his published edition of them feels that the historian is put into a strait waist-coat by the positivist formulae, but at the same time he is uncomfortably aware of the dangers of introducing judgments foreign to the province of history. He grants that 'historians, limited by the kind of apparatus they use and the concrete evidence on which they must rely, restrict their realm to what we might almost call the mechanism of historical processes; the tangible factors involved in an episode, the displacements produced in human affairs by an observed event or a specific influence, even the kind of movements that can be recorded in statistics'. This gives history a mundane and matter-of-fact appearance. But it is clearly necessary. It would not do for a student to answer every question in history by saying that it was the finger of God. Not until we have gone as far as most in tidying up mundane events and the human drama are we permitted to bring in wider considerations. It is when we have reconstructed the whole of human life and found it not self-explanatory that we must turn to religion. For the 'fullness of our commentary on the drama of human life in time, we have to break through this technique—have to stand back and see the landscape as a whole—and for the sum of our ideas and beliefs about the march of the ages we need the poet and the prophet, the philosopher and the theologian'. The Christian, and Professor Butterfield writes as a Christian, sees in society and government the effect of the Fall of Man, a consequence of human sin, which also is rectified by the action of Providence. Convinced of this as true, he is in a position to realize that 'there is a gravitational pull in history itself which tends to bring down man's loftiest dreams, so that over a considerable span of time a long-term purpose generally manages to mix itself into a lot of earth'. The historian and the theologian here join hands and expect to find self-righteousness peering out of past human faces and bringing its own doom. Not only morality therefore is inextricably bound up with the historian's outlook, but definite Christian beliefs are verified and to be watched in the pages of history. After this admission, however, Butterfield adds, 'I am not sure that . . . the historian can justifiably go any further'. He feels, that is, that though the historian cannot avoid moral judgment and the sense that sin brings doom he is not in the position to allocate blame and to take upon himself a judgment reserved for the Last Assize. The great human systems come and go, and their doom may be delayed by the skill of a great statesman, but the cupidities of man are always caught up with in the end. This kind of historical judgment is fair and in accordance with the evidence. But even here we have to be careful, for the secular historian may dispense with the idea of Providence or Christian thinking and attribute what happens to causes imbedded in the nature of man and the universe.

Nevertheless Butterfield does go further. He appeals to the practice of historians and reconciles the historian and the historicist by means of what he calls 'myths'. Lewis complained of the habit of historicists of seeking for patterns. He compared them in their futility to the practice of reading faces into a fire. Butterfield agrees that 'the word pattern itself is too hard to be applied to anything so elastic as history'. Better is it to use the word 'myth' as typifying 'an essential process in history'. He points out that we do have recourse to these myths. Galileo, for instance, introduced a new myth and opened up the way to modern science. The view of Marx that history is determined by a conflict in terms of thesis and antithesis is bound to be of interest to the historian. It may never be applicable in its purity, but as a suggestion for dealing with the intractable data of history it is an improvement on a linear theory of development.

Toynbee's hypothesis of 'challenge and response' may mark a still better interpretation of the essential processes of human life. Such myths will not tell us all, but they serve at least a useful purpose and have some relation to the truth. Many of the so-called philosophies of history, of course, do not deserve the name of myth, because they have little or no relation to fact. But this obsession with patterns and symbols reveals the way in which the historian is almost obliged to treat his subject matter. Some people, as Butterfield remarks, see the course of history as a spiral; others as a mechanical system; others, again, as an evolution parallel to the growth of forms of life, and recent thinkers have played with the words 'democracy' and 'progress'. Butterfield holds that all such theories and symbols depend upon too rigid a pattern. He himself ventures a myth not unlike that of Gerald Heard. 'If we want an analogy with history we must think of something like a Beethoven symphony —the point of it is not saved up until the end, the whole of it is not a mere preparation for a beauty that is only to be achieved in the last bar.' In such a musical work the parts have their own beauty and significance even before the end has been heard; similarly each generation and also each individual can be examined and to some extent understood without a general theory of the universe and before the history of man closes. History is a live thing and the image of the symphony can be completed with that of the composer, 'who composes the music as we go along, and, when we slip into aberrations, switches his course in order to make the best of everything'. This 'switching' is not unlike Vico's rectification of the errors of man which Providence is ever performing. Butterfield's idea allows for the unpredictability of history and at the same time for that degree of fixity which all must acknowledge.

Butterfield, therefore, ignores the embargo which writers like Lewis would impose on historians. But he moves cautiously, and it would seem that he does no more than admit the workings of Providence without venturing to explain them in any particular instance. The doctrine of Original Sin is justified by historical evidence, and sin catches up sometime or other on a nation or society. There are myths which give us clues to the meaning of human progress, its successes and setbacks, and the more we use myths or patterns which bring out the personal element the closer do we come to a true explanation. In a more recent work, *History and Human Relations*, Butterfield appears to give up some of the ground held in *Christianity and History*. He is no longer convinced that philosophizing on history can throw any light upon it. Better is it for the historian to stick to his last and pursue the empirical methods now canonized. Even moral judgment should be forsworn. We are all under sentence of sin and our judgments are vitiated not only by lack of perspective but by prejudice. 'The kind of ethical judgments which historians like Lord Acton have been anxious to achieve are possible only to God.' Each side when there is conflict believes that it is in the right, and it is not for us to decide between their claims. The most the historian can do is to be scrupulously fair in setting out the evidence of both sides.

If this be all that the historian can do then history so far written must be purged of some of its most interesting pages. It can have no lesson for the budding statesman. A certain policy may contain in it dangers as serious as the potentialities of the atom bomb; yet like the scientist, the historian must work upon it and state it as dispassionately as the scientist. The question may well be asked whether this be possible, let alone correct. In science the subject matter does not call for moral judgment and the emotions of the scientist are not engaged. But the subject matter of history is human conduct. Moreover the historian cannot divest himself entirely of his feelings and beliefs, and, if he were to try to do so, he would blind himself to what is the nature of human action. The more all-round the historian is, the better equipped is he to understand the variety of human nature. Nero is probably unintelligible to a man who lacks understanding of the artistic temperament, and no one can have an inkling of the power of the motives of, let us say, the Covenanters, who is without any appreciation of the force of religious enthusiasm. Again the medieval or Islamic mentality must be a closed book to the purely positivist historian. Nor is it sufficient to be aware of the strength of morality and religion as a motive force. There must be present also, actively assessing values, a fellow-feeling and sympathy—and where these are active it is impossible to refrain from condemning what is false or sycophantic or hypocritical or base, and praising what is judicious, fair-minded and magnanimous. The truth about the past is what the historian must have for his aim and ideal, and any limitation put on this ideal is a blunder and a hindrance to wisdom. This is likely to be forgotten at a time when departmentalization is so useful, and when history can be studied under so many aspects. We fail, as a result, to notice that poetic drama, for instance, can supplement the work of the prosaic historian, and that Homer and Vergil and Shakespeare have thrown a light upon history which the professional historian does well to study. Ensnared by the ambition to be precise and sure historians wish to treat human material as on a par with the impersonal subject matter of the physical sciences. This is an error denounced centuries before Christ by Aristotle. It is abetted by the anxiety of the historian to do justice to the evergrowing complications of the material with which he is presented. This makes him the slave of his material instead of the master of it. As has been well said: 'No longer a master-builder, the historian has become scarcely more than an articled craftsman (with special trade journals to contain each article of his craft). He has held countless inquisitions and post mortems. He has been indefatigable. But the question he has rarely found need for time to ask himself during the past half-century is, what has become of history?'

But if history be unlike any other subject of research in that it deals with human affairs and human conduct, we are back in the predicament recognized by Butterfield in the first of his two books. Human beings cannot be treated as measurable things and the course of history cannot be predicted. Freewill, morals and religion have all to be taken into account, and if we believe in God we are bound to think of Him as not only creating man but directing man to that end for which he was created. Providence therefore is behind and in history. The historian seeks for truth; that is to say, he must search diligently for what may provide a key to the meaning of what men have done, are doing and will do. We must not in advance lock up certain doors and put up a sign of 'no entry' or 'private'. That is the charter of freedom for the historian. But when the historian tries to act upon this charter, he seems to lose his way. The more positivistically inclined are tempted by the apparent fatalism in historical processes to reduce the story to a series of causes materially determined. The trained mind confines itself to a small patch and by cultivating that is able to eschew generalization, while the moral or theological historian lays his emphasis on non-naturalistic motives or on Providence. *La Scienza Nuova* of Vico may justly be considered the best attempt to press every kind of knowledge into the service of history. Having determined at the beginning to set no limits to what might help him in his search for truth, and having a clear idea of what precisely is the subject matter of history, he draws his evidence from the empirical sciences, from language, from anthropology and from theological doctrine. All is grist to his mill, and he claims that he never deserts the methods which are appropriate to historical study and that his use of Providence is no *deus ex machina* but derived from the evidence before him. No one would claim that his work was entirely successful, but it has the merit of showing the way which historicism is justified in taking.

Butterfield for a while appeared to be following on the trail blazed by Vico. But as already stated, he has shown a growing inclination to reserve judgment on deeds of the past. The reason for this may perchance be that he is well acquainted with some recent trends in Christian Protestant theology. This trend is best known under the name of its chief exponent, Karl Barth. In his voluminous works Barth has repudiated not only the idea of liberal theology but also any affiliation between the Christian faith and human progress. In so doing he has raised a fundamental question about history and the relation of Christianity to it. If he is to be believed, it is useless to look for any religious meaning in history. He cuts the ground from under the feet of the philosophers like Bossuet or Vico by denying the relevance of faith to secular developments. The two cities of which St. Augustine wrote exist, but there is no intercourse whatever between them. Scandalized by the liberals' repainting and redecorating of the Christian Revelation, Barth has swept away all human comment on the word of God, as Christ drove the traffickers from the Temple. God's Revelation is a *mysterium tremendum*, and there is no human medium in which or by which it can be comprehended. Faith is a pure gift, ineffable and untranslatable, and God chooses without any consideration of human merit His elect, to whom He gives this divine gift of faith. There is nothing, therefore, in human life or effort, nothing in human history, in its institutions, moral order or spiritual aspirations, which can serve as a *point d'appui*, or point of contact, with the mystery of the kingdom. He who is justified in Christ and one of the elect is, in St. Paul's language, a new man. Before justification he may have had every human virtue, but this now counts for nothing. He has thrown off the old man to enter a new life.

This uncompromising view stands out as a corrective of the too humanist and secular views dominant at the end of the nineteenth century, and it serves to restore the sense of the majesty of God, whose ways are not like our ways. It rightly assigns all in the supernatural order to the action of God. Nevertheless, if expressed intransigently and without qualification, it snuffs out all human effort and makes naught of the Christian message. Try as we may, we cannot abolish altogether the human element because the divine revelation has to be couched in human speech and in the writings of the evangelists and St. Paul, from whom incidentally Barth has drawn his teaching. Even Christ Himself would be lost to us because the Word was made Flesh and dwelt amongst us in a human nature. That such must be the conclusion of Barth's views was at first thought to be necessarily correct. But Barth has written at enormous length, and in his later writings the severity of his tone has been softened. He has tried to bridge the gulf he has made by means of what he calls 'tokens', without at the same time yielding any of the positions he has taken up. All comes from God, and Christ reconciles us to Himself, and 'only as he beholds the reconciliation that has taken place between God and man, can *Man* know *God*. Anything that man may imagine he knows about God apart from reconciliation, that is to say in his "natural" position as a rebel against God and consequently under the wrath of God, is in truth but the idol of his own heart.' But because of Revelation and because of the reconciliation man may be able in his new state to discern tokens of Revelation. These tokens are in created things, and 'Jesus Christ Himself has instituted and established and determined them, in order that, according to God's good pleasure, they may serve and be effective as tokens of Revelation; in order that they may be witnesses and testimonies to Jesus Christ for the purpose of calling men to faith in Him'. These 'tokens', however, do not mean that human life has been lifted up into association with the divine or that the divine is made convertible into human terms. The gulf remains; our thoughts, actions, and history are too human and contaminated by sin. There is, moreover, another reason why history is devoid of eternal significance. Barth fastens on to the eschatological passages in the New Testament. The mysterious statements about the end of the world and the second coming are identified by him with the advent of Christ who 'fulfils all things'. Christ is the consummation promised in the Old Testament, and nothing that matters can happen in the time which succeeds that coming. So far from history having a Christian meaning it is a waste-product, a kind of Limbo which Christ has passed by. Those who have to live in it live by faith in another kingdom, and their true life is not of this world. As R. Mehl, one of Barth's followers says: 'The new man is quite different from the historical, Christian type, which psychologists and moralists are very well able to describe by contrast with the ancient sage or modern citizen. The Christian type bears the mark of Christianity—but in so far as it is a type of civilization, it gives us no likeness of the new man. The latter is not to be verified in experience.'

If Barth be right then any hope of finding a Christian philosophy of history must be abandoned. The strength of his argument depends on two points, one, that the Christian Revelation entails a denial of all human values, and two, that, after the fulfilment of all things in the coming of Christ, later history has no ultimate sense; 'life is but a shadow . . . a tale told by an idiot, full of sound and fury, signifying nothing'. Such a disconcerting conclusion invites an immediate denial, but that would be unwise, because there is an important problem raised by Barth's abrupt dismissal of human values. Both the unworldliness and the eschatological outlook are implicit, if not always explicit in Christian teaching, and cannot be dismissed as of secondary value. It belongs to the very fabric of Christian belief that all things begin and end in Christ, that history leads up to His Coming, and that in some sense finality is reached in His advent and Redemption. There is a soaring expression of this doctrine in the liturgy of the Church, especially in the antiphons of the Office for Christmas and the Epiphany. Again, all Christians must admit that the life of grace is invisible and that in the new kingdom of Christ God forestalls, initiates and does all by His grace freely given. Man is incapable even at his best morally and spiritually of eliciting a single act in the supernatural order by his own effort or merit. True also is it that in the New Testament the old man or the world is set in sharpest contrast with the new man and the kingdom, which, as Christ said to Pilate, is not of this world. All this has to be admitted, and Barth excites attention by shouting it from the housetops and without any qualification. He cannot, therefore, be accused of a new and outrageous view of the Christian teaching; what he fails to do is to do justice to the balancing doctrines. It would seem in vain that the Fourth Gospel deigns to use the human wisdom of the logos and Greek philosophy, and that St. Paul tried to talk the language of the Athenians at the Areopagus. In the main tradition of Christianity from the beginning, the truth which Barth emphasizes is woven into another which is equally part of the Christian creed. The Incarnation of the Son of God is an historical fact; it is also a vindication of the dignity of human nature; its password into eternal life. The Son of God could be seen and handled, and the society He founded is a visible Church, the dispenser of graces. The millions of Christians, who have helped to make history, have consolidated their spiritual life in family duties and amidst social institutions, in the happy belief that everything belonging to human nature could be sanctified and consecrated to Christian ends. Barth cannot ignore these facts, and they create a problem for him. How can the 'elect' who are alive upon this earth have their 'new life' expressed wholly in another dimension from that of History? From certain statements he makes it would seem as if he approached the Catholic answer. He says that the future world is already here but in mystery and sacramentally. The Catholic might subscribe to this formula, though it is to be feared that it would mean much more to him than it appears to mean for Barth. Barth's meaning is that the Redemption has restored the world and that there are reflections of this new glory to be found in the works of man and of civilization. But the restoration belongs to another plane and will not be revealed until the last day. Till then it is hidden in God with Jesus Christ. The best that can be seen in the world is a reflection like the light reflected on a pool or mountain-side. Culture, he says, has its own worth and dignity, but it is 'an exclusively earthly reflection of the Creation, which itself remains . . . lost and hidden from us'. There 'is no continuity between the analogies and the divine reality, no objective relation between what is signified and what really is; no transition, therefore, definable in terms of any progress, can be made between one and the other'. Such an inflexible verdict rules out any hope of relating heaven and earth, grace and nature. History can never be more than a pastime. When the last trumpet sounds, all the works of man will fade out; they have no bearing on what then is to be revealed.

The import of Barth's views has been widely realized, especially as these views are in accord with a new trend in Protestant theology. They confront us with a new view on history which to many is unpalatable but cannot be ignored. The result has been almost a spate of ideas, some favouring, others discountenancing Barth, but all to some extent affected by his winds of doctrine. Rightly has this change been called the 'theology of crisis', and the work of theologians like Oscar Cullman and Reinhold Niebuhr, not to mention Emil Brunner, and many others, centres round this critical problem. Most have felt that the stark rejection of history is inadmissible. The Christian religion has been founded by God made man, and the reverberations of the divinized humanity will be heard down the ages to the end of time. Nature and the supernatural action of God have been wedded together, and to divorce them is, however salutary the purpose, a desecration. The task of the Christian thinker is, therefore, to do justice to the marriage, while accepting the very different roles and even temperaments of each member. The Protestant has his own problems due to the competing influences of Calvinism and liberal theology. The history of Catholic thought, however, bears witness to a corresponding problem, as the scales can be seen to have moved up and down, now weighted in favour of a severely ascetic view, now inclined to what may be called a sacramental outlook on nature and life. Because of the different interests in past ages both schools had in mind rather the question of the worth and use of earthly joys and loves than the more general subject of history. Clearly, however, the two subjects are closely interconnected. If what men do and think as individuals and in society is worth while for its own sake and gives body to spiritual purposes, then the record of man's acts and experiences will have significance even by Christian standards. On the other hand, if it be a world in which the Christian should take no part, it would seem to be no more than a ladder or scaffolding to be discarded after use.

That the scales can go up and down is confirmed by a recent discussion of this very topic of nature and history and grace by some distinguished Catholic thinkers. The 'ascetic' standpoint can be found in an article in the *Nouvelle Revue Théologique* for March 1949 by Père Léopold Malevez. He begins by quoting a Thomist, Père Y. Congar, O.P. Père Congar is ready to admit that there is a connection between the progress of the world and the final reality of the Kingdom of God. But he immediately qualifies this statement by saying that 'there is no continuity between one and the other. It is not human effort which gains for us the Kingdom of God. The latter does not come as the fruit of the world's progress. Biblically it appears as a gift, as resting essentially in God's dominion. Neither the world nor even the Church bring it about. It is given from on high; it is Christ who will bring it about by His own power.' In further explanation of this somewhat mysterious olive branch he adds: 'Human effort, natural and temporal though it be, does search for the answers to the questions of which the kingdom will be the final solution. Man labours at an answer, and he ought so to labour, but he will never entirely reach the answer. And the reason is that we are in a world of mishaps and reverses, in a world too that is sinful, whose character it is to set questions and not give answers. The sense of history, the consciousness of human effort, mean that we are struggling towards the kingdom; that is, struggling for perfect knowledge, perfect justice and happiness, for a complete mastery of good over evil, of life over disease and death and all that goes with death or leads to it; a striving for power and the victory over matter by spirit; a continuous struggle to overcome what is heavy and thick, darkness and time. All these struggles are attempts to achieve a state and an answer which only the kingdom can provide.' 'What position then exactly', Père Congar asks, 'does this world hold relatively to the kingdom?' His reply is that progress represents a series of preliminary sketches, necessary, indeed, but such as will be superseded by the ultimate version. These sketches are like to the efforts made by a class of students to whom the master has set a task beyond their powers. They improve steadily, though all their attempts are inadequate and fall short altogether of the true answer.

The attempts, nevertheless, are necessary if the students are to reach the stage of appreciating the answer when it is given.

After thus quoting Père Congar, Père Malevez points out the prima facie likeness of his view to that of Barth. He does not, however, believe that the likeness goes deep. To Barth this world is an exile and has no communication with the world of faith, whereas to Père Congar, as to all Catholics, Christ is to be with us all days and the kingdom comes to be secretly perhaps, but sacramentally, and it is ever operative in the souls of the just. The human Body of Christ continues to be present, and the Church is the extension of Christ in time. The Holy Ghost, the spirit of truth, dwells in the Church and in the hearts of the faithful and confers upon human acts a divine and ultimate value. So far from being waste products, our human experience is the dough in which the yeast works; divinity shapes our ends, rough hew them as we may. If then it be true that we can be already citizens of the heavenly city, the merely external relation which Barth posits must be replaced by a most intimate one, and whereas Barth regards it as arrogance to attribute any salvific value to human acts, the Catholic believes that God's grace can so activate his life as to make what he does spiritually meritorious. Père Malevez is at pains to make this contrast, but having done so he proceeds to qualify the Catholic assurance. According to St. Thomas Aquinas man does not merit eternal life because of his human choices; it is the grace of the Holy Spirit within the soul which gives those choices their worth in the sight of God. If, says St. Thomas, we envisage the substance of the human act just in so far as it is the outcome of our free will, it falls short of con-dignity to the supernatural reward. We can speak of a con-gruity, and that is all. This congruity can be described as a certain equality of proportion. That is to say, it is congruous or fitting that when a man's acts are humanly virtuous God should reward them in proportion to their excellence; if how-ever we have to speak of meritorious acts according as they proceed from the grace of the Holy Spirit, then those acts merit eternal life *ex condigno*. What is meant by *ex condigno* St. Thomas explains in one of his answers to difficulties. 'Though the grace of the Holy Spirit, which we have in our present life, is not equal to the glory to come, it is, nevertheless, equal to it virtually; even as in the seed of the tree the whole tree is virtually present. Similarly the grace which is present in man comes from the Holy Spirit, who is the all-sufficient cause of life eternal; wherefore it is said to be the pledge of our inheritance.' Père Malevez infers from this passage that St. Thomas severs all connection between the values of this world and those of the kingdom of God. If this were true, human history would be in 'outer darkness'. But it may well be argued that the distinction made by St. Thomas is necessarily abstract and that he would be the first to acknowledge that the distinctions he makes fall within the same subject, man. Our acts remain ours when graced as well as when they are merely human, and the union of grace and nature is indivisible. Here indeed we walk in mystery, and it is difficult to apply distinctions accurately. It is human nature which is graced, and it is the person who acts. At the same time what is given to us and engrafted on to our nature is a pure grace, given freely, one to which we have no right. By this alone is our life privileged to have a family likeness to the divine, and we dare not make any boast about this grace, as if it were ours by right. Not so unreasonably, therefore, Père Malevez writes: 'The continuity of our present life with the kingdom of the reward, authentic though it be, is not absolute; nay it is inexistent if we consider our human condition for what it is apart from grace and as that of a creature.'

As if this were not enough to check enthusiasm, other serious limitations have to be mentioned. Grace elevates human nature, but the theologians tell us that the union of God with the soul, is in the highest part of the soul, and so light, if profound, is God's touch that we have normally no experience of it. We live by faith and not by experience, and we are left conscious only of our loneliness and vulnerable state. What is even more perplexing at first sight, there appears to be no change in man's condition despite the coming of the kingdom of Christ; Christ's victory over the effects of sin is not consummated here on earth. This, in truth, looks like a setback, after the certain news of what the liturgy calls the *copiosa redemptio*. Though so much more generous than the original gift to Adam of sanctifying grace, the Redemption does not repair human nature so as to make it comparable in its integrity with the state of man before the Fall. Human integrity is not restored, and there remains, as is only too obvious, a resistance to grace and a rebellion of the flesh. No Catholic theologian would call our human nature corrupt, nor would he follow Barth in describing history as branded by sin. His word is 'bias' or 'inclination', a bias towards evil, and this is enough to throw doubt upon any equation of the best in this world with the kingdom of God. For this reason Père Malevez says: 'Not only is the continuity of our life with eternal life incomplete by reason of our divided self, but also for this further reason that our self is not in accord with righteousness.' This he would say is borne out by experience: every one is aware of a sickness of soul, and not even the Church in its human and historical record has kept free of the taint of worldliness and sin. That is why in the Council of Trent the emphasis is laid not on man's good works but on the righteousness of Christ. The Church rests its hope on the divine assistance, ever mending the weakness of man, and our merit does not come from our justice, but from that of Christ who sustains us. Like Barth and every serious student of the New Testament, the Catholic theologian turns to divine grace and the act of God whenever the rehabilitation and perfection of human nature are in question. Only a hairsbreadth seems to separate the differing views, and yet we know that such important consequences follow from that tiny difference, it must be more decisive than it appears. To the Barthian God is withdrawn; He is not to be found in the world which is given over to sin. To the Catholic the supernatural is present, but we are not so endowed that we can point out its presence or feel it. Hence Père Malevez has to repeat the bewilderment of Job: 'The philosophers ask themselves about the meaning of history; what is the meaning, the plan, the absolute explanation of our individual lives, with their disconcerting alternation of joys and pains, grandeur and degradation? And what is the supreme intelligible law which governs the procession of civilizations and the rise and fall of empires?' In the end, he owns, we are left baffled and have to fall back on faith, on the presence of Christ and the workings of the Holy Spirit.

So far Père Malevez has been dealing professedly with the question of human moral and spiritual fitness for eternal life and the relations between them. He enlarges the question now so as to embrace that of the ultimate significance of progress in science and learning and the development of civilized life. It does not seem credible to him that God, who has taken human nature, should not take into consideration that world of which human beings are a part. In Christ is perfect humanity revealed and honoured, and everything is reconstituted in Him. It follows that the best of man's products, his science and culture, have a place in the Christian dispensation. This line of thought, if followed out, would take us far from Barth. Père Malevez, however, is content with Père Congar's striking image. Man's efforts are similar to the attempts of pupils to answer a problem which is beyond them. The master knows that the problem is beyond their capacity, but sets it because it is good for them to try, and their answers may gradually approach the true solution. 'Precisely in this way,' says Père Malevez, 'are we to think of the immense, pathetic history of man in relation to that destiny to which God is leading him. It would be blasphemous to imagine that our profane culture can ever, by its own strength and out of its own isolated resources, create our heavenly state. Too true is it rather that its highest accomplishments . . . do not win for it the slenderest right or claim in regard to the "new man"; in the end its most outstanding successes will pale and disappear at the dawn of the last day; materially nothing will remain of the discoveries of man's genius. Thereby the difference and discontinuity of the future life with the present are safeguarded, and, also, due regard is paid to contemporary Catholic theologians who favour an eschatological answer. But all this does not prevent our finding room for perfectionist tendencies. . . . All the victories of thought and art over matter and its clogging and opaque nature are to that same degree the works of Christ Himself. Of Him Scripture says that all was constituted by Him, and His Lordship reaches beyond the frontiers of the Church and what, in the strict sense of the term, is called His Body, to exercise itself over all the powers of the entire world.' This belief gives significance to our occupations and requires that we should put our best into all we do, and it gives that zest for learning and discovery which has been such a notable mark of Western civilization.

The answer, therefore, of Père Malevez to the problem of the relation of the 'two cities', the heavenly and the earthly, runs along the lines set by Père Congar. Human history has no continuity with the final truth which will be revealed at the last day by Christ. But that does not mean that the growth of civilization and the attempts to understand the history of man are valueless. We have a problem which is beyond our powers and all human answers will fall short of the final truth. Nevertheless we are keyed up by the effort to know and to achieve greatness, because our tentative and defective essays help us to appreciate the far-off, dim trans-stellar kingdom and to apply ourselves still more ardently to prepare our minds and will for it. This, in contrast with the absolute veto of Barth, offers a measure of reconciliation. It may not, however, seem to amount to very much. That we should be thankful for such small mercies is suggested by Père Malevez's reference to one hitherto little-mentioned difficulty. This difficulty is so serious that many take it as decisive. How, they ask, can we think of any continuity between this world and the Kingdom of Christ when the basic teaching of Christianity harps upon discontinuity? 'I preach Christ crucified.' The Christian religion is one of self-denial and the rejection of this world. The Incarnation is followed by the Cross, and from the Apostolic times onwards the theme of Christian writers has been that power and riches corrupt and that the kingdom of God is won by violence, the violence of self-sacrifice and hatred of what this world offers. Père Malevez contents himself with a short answer, which comes to this. Self-abnegation cannot be made into a principle which will exclude all human values. Such a use of it would be suicidal and make Christianity a foe to the advances of medicine, the alleviation of pain, the improvement of social conditions. The Christian balance is preserved if we practise such detachment as will save us from appropriating success to ourselves and exaggerating the worth of what we do. There is a more ultimate principle under which that of self-denial falls, namely, to seek first the kingdom of God. The remark of Charles du Bos on St. Augustine excellently exemplifies this: 'Il semble qu'il-y-ait chez Saint Augustin une delicatesse suprême qui l'incite à parachever et comme à caresser par l'expression les choses dont il faut qu'il se détache au moment même qu'il va s'en détacher.'

A more positive view of the value of history and human endeavour has been put forward by the Abbot of Downside in an article in the *Downside Review* of 1950 (Summer Number). There he raises the question explicitly: What is the value of science and humane history to a Christian? Within the unity

of Catholic belief he recognizes that there have been two different tendencies, the one leaning to detachment and in recent
years sometimes formulating itself in terms of eschatology; the
other more humane and conciliatory. In its rigorist form the
first commits itself to the discontinuity of all history with the
kingdom of God, taking as its support the words of St. John:
'We know that we are of God, and the whole world is seated in
wickedness. And we know that the Son of God is come. And
He hath given us understanding that we may know the true
Son. This is the true God and life eternal.' This text and others
of the same trend are interpreted to mean that this world of
wickedness is in the power of the evil one, the Adversary; the
Christian has to shun its deceits and have his conversation in
heaven. Christ came not to bring peace but a sword, and the
sword signifies separation and sacrifice. We have to live in the
world as if not belonging to it, to use what is necessary in it as
means to the sanctification of ourselves and of our neighbour.
Even the highest values in the world must be given up; the
'sweet sound that breathes upon a bank of violets', the beauty
that is too dear for our possessing, laughter and the love of
friends, to all these we must bid good-bye save when they can
profit us in our spiritual athleticism. 'Our work', as Abbot
Butler says, according to this view is 'not to embellish the
world, but to confront its hostility, and we pass from our
divided world to God by a *salto mortale*.'

Uncomfortable and uncomforting as this teaching is, there
can be no doubt that it has a place, if not the primary place, in
the Christian faith. Renunciation and self-denial are the constant refrain of the preacher, and he has abundant texts from
Scripture on which to draw. Holiness and asceticism go together. There is, moreover, an unearthly beauty in this ideal
when practised and in the increment which it gives to earthly
loves. Humanism is made to look coarse and even vulgar when
it falls upon a comparison. Its limitations can be clearly seen,
for instance, in the disdainful remark of Goethe after his visit
to Assisi: 'I left on one side with a feeling of aversion the
enormous foundation of the Churches crammed side by side
in a Babylonian fashion.' His tastes did not include the heaven-
lit beauty which St. Francis bequeathed to the Umbrian hill-
side. As men cannot help rating the rare and the refined above
the common and the coarse, so to Christian eyes at least the

sculptured St. Bruno and the elongated figures on the portals
of Chartres may more than make up for the natural perfection
of a Greek Apollo.

And yet! and yet! 'Dost thou think because thou art virtuous
there shall be no more cakes and ale?' Shakespeare, if it be true
that in these lines he is tilting against the new Puritanism,
thought the old Catholic ideals smiled on God's good gifts.
Abbot Butler, taking his cue perhaps from St. Thomas More,
champions a Christian humanism. It is an alternative which
also has a long pedigree, and its fruits are to be seen in the
medieval and early Renaissance world. History is not the son
of a bondswoman, to be cast out. All human action prepares
the way for the coming of Christ's kingdom, and above all
Christian activity. Those who are in grace have an interior
quality which makes their work anticipatory of what is to
come. Life is thereby gradually disposed through the ages to
receive and fertilize the good tidings of the kingdom of God.
Time is the flower, and eternity the fruit. Since the Incarnation
Christianity has bestowed many gifts on man, giving him a sense
of eternal life, of a living Providence, of the dignity of human
nature and its products. In fact, Christians are heirs to the
kingdom, and what they are and do has a certain condignity
with eternal life. The difficulty remains, notwithstanding this
plea for human values, as to how they can be reconciled with
the hard sayings of the Gospel and tradition, and it is here that
Abbot Butler's view becomes noteworthy. He does not burke
the difficulties, but first he bids us beware of taking texts from
the Scriptures and using them as scientific formulae. The
Hebrew genius has a prophetic type of writing which has its
own special rules of interpretation. Passages which seem to lay
down a law, such as that of turning the other cheek, taking up
one's cross daily and hating one's father and mother, do not
belong to the same genre as the canonical prescriptions to fast
and abstain and to keep the Sabbath holy. Again, the Gospel is
a dynamic force most fittingly described in terms of a new birth,
or, in a favourite Pauline image, the making of all things new
in Christ. As a result the early Christians were vividly and
defiantly conscious of the change, the newness, and of its contrast with the old. The old seemed dead—it was done with—
and the present novelty of life struck them so overwhelmingly
that it left no room for past or future. In their end was their

beginning, and the coming advent of the Lord left them with no thought of the morrow or the affairs of this world. This view contains the eschatological element in Christianity, a permanent truth, whose connections with other truths needed time and experience to determine. At first the realization of the new birth tended to be joined with the anticipation of the Last Day and to coalesce in their experience. As time went on, however, the gap began to widen, and scope was given to develop the implications contained in the fact that the time of anticipation was indefinite. One momentous implication attendant on time for its realization was that Christ continued present in life as generation succeeded generation. The Incarnation touched different places and different times and peoples, and this new power gave to all a new consecration and mystery. Christ was present in hidden form in the Eucharist and in His visible Church, but Christ was also favouring and gracing all that was being drawn into His orbit. This must mean that the period of anticipation before the end of the world, a period very prolonged and indefinite, must be taken seriously; it belongs to Christ and is an extension of His first coming, the while He grows to His full stature. The presence of Christ in the Church and in the Eucharist was recognized to be real though different from His mode of living before His death and Ascension. The next step is to extend the use of the word 'sacramental' to cover in a more general sense what goes on in the years which are described as 'the years of the Lord'.

Thinking along these lines Abbot Butler holds that the period between the two comings—the Incarnation and the Last Day—has a special mark like that on the doorpost of the Israelites the night the Egyptians were smitten. Humanity received a new birth at the advent of God, and this new birth is not stillborn or smothered in infancy. It is to be regarded not as a shadow fading away before the Second Coming, but as a real, unparalleled anticipation of it. The change can be described in terms of a prevenient grace, which prepares nature and dresses it for the time when all things shall be made new, nature as well as what is experienced in faith. We ought not, therefore, to leave history in the ditch while we travel with our hidden treasure to our last end. To think in this way is to undervalue the Incarnation. The new Adam, like the old, gives a name to creatures, a new name, and His re-creative act has become part of the texture of history. It does not abolish but transfigures historical values. The harvest to be reaped at the end of time is homogeneous with the historical seed, and in its growth that seed exercises its mysterious, biological alchemy on the inanimate matter wherein it has been placed. In this sense we are justified in interpreting the words, 'the Kingdom of God is at hand'. We are not undergoing the baptism of St. John, for Christ has already had His heralds and His prophets, and His reign to which there will be no end, has already begun. Hence St. Paul adds to his warning that we are dead with Christ the good news that we are redeemed in hope. In this hope the Christian looks on the kingdom of God as sacramentally present and as subject to the vicissitudes of history, though triumphant over them. It is the object of violent struggle, the pearl of great price, the hidden treasure, and also it establishes and renews on an eternal basis every human value.

That a Christian should be told also to lose his life and to be crucified to the world is compatible with such a sacramental view of nature and history. These and similar commands convey the sense of newness, the passing of the old and the need of deliverance from it. But newness does not mean mere denial. As nature and evolution show, the old is taken up and persists in a new form. Without doubt much which so-called humanism offers has no place in the kingdom of God, for it is subject to human vanity and is false. Original Sin casts its shadow over the boasted works of man and gives the glitter of Babylon to what might otherwise have belonged to Jerusalem. But the diseases of the body do not render the body evil, and similarly the stains on nature and human effort do not affect its ontological worth. They remain good and may be reorganized into a diviner scheme. As it is said in the Epistle to the Romans: 'Created nature has been condemned to frustration not for some deliberate fault of its own, but for the sake of him who so condemns it, with a hope to look forward to, namely, that nature in its turn will be set free from the tyranny of corruption, to share in the glorious freedom of God's sons.' In other words, nature too struggles in hope, and 'every human achievement, at every level of human interest that is done or preserved in grace will find its apotheosis in the post-historic reign of God.'

In saying that history is the flowering of the seed whose fruits will be garnered at the end in the kingdom of God, Abbot

183

Butler brings together as closely as possible human life to its supernatural end. No longer have we to accept the discontinuity laid down by Père Congar and Père Malevez. The Christian has not to arrive personally safe but without luggage; he has to take with him all that he acquires on the road. There is no misanthropic unworldliness here! Even the image of the pilgrim with his staff and scrip hastening past Vanity Fairs or valleys of tears must be dropped. We are so accustomed to what Abbot Butler might call the cautionary tales or necessary moods of spiritual writers that we may be at first timid in accepting this challenging and heartening view. In *The Imitation of Christ* by Thomas à Kempis, for instance, there is little concern about the values of this life. 'Thou errest greatly if thou seekest any other thing than to suffer, for all this mortal life is full of miseries and is all beset about and marked with crosses.' In one of the first documents of the Christian era the letter of St. Ignatius of Antioch to the Romans the same note is to be found: 'For alive as I am at the moment of writing my longing is for death. Desire within me has been nailed to the cross and no flame of material longing is left. Only the living water speaks within me saying: Hasten to the Father. I have no taste for the food which perishes nor for the pleasures of this life. I want the Bread of God which is the Flesh of Christ, who was the seed of David; and for drink I desire His Blood, which is love that cannot be destroyed.' So long and strong a catena of passages can be made down the ages with the same import that even those who are won over by Abbot Butler's argument may well feel qualms. They may wonder whether both views must not in some way be maintained, if that be possible. Newman in his *Parochial Sermons* felt the pull of both sides. 'Religion', he says, 'has (as it were) its very life in what are paradoxes and contradictions in the eyes of reason. It is a seeming inconsistency how we can pray for Christ's coming, yet wish time "to work out our salvation" and "make our calling and election sure". . . . And so it is a paradox how the Christian should in all things be sorrowful yet always rejoicing, and dying yet living, and having nothing but possessing all things.' It would look as if one of the supreme paradoxes of Christianity is the sturdy belief in matter, in work, in vocation to all the tasks which enable life to be carried on, and at the same time in its call upon all to renounce the world and all its pomps from the very moment of baptism.

Since by history we mean in general the record of man upon earth so far as it is sufficiently known, discussion of it has perforce had to combine many problems which should be kept distinct. Every individual, for instance, has to go to school with Christ, to turn over a new leaf in the manner demanded by St. John the Baptist, and all his life has to be regulated by a new directive of love. How he regards other loves and the world in which he has to live will be controlled by this. In comparison with this new force of love all else is secondary and may be spoken of as of no importance. Nevertheless his life is full of duties and he has his human ties, and in working with and for others and his community he has to reverence nature and human life and create something perfect, whose value is not negligible. Because of this the individual's spiritual ideal cannot be entirely separated from the more general problem of the value of his works, especially when they are seen as part of the general human effort which issues into civilizations. Have truth, as shown in pure and practical science, and philosophy, and beauty, as manifested in nature and works of painting, poetry, music and architecture, an intrinsic value on which we can linger, or are they to be treated as sheer scaffolding to lift us up into a spiritual world beyond them? Newman evoked criticism when, in his *Idea of a University*, he emphasized the intrinsic value of higher education. His own belief even in his early ministry was that 'the Creator of the world is none other than the Father of our Lord Jesus Christ; there are not two worlds, one of matter, one of spirit; one of the Law, and one of the Gospel. . . . We must not give up the visible world as if it came from the evil one. It is our duty to change it into the kingdom of heaven'. And in another of the *Parochial Sermons* he observes that Scripture and spiritual writers emphasize the world's dangers and evil because we have to 'unlearn false notions of its excellence and be saved the disappointment which follows them. And, therefore, it is that Scripture omits even what might be said in praise of the world's pleasures— not denying their value, such as it is, or forbidding us to use them religiously, but knowing that we are sure to find them out for ourselves without being told about them, and that our danger is on the side not of undervaluing but of overvaluing them. . . .' This view he kept all his life, and in later days in a magisterial passage he sums up what he has to say on 'God's temporal blessings'. 'All the beauty of nature, the kind influence of the seasons, the gifts of sun and moon, and the fruits of the earth, the advantages of civilized life, and the presence of friends and intimates; all these good things are but one extended and wonderful type of God's benefits in the Gospel. Those who aim at perfection will not reject the gift, but add a corrective. They will add the bitter herbs to the fatted calf and the music and the dancing; they will not refuse the flowers of earth, but they will toil in plucking out the weeds.' (*Sermons of the Day*, pp. 123–4.)

It is this second problem which leads us directly to the question of a possible Christian philosophy of history. If, as Newman thinks, God's creation, the world, is so disposed that it can collaborate in the making of a significant society upon earth, and if the works of this human society are not bleared with sin so as to make only mementoes of mortality, then can we hope for some continuity between the fruits of time and the supernatural kingdom? Good as this earthly life may be, the best that this world can offer may by comparison be vanity compared with what is to be, or at best a foretaste. When Donne tells us that Methuselah, the Four Monarchies, and 'all the powerful kings and all the beautiful queens of this world were but as a bed of flowers, some gathered at six, some at seven, some at eight, all in one morning in respect of this day', he is not only belittling time in contrast with eternity but emptying its fair products of ultimate significance. In this our human life the Providence shown will be pedagogic but not revelatory. Abbot Butler, as we have seen, firmly holds to the belief of continuity between this life and the next, time bringing the flower and eternity the fruit, but to Père Congar human life is at best an exercise in patience and a trial expedition to an Everest which is beyond our strength. No one can deny that pain and effort are ingredients of human happiness in this world. 'They that sow in tears shall reap in joy. Going they went and wept casting their seeds, but coming, they shall come with joyfulness carrying their sheaves.' The theme of philosophers and poets is the fragility of love and life; not only the glories of our blood and state are shadows not substantial things, but beauty is like a flower which wrinkles will devour, and death takes everything away. So overwhelming is the contrast between the flickering half-lights of time and the radiance of eternity that it is hard to believe that one can prefigure the other. But perhaps a more delicate and subtle sense may see in the melancholy of loss a proof that time anticipates as well as takes away. Newman, who from boyhood, as he said himself, felt that the spiritual world was alone real, nevertheless was persuaded that the glories of nature are types of what is to come: 'To those who live by faith, everything they see speaks of that future world; the very glories of nature, the sun, moon and stars and the richness of the earth, are as types and figures witnessing and teaching the invisible things of God. All that we see is destined one day to burst forth into a heavenly bloom, and to be transfigured into immortal glory.'

Chapter VII

THE CRUCIAL VIEW OF HISTORY

At the beginning of the section on Christianity and History I made reference to three ideas, the eschatological, the other-worldly and the providential, which must enter into any Christian theory. All three are like angels with flaming swords barring the way to any entry into God's mind and the meaning of the Christian dispensation of history. C. S. Lewis expressed himself entirely sceptical about the possibility of any historicism, as he calls it, because of our present and incurable lack of knowledge of the past and future. All hope of anticipating providence seemed to him vain. God is the composer of an age-long drama, and we who are actors in it and unaware of the design even in our own small parts, would commit an act of contemptible folly in trying to explain what will only be intelligible at the end. To this an answer is given both by Heard and Butterfield that in an artistic composition the parts may have intrinsic worth and meaning and we can at least try to extend our knowledge from what we know to the whole. This argument is sufficiently plausible to allow us to try. Our efforts may not be final, but they may provide us with some principles and give us an inkling. When we turn to the historic religion of Christianity we are faced with the second problem, namely, the apparent conflict of its ideals with human progress and secular happiness. The eschatological problem is closely associated with this doctrine of unworldliness. If the Christian is to live in expectation of the second coming of Christ, he is not likely to be overmuch interested in time and the affairs of man which make history. On the other hand the Scripture texts are so rich in mystery and so firmly embedded in the whole Christian Revelation, it may be that they will prove to be like pillars of fire by night in our search for a Christian philosophy.

C. S. Lewis in his attack on Historicism introduces a line of thought which he does not leave himself space to follow out. 'Each man finds in his own life every moment of time is completely filled. He is bombarded every second by sensations, emotions, thoughts, which he cannot attend to for their multitude, and nine-tenths of which he must simply ignore. A single second of lived time contains more than can be recorded. And every second of past time has been like that for every man that ever lived.' Now the obvious, but superficial answer to this is that every individual knows most of his experience is not recorded because it is not worth recording; what he selects and chooses and makes known in action is the juice of the orange. Self-criticism is, however, notoriously faulty, and, what is more important, much of the lost vital history of a soul can never be made public. The interior life is a world apart and external behaviour gives us only a far-off glance at it. Now history has to by-pass all this hidden experience, and it can do no more than describe and interpret individuals in their public relation to events and movements in various societies. As such they become like thistledown and

> *Gaily these ghosts of flowers*
> *With rise and swirl and fall*
> *Dance to their burial.*

The historian has to be content with these ghosts, and he is seldom fully aware of the fact. He is the manager of the appearances of human beings on the stage, and because these persons do obey certain rules and fit in with other characters and with a general human behaviour, he tends to think he understands the individual and is interpreting the whole of human nature. The more he falls under the spell of history-making the less can he do justice to the uniqueness of each individual. The spiritual is unconsciously transferred into semi-materialistic bondage; human beings become numbers without a name, what Hegel calls 'moments' to be subsumed in higher unities. They are led to the top of the hill and then led down again; they are a group under a leader, a class which is being freed, a nation which is growing or decreasing in power. The multitudes of obscure individuals flit into history and out again; they grow into vast hordes in the East, building the Pyramids or crossing the Hellespont; they die in their thousands in the plague of Athens, in the mines of Syracuse or at Lake Trasimene and Philippi; they storm the Bastille, gather outside the Palazzo Venetia or perish in concentration camps. Even those whose portrait is finely drawn and who peer out at us in the pages of a skilled historian are necessarily stylized and remain as reticent and mysterious as the Mona Lisa. Even our own composed judgments on those we know skip the mystery which every individual life enshrines. We like the silhouette more than the frightening reality, or we cling to the tangible image because it is more easy to manipulate. We treat others as things, take on the ready-made ideas of our time and submerge ourselves in their current.

As then a glass of water to the unassisted eye hides the innumerable lives active within it, so history has to conceal as much as it reveals. Furthermore those who appear in the pages of history belong to time and are part of its process. That this is not the Christian estimate of individual life strikes us at first with surprise, but the Gospel makes it clear, and the eschatological language is decisive. Whereas we tend to take for granted that ripeness is all, that we develop, come to be ourselves in time, play our part, and are then judged on our slowly improving record, it is an ever-present 'crisis' and our response to it that the Christian religion seizes upon as of importance. How different the two outlooks are can be seen from this: that on human estimates the inscription on the tombstone which says that Everyman has lived a good life and therefore is now receiving his reward is so true as to be commonplace; whereas the Christian knows that one deathbed act of love or hatred can decide a man's eternity, that Dismas, the good thief, has his portion in paradise, and that any moment a vital decision may be required of one. The difference here goes deep. In the Christian philosophy persons are not just processes. We do indeed develop, and in the first stages of our life we are not sufficiently ourselves to be fully accountable for our thoughts and actions. But once we have grown to human estate, are in possession of our minds and wills, and can reflect and act independently, we have to be treated as persons and not as things or processes. We continue to change, but this change is one peculiar to human beings. At each moment we remain identical with ourselves, and it is because of this prerogative that we are not to be judged as an incomplete growth until some far-off end or perfection is reached. At each moment we are in a true sense complete; the string of our being each time it is 'plucked finds tongue to fling out broad its name'. The self dwells in loneliness and grandeur, and its thoughts are true or false, its acts good or bad, by absolute standards. This is the reason why the Church teaches that at any moment of our rational life we can decide our fate in eternity by an act of choice.

So to think of ourselves is not to deny that we can and do make progress. The kind of development, however, is peculiar, and it was diagnosed correctly long ago by Aristotle. He pointed out that a rational being developed by acts of knowledge and choice, and each of these acts is complete in itself, what he calls *teleiai* in order to distinguish them from processes which reach perfection only at the end of the process. An experiment, for instance, in chemistry or physics may take a long time and have many phases until it is finished; the embryo in the womb is at first an imperfect and undeveloped child. The intermediate stages in these processes draw their meaning and value from the end. To give an artificial but plain example, a dancer in the period of training is in process of becoming the complete dancer; the work in the studio is preliminary work. But when she has passed her tests and is accepted, each of her public performances will be judged on its own merits. This truth, less noticed in its bearing on human development and in history, is familiar to all in morals, in the statement that human beings are to be treated as ends and not as means. But though accepted when expressed in this form, it is too easily forgotten in the associated problem of the individual in relation to the community. The community exists to promote the well-being of the individuals who compose it, and all legislation must have this in mind. As, however, the individuals have their obligations to the community and in the light of the common good have to subordinate what might be privately but selfishly advantageous, some writers have coined the distinction of individual and person to suit the double role everyone has to play. The individual is one among others, one of the population who has to pay his taxes and undergo military service. The politician and the historian are thinking of this mass of individuals when they talk and write about society, future generations, the growth of civilizations and culture and democracy. Outstanding individuals are studied and their historical character and significance criticized; nevertheless in doing this the historian is primarily concerned with the general picture of causes and events and not with any one individual as a person. He accepts, though in a less degree, the limitations which all specialists, such as biologists and doctors and sociologists, accept. If challenged and criticized for so acting he could defend himself by saying that if every person is an image of God, unique and a prince *in petto*, he shows little trace of this glory in public records. The kind of man of whom the historian has evidence often behaves like an animal, is a creature of his environment and heredity, blind to his own best interests, full of prejudices and corrupted by power. It is not his duty to correct this version of the individuals met in history, but it is not the full truth as the philosopher and the Christian should know. It ignores the lonely, conscientious struggles of the individual person and his existential predicament. What Doughty said of the Arab, that his feet were in a cloaca and his brow touched heaven, is true of every man. In just perspective the nondescript and ne'er-do-well are equally with Alexander and Newton images of God, and in each successive age the multitude of voices, each with its own incommunicable 'crisis', is the touchstone of truth. They with their living experience cannot be caught in the mesh of any historical explanation, and while alive they alone matter. Their response to their Maker is more important than what may happen after they are dead; that 'crisis' is the day of the Lord and the end of the world for them.

The mention of the 'day of the Lord' recalls the eschatological Christian belief in the advent of Christ, and brings us up against the doctrine of what is called the Parousia. In the first century of the Church, and sporadically for a long time after, many Christians supposed the advent of Christ to be very near in time, and with this advent the world would come to an end. This view was a naïve reaction to a profound and apocalyptic warning in the message of Christ. Apocalyptic sayings have their own rules and have different layers of meaning. The Apostles knew that they had to live in expectation; they knew too that at the coming of the Son of God, the Alpha and Omega, the world reached a consummation. Salvation had come and all that remained was for its effects to be realized. All the past had been completed in Christ and nothing new could supersede His coming. If then there had to be a future it could not be one of indefinite progress to an event or occasion, human or divine, yet to come; rather should it be compared to the ripple of a divine arrival in the waters of time. As the Church sings, 'the Spirit of the Lord fills the whole world; the whole frame of created things recognizes the accents of His Voice'. Time now spells the opportunity of everyone in every generation to encounter the Son of Man and to know by 'crisis' the day of the Lord. This new view has naturally been ignored by the empirical historian; it has also been missed by most, if not all, philosophers of history. The modern scientific historian and historicist have been distracted by the enlarged size of the universe disclosed by many sciences, by the long aeons of inchoate and early life and the prospect of thousands of years yet to be. Man has retreated from the central position in the universe to be a tiny spectator of a world with illimitable horizons. Even the Christian thinker falls into the way of contemplating a slow advance towards an epoch of peace and happiness which could be an antechamber to heaven. True the Christian can never quite confuse the world's progress with the last day and his vision of heaven, but he can share with Marx the expectation of a terrestrial happiness in some dim future. Marx, being a Jew by race, thought messianically of his class-less society. We blame him for such a foolish as well as incon-sistent belief, but are we any wiser in substituting for the arti-ficial creation of Marx the gradual emergence of an almost equally perfect society from the womb of time? The early Christians saw everything too near; we suffer from the opposite defect and see everything too far off. They paid too little atten-tion to time; we pay too much.

The doctrine of the Parousia has to be pieced together from various texts of Scripture, and its full meaning transcends human understanding. Nevertheless we can learn enough to see that it capsizes a naturalistic explanation of history and gives a new and startling meaning to the conventional descrip-tion, *annus Domini*. The Son of Man was born in a certain year and lived a definite number of years, but he was also God and by right and by virtue of His mission the head of all things. His advent, therefore, must impart something new and mysterious to time, and this is borne out by the sayings, like lightning flashes in clouds, which concern the future. They belong to the prophetical and apocalyptic type used to convey the intentions of Jahweh. The Parousia is more powerful and comprehensive than any world-event; it is now justice and punishment, now mercy and love; it is instantaneous and has the effect, as it were, of ricocheting in time. The coming of the Lord is now here, now there; it is the end of one dispensation, the fall of the old Jerusalem, and the beginning of another, it is the gift of grace and faith; it is in the 'crisis', the test, wherein and whereby we are found ready or wanting, it descends upon us without warning, 'like a thief in the night', and from the direction least expected. It is, again, at death that the Lord Jesus will come; it is in the Church that He is met, and He will come again at the last day.

These various re-echoes of the Coming become more intelligible if we set them alongside what has been said about the significance of each human being. The life of the individual is like that of Jacob after he had wrestled all night with an angel: 'Thy name shall not be called Jacob, but Israel.' Each one's life is that of the cosmos in miniature. As a rider to the Gospel saying: 'What doth it profit a man if he gain the whole world and suffer the loss of his own soul', we can add that each man has the whole world as his arena, test and cross; it was made for him, and its welfare is dependent upon him, as Israel on Jacob. He is there, an immortal being, the likeness of God, to face his destiny. Free by nature and, if he so will, anointed in grace, he has in the seeming loneliness of his soul to take sides and make a choice. Now is his testing time, and though he know it not the test lies in his recognition and response to a sudden visitation, a 'dark descending', the Coming of Christ. The Jewish people are the prototype and symbol of that choice. Their prerogative it was to be prepared in an especial way for the Coming of God, and they had the Life of the World in their midst, and knew it not. Everything in their history led up to this, and their future and all history turned on whether they would accept Christ or reject Him. They are the symbol of what is crucial, the great Divide, in the life of every human being. The theme of this encounter, hinted at in myths and felt by poets like Milton, lies outside the purview of the historian. The historian has to treat past and present and future from a detached standpoint; they stretch out before him and he can discern in them the figures of men and their behaviour towards one another. Time

to the historian is a thing seen; to the individual it is an experience lived, and it is each one's present experience which is real
and primary. The past and the future are made real and have a
meaning to us because they can be reproduced or foreseen by
our minds here and now. When we are interred, the future too
is interred with us; it is to others alive when we are dead that it
will be present. The long temporal series condenses itself into
a here and now, a lived moment which is or should be a flashing
off of personality, a reveillé, a commitment. It is the 'time of our
visitation'. All life is an expectancy, the tense awaiting for the
knock on the door and the sound of a voice saying: 'It is I';
and because this Coming is decisive and felt to be final, it is
described by apocalyptic writers in terms of judgment, sudden
call, catastrophic change, ultimate separation or union, and it
is localized in the coming of faith and grace, the Church, death,
the passing of a generation and the last assize.

We may say then that the Christian view shows that in
history there is a play within a play, or rather innumerable
plays; or to change the image slightly, all the extras of the play
come on to the stage as well as the chief actors, and have the
spotlight turned on them. From another angle we can describe
the Christian era as a continuous present; and this it is which
explains the paradox that in the coming of Christ history
reaches its fulfilment and termination and nevertheless does not
stop as many of the early Christians expected. The small world
that knew Christ has to grow like the mustard seed till 'all the
world has knowledge of His voice', and every generation has to
undergo the test and have a similar experience to that of the
Jews in making its choice. Each generation passes away; death
ends the experience of each of its members, and that without
metaphor or exaggeration means the end of the world for them.
Most men and women are so immersed in the events around
them and share so deeply the common experience of their
contemporaries that they take to heart the far-off *consequences*
of present mistakes and successes. They project themselves into
the future, expressing bitter resentment against rulers and
statesmen who will damage the world they know and love. It
does not matter that the effects foreseen will not be felt for
decades after they have joined their fathers in the grave. Their
own decease and insensibility are hidden from them in the
illusion of a false immortality. This illusion hides from them the

split moment in time when their decisive part has to be played; and so it does not occur to them that the 'day of the Lord' is upon them now, and that, in Pauline language, the 'time is short', 'the fashion of this world passeth away', and that afterwards comes the end when Christ 'shall have delivered up the kingdom to the Father'. Age succeeds age, and it is convenient to think of a series strung together in time and united by a kind of rhythm or spiral of development. Greece takes over from Persia and Rome from Greece, and a tradition of learning and political wisdom and morals is handed on, sifted, and partly lost and improved, an inheritance containing the promise of a perfect society. What truth there is in such an evolution it is for the historian to examine. The Christian philosopher, too, may ponder on it, but his will be the duty of reconciling it with the doctrine of the Parousia.

In the Scriptures the Coming of the Lord has a special mark, and, therefore, to complete the account of it something must be said of this. The symbol of the Christian religion is the Cross, and it is natural to turn to it for the clue. The clue is obvious, but notwithstanding it is constantly missed. There are, for example, many Christian thinkers who write as if the one condition of peace and permanent prosperity were a return to Christian principles. At the end of the First World War they made it plain that 'the war to end wars' could achieve its result and that the world could live in a 'tranquillity of order' provided that the truths of the Christian philosophy were applied to the domains of social and national life, industry and science. Many youthful crusaders at the time felt that the West had learnt a lesson and could not but profit by hearing the truth, and their aim was to proclaim that truth from the housetops. The catchword was Christian humanism. Optimism is always to be received with affection, as the Christian religion is profoundly optimistic. But happiness has to be bought with a price, and the ground of hope rests on a 'hard saying'. Chesterton's poem, *The Ballad of the White Horse*, is like a parable of this saying in its first part. King Alfred is made to walk through the Wessex fields in the utmost dejection of mind. He is being hunted like a fox by the Danes, and he seems utterly defeated. Suddenly, standing in a blue mantle in a field of corn he sees the Mother of God, and he asks her for help and hope. She answers: 'I say naught for thy comfort and naught for thy heart's desire, save that the sky grows darker and the sea rises higher.' The message sounds cheerless, but Alfred recognizes in it the sign of the Cross and becomes happy again with hope. In Gerard Hopkins's poem, *The Wreck of the Deutschland*, the same idea is to be found, and the paradox is the key to the poem. The poet is baffled and tormented by the news of the tragic death of five Franciscan nuns in a wreck at sea. He asks himself, where in such a cruel fate can God's Providence be found? It is easy to perceive the work of God in what is fair, to greet God in the heaven, in the 'stars, lovely-asunder starlight, wafting Him out of it', and also in the 'dappled with damson west'. But he is made to realize by this apparent tragedy that though God is 'under the world's splendour and wonder', His mystery must be 'stressed' in a special mode of coming. 'Not out of His bliss springs the stress felt nor first from heaven (and few know this) swings the stroke dealt. . . . It rides time like riding a river (and here the faithful waver, and the faithless fable and miss).' That many, even of the good, should miss this divine approach shows how mysterious and unexpected it is. And no wonder; for Thou hast 'thy dark descending and most art merciful then'. The explanation why God makes this 'dark descending' is 'the dense and driven Passion'. As He 'came unto his own and his own received him not' and the redemption was won through pain, his coming is 'lightning and love, a winter and warm'. The second Adam, the new head of mankind, draws the world to him in his Passion, and therefore his members meet him in a wreck such as that of the *Deutschland*. The soul being 'hard at bay', calls: 'O Christ, Christ come quickly: The cross to her she calls Christ to her, christens her wild-worst best.'

This is the interpretation of the Parousia which comes out of the Scriptures, and we can confirm it from the evidence of history. It serves to explain a curious fact which must strike all who read old biographies and sermons. The writers and preachers of every age are persuaded that their times are exceptionally awry, that the age is critical, and that never have there been so many threats and evils to contend with. Most of them, also, write as if round the corner, once they have escaped their present plight, there must be a long shining road of happiness. The expectation never dies, and it can be heard today on the lips of many speakers who put their faith in democracy as the panacea of all evils. Once long ago poets and orators looked back to a supposed golden age and sighed for its return; in later ages as scientific history took the place of myth the future was exchanged for the past, and on it hope rested—halcyon days when peace and universal contentment would reign. It is the mirage, the ignis fatuus, the Garden of the Hesperides, the better world which Ulysses thought it was never too late to seek; and it is a form of escape from the gnawing truth that 'sufficient for the day is the evil thereof'. If we turn to the history of Christianity, the same spectacle of desperate struggles with adversity meets us. The blood of the martyrs is the seed of the Church. The Church has rarely escaped persecution of some sort, and when it does enjoy prosperity evil itself is felt in a more subtle and corrosive manner, so that the Peter Damians and Savonarolas declare the judgments of God on the slackness and iniquity around them. From time to time religious revivalists or founders of cults have arisen confident that they have the key to a life of unassailable virtue and peace. I fear hopes are unvaryingly disappointed, and troubles and storms are met instead of calm skies. As the poet said, 'few know the mystery', and 'here the faithful waver, the faithless fable and miss'. It is when we are at bay, when we can no more, when we are tried by enemies within and without, when the devil, the world and the flesh are in full hue and cry, and we hear our hearts 'grate on themselves', and 'it kills to bruise them dearer', it is then that the kingdom of God is at hand and death is swallowed up in victory. We know from the New Testament and in theory that life is a warfare, that blessed are the poor in spirit and those who suffer persecution for justice' sake; we are told to take up our cross daily, but the truth is glossed over in a world which is deceived by promises of easier times and humaner conditions. 'The disciple is not greater than his master', and if He who is the new head of the human race, has to win life through death and wear thorns as a crown, must not all those who come after, so long as history shall last, also be marked with the stigmata of suffering and rule as from a cross? The mystical union of the Head with the members, of the new Adam with his offspring, ordains that in the new dispensation of the world human beings must reproduce in some fashion the manner of life of Him who first entered into the Holy of Holies. It 'behoved Christ to suffer', and as He is the way and the life as well as the truth, it needs must be that the coming of His kingdom should be in suffering and by trial.

There was a time perhaps when St. Paul had to have the lesson fixed in his mind by a drastic experience. It looks as if he once hoped for an alliance on civilized terms between the Gospel and the humanism and secularism of his day. He certainly took immense pains to win over the learned at the Areopagus in Athens. There the new Logos met the old wisdom, and the occasion was propitious. Nevertheless he failed, and after that failure he never held out hope that the new wine would fit perfectly into the old bottle or that a world would arise sunlit with Christian peace. He had only one thing to say: 'I preach Christ and Him crucified, a mystery which must look like folly to the Gentiles.' In the book of the Apocalypse the same note is struck. The scene which unrolls itself before the prophet's eyes is one of continual tension and stress. There is war, and the elect are always in danger of destruction, and the powers of evil are not cast down until the end. 'And I saw the beast and the kings of the earth, and their armies gathered together to make war against him that sat on the throne and against his army.' It is only at the very last that all tears are to be wiped from the eyes of men. In the prophecies of the Old Testament and in the apocalyptic literature it is true that the coming of the Lord is often announced as triumphal; and it may well be that the effect upon the world of God's redeeming work was not decided until He who came unto His own was finally rejected. If this be true, then the Jews, chosen out and prepared for centuries to make a decision which would affect for weal or woe the whole future history of mankind, closed by their cosmic and representative choice one way of salvation and forced upon all future generations the hard alternative. The glorious reign which Micah foretold changed into a dark day; 'the Day of the Lord will be darkness, not light, even very dark and no brightness in it'.

If this be true, then history might have followed a different course if the Lord of the world had been accepted and not rejected by His chosen people. Obviously the hypothesis lies outside the bounds of the empirical historian, being further away from verification even than the choice of Adam and Eve and Original Sin. The second choice follows on the first and is caused by it. The evidence for the first is primarily theological, being based on the story in Genesis that at the beginning of history a choice was made which determined the entire future life of man. It was a choice between good, with supernatural rewards, and evil. Straightway after that fatal choice it is recorded also that a promise was given, a promise of salvation and recovery. Then, after a period, a people was chosen out, and it is made clear that in some strange way the fulfilment of the promise would depend on them. This must mean that they would have to make a choice. This explains the otherwise extraordinary story of God's apparently almost exclusive interest in and dealing with the Israelites, and His severe manner of preparing and disciplining them. He was preparing them for a second choice which in turn would be decisive and involve all mankind. But this second choice differed in one essential point from the first; this time failure was ruled out; the choice could not be between good and evil, for God's salvation could not be circumvented. The prophecies in the Old Testament, therefore, one and all, look forward to a time when God's kingdom will be established; but at the same time they show a strange ambiguity in their forecasts of what is to come. They are at times joyous: 'Then shalt thou see and abound, and thy heart shall wonder and be enlarged; when the multitude of the sea shall be converted to thee, the strength of the gentiles shall come to thee'; but they are also at times sombre, for if the Messiah is 'to see a long-lived seed', and if the will of the Lord is to 'be prosperous in the land', it is because the Servant of Jahweh 'has laboured' and 'shall bear their iniquities'. These prophets imply that the chosen people have a momentous part to play, and on their choice the future hangs. When therefore the Saviour comes He makes no advance to the Syro-Phoenicians, to the Romans or other peoples of the world; He presents Himself only to the Jews: 'I am not sent but unto the lost sheep of the house of Israel.' Such a statement from One who claimed to be the saviour of the whole world is so astonishing that it forces us to look for a special role which must be played by Israel. The Jews had not been trained with such unremitting care for nothing. In the first and fatal choice at the beginning of history the Bible makes it clear that God respects the will of man and will abide by his choice, even though the divine will is never frustrated. With the most sedulous care we see again

God preparing a race once more to make a representative and cosmic choice. His purpose is to prepare and make them ready for His coming; so that in the Gospel narrative we watch Christ making every effort to win the Jews. He rejoices when He finds faith and laments the darkness which prevents the Jews from seeing the light. His parables are for the most part first concerned with an invitation to the chosen people, and reveal the disappointment their hardness of heart brought Him. As His mission draws to an end His feelings are sadly expressed in the cry: 'Jerusalem, Jerusalem, which I would have gathered as the hen gathers its chicks, but thou hast not known the time of thy visitation.' This 'visitation' was His coming, his Parousia, and it was not recognized. Not only was it not recognized, but His living visible presence was removed from sight, His body disfigured and hidden in a tomb, *Aestimatus sum cum descendentibus in lacum; factus sum sicut homo sine adjutorio, inter mortuos liber,* as the Church sings in Passiontide. No refusal can thwart the divine intention, and no tomb could seal down the living Christ, but His victory is completed in the context of His reception. In His risen life He is not easily recognized even by His own apostles and disciples, and by the unbelieving people He is never seen again. His coming abides, His presence is to be universal, but the visitation from now onwards has a 'dark descending'; it is a sword which separates, and its suddenness and mode is typified in the first famous conversion on the road to Damascus. Until He come again in glory time will be stamped with the Passion of Christ. The momentous choice of rejection once made could not change the divine promise of salvation, but could and did define the manner of the redemption, tilt the balance in favour of the sombre prophecies, leave concupiscence and evil still in apparent possession, stage life as a warfare, and fix the coming of God and His trysting place in the Gethsemanes and Golgothas of the soul.

This view must now be considered for any light it may throw on a philosophy of history. It can be called the eschatological or apocalyptic or crucial aspect, with its insistence on the stupendous importance of the individual and the 'crisis' which decides his eternal destiny. The conventional and accepted standards of historical judgment are not of the sort to do it justice. All turns on the readiness of the individual, living each moment at the top of his bent, to know and accept the advent of God. The works of man recorded in history fade into obscure remains stretched out along the sands of time; they are like the effigy of a knight lying on his tomb compared with the live person looking down upon him. Worse than this: the historian can deal with masses, important groups and influential persons and the quasi-individual is always swamped by detail. But on this new view democracy becomes only too real, and the millions of human beings, who have to be mentioned in the mass, if they are mentioned at all by the historian, come thronging out of their graves as in the promised resurrection of the dead. Not one of them is insignificant; they have all gained their immortality at a price, and that price was worth more than all the treasures of the universe. In the *Book of the Apocalypse* St. John writes of a multitude without number; in the final and true account of mankind they will not only be numbered but named and singled out. If then the eschatological view were the only clue given us by Christian Revelation, there would be reason for despairing of any hope of a philosophy of history. The scepticism of Mr. C. S. Lewis would be more than justified. Fortunately for our purpose this clue is not the only one, and it remains to investigate the others.

But before doing so a word must be said about the other aspect of the Parousia, namely the rejection theme, the resurrection by death motif. This does provide a positive suggestion and is not too remote from a supposedly empirically based hypothesis, such as that of Mr. Arnold Toynbee. On his view, as we have seen, man progresses by struggle, by meeting the challenge of the Mephistophelian principle and enjoying the spoils of victory. Again, as has been already noted, the reaction of man to life has usually moved between two opposites. He has been either too sure of himself and of progress or too cynical and pessimistic. In the heyday of the last century the future was seen in a rosy light; the conditions of life were being changed by the application of science; life was becoming more pleasant by the discovery of drugs and anaesthetics and the neglected masses were winning their rights to education and a full life. The theory of evolution, too, supports the belief in a steady progress. This optimistic view still prevails in many quarters, but it has been badly shaken by the events of the last forty years. The prevalent philosophies today, which are to some degree a pointer to the mood of the age, are cheerless.

When the living God is no longer acknowledged, thought moves back to the idea of fate and the futility of human systems and human endeavour. This is expressed in the law of diminishing returns, and in the fear of a universe indifferent and implacable. Free will is surrendered and man suffers himself to be conditioned by causes, physical, economic and psychological. The most candid statement of pessimism is to be found in the description by Guyau of the history of man. 'There was a woman whose innocent folly it was to fancy herself engaged and on the eve of her marriage. In the morning, on awakening, she asked for a white robe and wedding garment and, smiling, got herself ready. "It is today that he is coming", she would say. By evening sadness seized her after her useless vigil; she would take off her white dress, but in the morning with the dawn, her confidence returned. "It is today", she would say. And she passed her life in this state of confidence ever balked and ever alive, taking off only to put on again her robe of hope. Humanity is like this woman. Forgetting all the deceptions, it awaits each day the coming of its ideal. For hundreds of centuries probably now it keeps on saying: "It is tomorrow"; each generation turn by turn puts on the white robe, but the mystic bridegroom always delays.'

In the Christian view the bridegroom does not delay; he comes not out of the 'dappled with damson west' but in the stress and the storm as the nun in the wreck saw. No easy optimism befits the life of men in their chosen course; nor again the pessimism of the defeated or the unexpectant. Somehow or other the secret of true living and of strong hope is wrested from hardship and disappointment, from the *durus labor* to which man is committed, and this is done in the Christian view by enlisting on one side the Lord of Life who through sacrifice 'bringeth all good things to their golden end'. This at least is one truth which the Christian philosopher can bring to his study of history.

Chapter VIII

THE TWO CITIES

The eschatological outlook is not the only one presented by the New Testament. The Gospel contains the promise of a new kingdom, and this kingdom is to grow and to cover the earth. This no doubt refers to the Church, to the growth of the Apostles and disciples into the body of the faithful, 'born again, not of corruptible seed, but incorruptible, by the word of God, who liveth and remaineth for ever', a 'chosen generation, a kingly priesthood, a holy nation, a purchased people'. These compose the kingdom, the city of God. But there are divers hints that the world itself is in some way to be brought into obedience to the divine designs. St. Paul in the letter to the Colossians, for instance, brings the whole world into the embrace of Christ. In Christ 'were all things created in heaven and on earth, visible and invisible'. The Father is 'through him to reconcile all things unto himself . . . both as to the things that are on earth and the things that are in heaven'. He tells the Romans, also, that 'the expectation of the creature waiteth for the revelation of the sons of God. For the creature was made subject to vanity: not willingly, but by reason of him that made it subject, in hope. Because the creature also itself shall be delivered from the servitude of corruption, into the liberty of the glory of the children of God.' These are mysterious sayings, and they have to be interpreted along with such texts as those at the end of the Apocalypse. There we read of a new heaven and a new earth; the first earth and heaven pass away; and the holy city, the new Jerusalem is seen coming down out of heaven from God, prepared as a bride adorned for her husband; and He who sits upon the throne says, 'behold I make all things new'.

From these texts and from the whole tenor of the New Testament the Christian Church deduced that there were to be two cities; they both would grow, and one had a celestial life and end and the other belonged to this earth. Owing to the fact that contrasts were needed, the earthly city came to be looked upon as the will of man in so far as it sought self-satisfaction in the things of this world. As such it was the enemy of the Christian ideal, and it had no share in the heavenly city. The ambiguity, however, in the use of the word 'world' and in the description of the city of man obscured the question whether nature and the good works of man were condemned to vanity or could be brought into relation with the supernatural order. For this reason such writers as Père Malavez and Abbot Butler can take opposing views on the place of human values in the kingdom of God. What is agreed upon by most who write on this subject is that man in the thousands of years he has been upon earth has matured and accomplished much, in self-knowledge, in scientific discovery, in wisdom and virtue, in poetry and art and in social advancement, which to human eyes is intensely valuable. Above all he had provided for himself the means for a happiness in accord with his nature. (The historicist is tempted to ask whether there is a law in this development and a pattern of perfection.) Those who believe in Christianity also agree that besides an eschatological interpretation we have the right to see God's purposes at work in time creating in and through the human situation a perfect society whose preparation is now and whose end is in heaven. The question arises whether there be any connection between these two societies or 'cities'.

The inquiry is not as clear cut as could be wished. This is due in part to the presuppositions of many of those who embark upon it; it is also due to the haziness which surrounds the subject matter. As we have already seen, Karl Barth, once he has made his conception of faith clear, is bound to deny all connection between the two worlds. There are positions also which are less extreme than that of Barth's which raise a barrier between the best this world can offer and the completely supernatural character of Revelation. Thought is declared impotent before the transcendent experience foreclosed in faith. These difficulties are not so pressing in the traditional Catholic outlook. There is no antecedent dogma or reason why an essay should not be made and a liaison found. What hampers and may altogether bar progress is the mist or cloud which obscures the subject matter. So much of human history is wrapped in mist, and the heights also of Sinai are lost in cloud. We are not therefore sure of the terms of comparison and likeness. What is there, for instance, in history which could be associated with the theme of the kingdom of God? The presence of evil in the world has proved a stumbling block for many to believing in the Providence of God. The question which lies at the back of Job concerns the goodness of life as we know it on the human level. If in answering this question we transfer the blame to man and admit that man has made a sorry mess of the world, we thereby seem to exclude straightway much of history from God's supernatural plan. And if we do this how much of history is left? Like joy and sorrow, good and evil make up the warp and woof of human life. A Christian may quote in answer to this the words *felix culpa*, but that takes us into such mysteries that philosophers, following the example of St. Thomas Aquinas at the end of his life, had better lay down their pens. Then besides the evil there is the imperfection which goes with all growth. Nor is this a contradiction of what has already been said of the perfection of the separate moments in the life of a person. The imperfection in question is seen in the gradual realization in time of an ideal according to which men should live, and in the development of general knowledge and of the sciences. Even those who are sceptical of general progress must admit that with the help of experience and also of mistakes, by means of experiments and new theories of knowledge, an almost infinite number of errors have been corrected and we no longer take for granted bestial religions, savage moral systems and customs, crude ideas of medicine and psychology, naïve beliefs and superstitions. The laws governing these chequered advances, if they could be discovered, might help us to safe generalizations about history, but it is hard to see what this tale of mistaken ideas, abortive efforts and temporary hypotheses has to do with the rounded supernatural perfection which must belong to the heavenly society.

To this I can see only one answer. Those who raise the difficulty make the mistake of supposing the heavenly society or city to be already formed or to come into being at the end of time. This view ignores the fact that the society or city is here and now in process of coming into being, that it was founded by Christ and that its citizens are composed of those who have been born into it in this present life just as much as those who live and die in this world. They are the same persons, and the relation, if it can be found, is not to be sought along the lines suggested above, but in the transfigured experience of this life. Such a defence takes us away from the broad picture of the spiral ascent of man in the purification of his moral and social ideas and the growing mastery of nature by the physical sciences, and throws us back upon ourselves; what each one of us makes of life and what riches each one of us accumulates in wisdom and spiritual experience. This may have been what Abbot Butler meant when he said that the Christian has not to arrive without luggage, but personally safe; he has to take with him all that he acquires on the route. We have, too, to take into account, the apocalyptic view which sees life not as a panorama, the past, that is according to the historian, but as a continuous present lived by each person. The long uphill journey of science is still far from ended, but moments of it may be precious to each climber. Archimedes' discovery of the 'spiral' and the pump was an incident in time and has long been surpassed, but the experience was a timeless one to the discoverer; and what is more, the timeless experience can be untouched by human progress, as when in their Anabasis the exhausted Greeks saw once again the sea.

But this answer needs examination, for it seems to take us back to eschatology and forgo the treasures heaped up in human history. If this were true, then the theory of the person and of his 'crisis', already developed, concludes all that can be said about the nature of history. This follows from the admission that, whatever the significance in the history of science the discovery of the 'spiral' may be, its only importance in the eyes of God and in the growth of the kingdom of God lies in the inner experience of the discoverer. And even here distinctions must be made. A scientific invention is a temporal event and it is almost certain to be improved, as an Indian catamaran gives place in time to the *Queen Elizabeth*. The human mind spends much of its time improving its resources, so much so that an ancient Greek or Roman, let alone a primitive savage, would be spellbound if he could be resurrected to visit a modern city or a Cavendish laboratory. In the sciences, then, the past is full of false starts, trial runs, of expedients, incomplete experiments and temporary hypotheses. Progress is made by correction. The same holds true up to a point in human relations. The rights of man take a long time to be appreciated and worked out into laws and institutions. Until man reaches a stage of maturity he behaves in many ways like a creature of nature; he lives by tribal instinct and custom and his moral reactions are dominated by his passions. He has to grow out of this condition and reach the age of reason. Once, however, reason emerges from the swaddling clothes of the instincts and impulses there is no longer the same story of advance to be told. Unlike the sciences the arts and the philosophy of man have an abiding worth. There are variations, there is good and bad thinking, but we cannot take for granted that a modern artist or philosopher is necessarily better than one who lived two or three thousand years ago. The *Odyssey* and the *Agamemnon* are not, like the Hippocratic Corpus, inchoate works. The Victory on the Acropolis, the stained-glass Notre-Dame of Chartres, the Giotto frescoes in the Madonna del' Arena of Padua conquer every age. So too with philosophy; the thought of Plato and Aristotle, though it is not free from the errors of their time on social and scientific matters, has not grown old and succeeds still in drawing youth into the ways of truth. Nor can modern times easily find a rival to Socrates in natural virtue.

The position, then, is this; much that is rated under history is only tentative. Our knowledge of nature, of our own bodies and even of the composite self which makes up our human nature, is always progressing, and what has been believed in the past is for ever under review and subject to revision. Such scaffolding can have little part in the final truth which the citizens of God are to enjoy. Art and philosophy have a better case; inasmuch as there is nothing to prevent a fully fledged system of truth arising at any time in man's history once he has reached maturity. That is not to say that perfection in art and truth in thinking have been ever in fact attained. From the histories of philosophy we can see for ourselves that the ground is strewn with corpses, that human ideas swing between extremes of sensible experience and disembodied metaphysics, humanism and theism, duty and pleasure, monism and individualistic ideals. At best, too, it might be argued, the truth of philosophy is but a map which omits most of the contents of life. So we must turn back again to the eschatological view that what alone is important is personal experience in so far as it is decisive. I say 'decisive' because the experience must be of the sort which has some relation to human destiny and the kingdom of God. But if this be so, then the rigorist steps in and will argue that those complete personal acts are confined to acts of virtue and spiritual decisions which bear on our last end.

Now few Christians would deny that our virtuous and religious acts, if performed in grace, have an intimate connection with the kingdom of God. But this is fasting fare, and not at all what those whose minds are touched by mortal things want. They need not, however, despair. The rigorist has overreached himself. If once it be allowed that virtuous and religious acts are not outside the kingdom of God, we have only to extend their range, and this is quite justifiable. We divide up our experience into various categories, intellectual, emotional, artistic, practical, moral and religious, and in accordance with these divisions we think of specific moral acts such as acting out of duty and of religious acts, such as praying to God. The rest we pass over as neutral. But this is a mistake; morality invades the whole domain of human activity, and it is possible for us to make religion do the same. It is the whole human person who is engaged in his business, study, in his pleasures and pains, on sea and land. What he is doing is either good or bad, and what is called neutral is, please God, for the most part good. He can never plead as an excuse that he was doing business or engaged on sport if his character or actions are challenged. Being moral is a whole-time job and there are no holidays. Conflicts may indeed arise between the claims of art or science. The artist is often made sore by the attacks upon him on the score of immorality. As a writer or painter he can give an answer by distinguishing between the claims of his work and his duty to respect the conscience of his neighbour. At times the true answer may entail much inner debate and anguish; what he cannot do is to dismiss the problem as unreal, unless, that is, the complaints are frivolous. How real the question is can be seen in the present anxiety felt about the atom bomb and other possible means of destruction of human life. The scientist is responsible for the discovery and elaboration of new lethal weapons. Can he rid himself of all responsibility by merely saying that he is a scientist and has no concern with the uses to which his discoveries will be put? Ought he not rather to argue that the legitimate or illegitimate *use* of his work is for others to decide, and that he is justified both because he is advancing knowledge and because the knowledge gained may have a rightful use? In this latter case the scientist, like the artist, is not shelving the question of morality; he claims that he is doing good and not evil, and thereby admits that the writ of morality runs in every human sphere.

Although it might be said truly that man is by nature religious, religion is not so all-comprehending as morality, and as it is Christianity which is in mind at the moment, we need not bother about religion in general. The Christian follows a definite form of worship of God and accepts a definite Creed. His ideal, however, is to see all things in Christ and so to 'supernaturalize' every moment of his life. In so far as he succeeds in doing this his religion embraces not only the time given to prayer and worship but all his actions and thoughts. Like morality, therefore, it is universal in its scope, and straightway we see that the conclusion of the rigorist mentioned above need not follow. If it be the ideal of the Christian 'to restore all things in Christ' we ought to be able to draw an opposite conclusion to that of the rigorist. These words quoted from St. Paul's letter to the Ephesians seem to invite us to believe that this world may somehow or other be christened and so made fit to share in the kingdom of God. It is customary to restrict this restoration to what is most spiritual in human life, but there is no conclusive reason for doing so. According to Catholic doctrine the grace of God qualifies all the recipient's thoughts and actions; he is raised to a new and higher condition of life, the supernatural life of union with Christ and divine sonship. Nothing therefore which is free from evil is outside the province of grace, and the work of a Christian consists in part in transfiguring human experience. Nor need the distinction made above between the actual experiencing and the deed cause trouble. The distinction can be made, and at times when it is a question of intention and performance, good desire and poor result, it is necessary. But ordinarily the two run together, as thinking and thought are one, and will and performance. The runner runs his race, the artist creates his work, and they are one. The works of man and not only the experience are to be transfigured. And this is what Christians in every age have taken for granted. The profane was annexed to the sacred, and as André Malraux has pointed out: 'The Christ in Majesty of the earliest portals entered into man's everyday life, transfiguring it, and the saints showed themselves on earth. Associated with specific handicrafts and places, they were far from being mere inglorious chrysalides from which was to emerge the butterfly of a wisdom perfect and unique; rather, were they witnesses to a holiness whose forms are as manifold as nature's. The saint is not saintly in so far as he supersedes or discards human nature, but in so far as he plumbs its depths. He is a mediator in the realm of forms (as in so many other ways), a light whereby the features of the dim people of field and furrow are revealed to us.'

The point here made by Malraux is valuable, and not only for the reason that it increases the range of what can be supernaturalized. The original difficulty, however, which forced us back on the eschatological answer, has not yet been solved. It arose when the question was asked, what in human history could be said to be the flower of which eternity would see the fruit in the kingdom of God? The example of the flower and the fruit was used both by Newman and Abbot Butler. Human history on examination showed itself to be a moving spectacle, consisting of human experiences, haphazard events, processes of nature, which are converted by science into ever corrigible hypotheses and truths of philosophy. The hypotheses are too immature and provisional to be lifted up into the glory of the city of God, and the truths of philosophy are too abstract and cloudy to serve in the presence of final Truth. But what if we surrender all claims to fitness and lay the emphasis on the very finiteness of our experience, on that humanity which makes the very imperfection, judged by absolute standards, precious to us? Toys in themselves are of no account, but to children they are so dear that they take them to bed with them; and when we go to sleep and awake to everlasting joy the toys of this life may well be part of our transfigured humanity. 'Take these imperfect toys, till in your heart they too attain the form of perfect things.' What we do now prefigures what we shall do with complete happiness, even as the doll cherished by the child is the first love of the future mother. It is not for nothing that every human being can be so deeply affected by apparent trifles which bring back to him memories and reminders of incidents which have made up the warp and woof of his life and endear the past to him. The green fields, of which we babble when dying, are linked in desire with the 'green pastures' to which we hope to go. In this respect the historical record is bound to differ from the story as told *du côté de chez Swann*, the public from the private memoir. The historian seizes on what helps to explain a social or national change of events, and in doing this he assigns varying degrees of importance to the chief actors. All human beings are to some extent public characters, and they like to play their part and judge themselves by their successes and failures. The Crossing of the Rubicon must have remained memorable in Caesar's mind. St. Anselm remembered all the details of the discovery of the Ontological Argument, and Dante of his first meeting with Beatrice, Galileo and Kant and Darwin felt sure that they were adding to knowledge and enrolling themselves in history. It is not that the private life stands over and against the judgments of history. The latter is an evaluation of the former and selects its materials from what is known of the lives of individuals. But as the author always knows more about his writing and his characters than the reader, so the individual life overflows the records and has a heart-beat which the mummy cannot reproduce. H. G. Wells said that every man has the sense of a mission, and special destiny; he feels that he is a prince in disguise and is to have his 'day'. His tragedy is that the 'day' never comes, and that life makes him walk in step and, like a policeman, moves him on. But, if the Christian revelation be true, and a higher pattern is being woven on the other side of secular history, Wells is right. The good is not interred in the grave, and the grace of an inconspicuous life is not lost. What history has to omit, the autobiography, the novel and poetry try to supply. They are windows which allow us to look in at what is going on at home; and this is why we cannot do without these supplements to our scientific records. What unites us with our fellows is our common humanity, the sharing in a life which is a skein of joys and sorrows, hopes and disappointments, births and death, pleasures and pains, laughter and tears. What the Greeks felt about these is to be found in the Greek Anthology, in the brief, tender verses and in their epitaphs. They needed some such expression, and their need has been supplied by the great plays and the growth of the romances into a poignant delineation of our human condition. The great novelist is sensitive to what we are really like, and he makes us see the changing face of our humanity in the mirror of his art. In reading Shakespeare we do not moralize over the characters; we are separated by art from their sins but not from their humanity. And it is the humanity of the young and the old, the kings, the dreamers, the maids and the fools, which touches us to the quick and shows us that this life, imperfect as it is, is the stuff of which we are made. When in love we do not calculate, and art has some of the alchemy of love. It enables us to see that the creation of a finite world is a blessing, and that it is not to the purpose to weigh it in terms of our own cold philosophies. It is not what the historian values, nor what the planner of future temporal happiness sets down on his drawing-board, but the human *Comedia*, the tangled mass of bitter-sweet experiences, in so far as it is not swollen and rotted with evil, which will receive a divine benediction.

The description 'bitter-sweet' was used deliberately. It applies generally to the experiences which everyone has when looking back on his past. In the tranquillity of old age the pains of the past mingle freely with the joys, like the sacred oxen in the streets of India. What hurt at the time so much, the loss of those we loved, ingratitude and the disappointments and failures, the years have healed. 'Suffering does not last, but having suffered lasts for ever.' But the description has a still more exact application to much that happens in this life. Pain and pleasure may oppose each other, but often pain of a kind is the very condition of the most sought-after pleasures. Even when we begrudge the pain at the time, the ensuing joy makes us glad that we endured it. What learning we have is sure to have cost us weary hours and strenuous application; still more the skill of the surgeon, the perfection of the movements of the ballet dancer, of the playing of the violinist, have been preceded by repeated attention to details and lessons, and in all these cases the end achieved is felt to be worth all the trouble. The very joy of mastery grows out of the painful process of acquiring it. Nor can one have that joy without the cost which it demands. The cost be it of Everest overcome, or a Kontiki saga or scar or wound—'there is no poppy in Castile so lovely as his open wound'—gives the special quality to human growth and life. They compose the refrain of the *Ecce Homo*. They are the sheaves brought into the new Paradise. 'They say that in the unchanging place Where all we loved is always dear, We meet our morning face to face, And find at last our twentieth year.' The pleasure of games is in a bloodless battle which is taking toll of one's strength and often fought out in conditions which keep the comfort-seeker at home. Every month we read of almost reckless expeditions, of battles with sea, the air, the mountains and the jungle. No one who reads of the attempts on the North or South Pole can think of hardship and joy as opposites, nor would he dream that he can have the special satisfaction of mountain-climbers by walking up the hill nearest to his house. The Kontiki saga cannot be shared by stay-at-homes. In brief, in the *comédie humaine* there is a special kind of happiness; it belongs to creatures like ourselves, who out of uncertainty of their own strength and in the desire to exercise their unfledged powers and to draw out of life what they ought, test themselves and in the testing refine their loves and joys. This being so we can see perhaps more clearly why so many hope that in the heavenly city what makes up the very substance of our humanity will not be absent. Without it our grace and beatified spirits will look so ghostly.

But there is a still deeper level on which pain and pleasure meet, and that is in sacrifice. It is by sacrifice that we insure ourselves against unhappiness. In another work I have tried to show that one of the two necessary ingredients of love is self-giving. The break with our centripetal and selfish dispositions is in anticipation hard, and costly in the act, but it pays the highest dividends. Not that lovers look to the reward; it is providentially inseparable from it. Human beings have always been aware when confronted with examples of sacrifice that they represent the best in our nature. We remember and put up monuments to the heroic, and to this day we keep a hold, if a slender one, on the Christian tradition of self-sacrifice for others as the standard of merit. We honour the professions whose professed aim is to serve the community, those who risk their health and their lives to nurse the sick, comfort the old and helpless, the Florence Nightingales and the Damians with their lepers. The Gospel reveals the splendour in such sacrifice, and in doing so gives us perhaps the clue to the way in which human events are transferred without loss to a new and golden background. It is when the just answer the King, saying: 'Lord, when did we see thee hungry and fed thee: thirsty and gave thee drink? . . . And the King, answering, shall say to them: Amen I say to you, as long as you did it to one of these my least brethren, you did it to me.' The clue given in this parable is in the transposition made in the recipients of the mercy shown. The act is not lost; it has its place in another setting, which was unknown in the experience and memory of it. This suggests that no philosopher of history now can perceive the plan which is being worked out in the story of mankind; that nevertheless that plan is in operation and it uses the same subject matter as the historian and the philosopher. We have the further hint that what in the heavenly city will prove to have been most important is the love of one's neighbour, especially when it is expressed in self-sacrifice. (This ideal of sacrifice has always been part of the Christian teaching, and it has become so much a part of our philosophy of life that it serves to correct our too human historical estimates. Not only is the heroic and generous act worth while in itself, but it continues on, doing good, whether above or under ground. It may appear to be a splendid failure, but that appearance is deceptive, and it does not fail to affect the future course of events. Suffering, too, and sacrifice, when borne for the sake of others, have a redemptive quality, whose power can be glimpsed, though not as yet, comprehended, and it is this belief which has helped to change the attitude of innumerable patients in hospitals and helped to explain the vocation of solitaries.) Now that we are learning more about the so-called 'collective consciousness' (a misleading description of a truth not yet sufficiently explored), the idea of persons being affected for good or evil by one another independently of visible and conscious action, no longer seems absurd. A community trades on its past in ways which cannot be explained in the counting-house of the rational self, and there is evidence, too, that those living in groups and united by tradition have modes of inter-communication superior to that of sympathetic magic. That striking statement of John Donne's is receiving new corroboration: 'Every man is a piece of the continent, a part of the main. . . . Any man's death diminishes me, because I am involved in mankind.'

Where then does all this argument lead? Not to any systematic Christian philosophy of history. It is, indeed, vain, as Lewis said, to try to formulate any theory which could explain satisfactorily in wider terms what the historian examines methodically and empirically. But we are not left with empty arms. First the eschatological point of view threw a light on the chief actors in history, the individual himself. Each individual is a miniature cosmos, and the whole earth and all time draw near him to force the decisive yes or no from him. Time in a sense stands still, because it has been fulfilled in Christ, and every individual and every generation lives at the end of the world meeting his destiny. This, it has been claimed, is the unique contribution of Christianity to the philosophy of history. But while it explains the individuals who compose history, it leaves out of account the growth which in time man and mankind has achieved in community, in nation and as a whole. The question can, therefore, be asked whether all the human achievements and the struggle and development are just a waste product or have they any everlasting significance. Do they enter into any scheme, whose nature can be seen or surmised? In another form the question comes to this: has the development of the city of man any abiding relation with the city of God? That there is a city of God which also is coming into being is guaranteed by the New Testament and by Christian tradition. It must be accepted as a truth just as much as the eschatological fact. At first the difficulties in the way of knowing anything about the ultimate character of the city of God and about the relation of human experience to it seemed overwhelming. But out of the mist came the light that we must look on human history as a kind of growth; a finite perfection, in which the joys and sorrows, ephemeral and inglorious as they may appear compared with absolute and divine perfection, are, nevertheless, the very heart and soul of our so limited perfection which God created and loved. Furthermore, the best that we can be, and what we prize most, is love which is heroic and sacrificial, the love which sees our neighbour as ourself. This is the secret of the hearth, of campaigning, of living together. And at this moment it may occur to the reader that such a joy and such a love have been already made familiar to us in the eschatological account of the individual. There the 'crisis', the immortal moment opened out to display a special character, that of life through death, the 'winter and warm', the mystery of man who must christen his wild-worst best. In this crisis or agony the self is face to face with the Son of Man who conquered death by death. It is the fulfilment of the commandment: Thou must love thy God with thy whole self. But in the history of man as he develops and tries to make a worthy city of man, it is once again love and sacrifice, which is the key, and this time the second commandment is fulfilled: Thou shalt love thy neighbour as thyself.

Chapter IX

HISTORY OF ISRAEL

To the Jew and the Christian alike the Old Testament provides a clue to history. They differ, however, in their interpretation. The historian keeping aloof from theological disputes can, however, compare it with the records of other peoples and mark down its special features. Now those features do set this historical record apart and provide the ground for the interpretation of the Christian philosopher. The story is, indeed a strange one, and, so far as is known, it has no parallel. The early Christians, as the New Testament shows, saw in Christ the fulfilment of a long succession of events and prophecies, and they and Christians ever since have taken joy in discovering in the Old Testament foretypes and images and events whose meaning is shrouded or ambiguous until the expected Messiah or Saviour is revealed in the person of Jesus Christ. The critical studies of the last hundred years have made questionable some of these readings of personages and prophecies, and scholars have tried to show that some of the principal ideas which appear in the early books were borrowed from the civilizations around them. Wellhausen, for example, denied that any expectation of a Messiah existed before the Babylonian exile. Herman Gunkel and Hugo Gressman, on the other hand, related the Israelitish idea of a Messiah to similar ideas in the Oriental religions of the time. Other writers, influenced by the work of Sigmund Mowinckel, have distinguished between the Indo-Iranian conception of the Son of Man, the expectation of a kingly Messiah, a prophetic or eschatological or transcendent one, between the hope of a glorious kingdom in some indefinite future and at the end of the world. Despite these criticisms the main lines of the history of Israel remain as clear and unusual as ever.

They are unusual as compared with what we know of the Oriental, the Greco-Roman and the Norse outlook on man and time. The Aztec, the Inca and the Mayas religion does seem to have a point in common with that of Israel, in that a hero appears, goes away, and there persists the expectation of his return. Amongst the Aztecs this is the Plumed Serpent, Quetzalcoatl, who became celebrated as the god of knowledge. The same story is incorporated, though not so strikingly, in the religion of the Incas. But the resemblance of this with the expectation of the Messiah and the coming of salvation is superficial. As with many other religions the sun and moon are divinized and made the chief objects of worship. The Oriental outlook has no pertinent relationship with history. Nor again can the Greeks be said to have conceived of the close connection between a divine Providence and historical events. Though generalizations are seldom without their exceptions, the verdict on Greek philosophy holds, namely, that it was, in keeping with its thinkers' genius for mathematics, more concerned with the static than the dynamic. The Word, for example, as Dr. Alexander Jones has pointed out, is in the Hebrew associated with action, whereas for the Greek it is 'an instrument and expression of thought even if the thought remained unuttered'. To the Psalmist it seemed natural to say that 'by the word of the Lord the heavens were made'. So again the Hebrews took for granted that the thought and word of God were directives and produced results. 'He sends His word and melts them; his wind shall blow, and the waters shall run. He declared His word to Jacob and His statutes and judgments to Israel.' God's word then is a continuous creation or corrective, an act which can almost be called the untemporal side of what in its effect is a temporal evolution. 'My Father works even until now', as Christ said, and this divine word and activity are seen in their clearest light in historical happenings. The Greek looked for the universal, the essential and unchangeable, and in so far as the concrete was subject to change it fell below the perfection which reason demanded. The Hebrew was at home with the concrete. Not for him the sharp division between the body which is corruptible and the spirit whose home is 'yonder'. Man to the Hebrew was created from the earth and a living spirit was breathed into him, and so it is that in the biblical history the human beings are like material beings formed in the hands of God. Time is all important in their advancement or failures. Solomon begins well but turns to evil. David is first shown to us in all the freshness of youth, and then the years take their toll, and he dies, all his lusting passion spent, to leave a strange progeny, from which, nevertheless will spring the Son who is to be the saviour of His people and the nations.

The Hebrew conception, then, of time is very different from that of the Greek. In the Hebrew language, 'to be', as a copula, is usually left out, and when it is used it serves to express a living existence or action of some sort. So too it dispenses with past and future tenses because action is looked at from the point of view of the speaker or writer as an action which is either complete or incomplete. God is everlasting, the creator and moulder of man. Man lives and dies, but the life of the people whom God has blest continues as a tribe or even under the one name Jacob. 'Therefore there is a judgment of the Lord with Juda and a visitation for Jacob.' Time reveals the intention of God and gives a meaning to history. 'Fundamentally', as Fr. Quintin Lauer writes, 'the temporal line of redemptive history is one and the same in New and Old Testaments, beginning with the first going forth of creatures from the hand of God and ending with the return of creatures to God. Creation itself is historical, but it is revelation which gives to this history its special structure. According to this structure history is a continuous line of events, but, unlike a history conceived apart from the divine plan of salvation, it is a continuous line which has a "mid-point", one central event, from which all other events, before and after derive their significance.' Such a view of time is opposed not only to the Greek or Oriental but also to that which has tended to prevail in Europe since the passing out of currency of the Christian metaphysic. M. George Poulet in a study of attitudes to time since the Renaissance has brought a wealth of evidence to show how shifting and uncertain the sense of time and even of personal subsistence has become in the last three centuries. God's action ceases to be continuous and conservative. To Calvin, 'each moment of faith becomes the foundation of all existence. I see myself continually flowing away; no moment passes without my seeing myself at the point of being engulfed'. God, however, sustains the elect. From the seventeenth century onwards the individual, if we are to believe the philosophers, has to struggle to keep his identity. 'I think, therefore I am.' Time is a chaplet of instants, and duration a succession of creations. Even a Bossuet can declare that 'there is never more than an instant between us and nothingness', a saying reiterated in other words by Boileau's 'The moment in which I speak is already far from me'. In the eighteenth century divine help departs, and in place of the 'I think', it is now 'I feel, therefore I am'. The individual has to be a 'man of feeling' and preserve his identity by memory. This condition of mind helped at the end of the century to produce the romantic agony, the longing to find some means of making the happy sensations permanent. With the nineteenth century the problem of time and permanence could be solved, so it was thought, by recourse to the idea of 'becoming'. This was the time when Hegel produced his theory of the dialectic, a process of becoming which superannuated the notion of being; and later Evolution was to reform scientific theory and give a new turn to philosophic thinking. 'To exist is to change, to change is to mature, to mature is to create oneself endlessly.' The optimism, however, which was engendered by the vision of indefinite progress, was not long lived. The shibboleth, 'to make and in making to make oneself' proved unrealistic, and reflection saw that the 'making' was 'out of nothingness'. In literature the problem of time and of the self remained unresolved. The Bergsonian *élan* gave no permanence to the self and led to the *A la Recherche du Temps Perdu*, and The Age of Anxiety and the *néant* of Sartre. Time has become only a heap of broken images; 'in and out, in an endless drift of shrinking forms in a circular desert'.

Far different is the Hebraic conception of time. It is the means and opportunity for things to grow and for man to live and fulfil himself. Such is the picture of Genesis, a work lasting six days; and another series of 'days' is required for man to grow to a higher sense of his destiny and to prepare himself for the midpoint of time, when the glory of God, the shekinah will be manifested. No matter whether we take the Bible story as it stands or, as some critics would maintain, a later sense of mission and of messianic hope be read back by later writers into the early story, the story has a character unlike that of any other known history. At the beginning man walks with God in an earthly paradise; he falls by his own choice from that favoured condition, but straightway a promise is made of reparation. Then in the figure of Abraham we have the prototype, the man who has a faith and believes in the promises of God. How deeply impregnated was the Jewish mind with this figure can be seen in the Letter of St. Paul to the Romans. He is arguing with the Jews about circumcision and the Law, and he takes as common ground of agreement the promises made by God to Abraham. 'For what saith the Scriptures? Abraham believed God: and it was reputed to him unto justice.' To Abraham were made the promises: 'For not through the Law was the promise to Abraham and to his seed, that he should be heir of the world: but through the justice of faith.' Israel is of the seed of Abraham and moves forward in the strength of the promises made to him. These promises are given to Abraham from the first: 'And the Lord said to Abraham: Go forth out of thy country . . . and I shall make of thee a great nation . . . and in thee shall all the kindred of the earth be blessed.' The promise reappears at the end of Genesis in the words of the dying Jacob to his sons, when he tells them that 'in the days to come the sceptre shall not be taken away from Juda, nor a ruler from his thigh, till he come that is to be sent; and he shall be the expectation of nations.' This promise was compared by the great prophets later to a spreading out in ever wider circles of God's goodness and mercy. The active word of God is like this living water as seen by Ezechiel, or the rain and the snow as seen by Isaias, which 'come down from heaven and return no more there'. 'So shall my word be, which shall go forth from my mouth. It shall not return to me void, but it shall do whatsoever I please and shall prosper in the things for which I sent it.'

Bound up with this faith in a promise is the belief of Israel in one God. This is equally remarkable. Polytheism was the cult of the nations around Israel, and if it be argued that Abraham came from a part of the East where the worship of one God was known, there is still a decisive difference between the philosophical theism of a minority and the national worship by the Israelites of a living God who spoke to His people with such predilection and intimacy. Moreover the Jewish religion was not intended to be a tribal cult; the Jews were to be missioners, and, despite the prejudices of the multitude, the worship of the true God was to take the place of all other cults and reach to all the nations. We know from the story of the

Jewish people how exposed they were to contamination from the cults around them. The religion imposed on them from Sinai was contrary to all their primitive instincts and habits, and they were for ever falling back into the worship of Baal and gods who satisfied their crude wants. They needed more than human strength to believe in a transcendent God, who was one, living and holy, and who imposed on them Commandments which were despairingly difficult and yet strictly to be observed. With justice has Père Hilaire Duesberg written that 'when one adds the almost irresistible attraction the surrounding world had for them, their continued vacillation between Baal and Yahweh—which Elijah picturesquely called "limping on both feet" (1 Kings 18, 21)—the infidelities of kings, the complicity of sinful priests and false prophets, one understands that their belief in the one and only God was not called for by any psychological tendency, any ancestral recollection, or any intellectual need. Yet this belief was held by them to the exclusion of nations older than they, who long before them had walked the ways of civilization.' Their faith in the future helped to keep them compact and faithful. The nature of the promise gradually unfurled itself before them in renewed promises and in the revelations of the prophets. Yahweh, too, who at the beginning had tempered the vision of the future to what they could understand and demanded of them what they could carry out, though with difficulty, showed them in the process of time the height and width of their vocation. That vocation was to usher in a new era and a spiritual and supernatural kingdom. This higher note is present, for instance, at the very beginning of the prophecy of Isaias. There we learn that 'all nations shall flow unto (the mountain of the house of God), and many peoples shall go, and say, "Come, and let us go up to the mountain of the Lord, to the house of the God of Jacob, and he will teach us his ways, and we will walk in his paths." ' This universality of the kingdom is echoed in Jeremiah and in Daniel and reaches its mysterious and culminating statement in the prophet Malachi, written in the year 445 B.C. The Jews were in a chastened frame of mind after their return from captivity. They had to begin again and restore their religious worship. It is at this moment that Malachi tells them that the altar of Yahweh is to be universal; 'for from the rising of the sun even to the going down, my name is great among the Gentiles; and in every place there is sacrifice and there is offered in my name a clean oblation. For my name is great among the Gentiles, saith the Lord of Hosts.'

Through their contacts with other civilizations and their experience of success and failure the Jews came to a better understanding of their unique religion and of their destiny. They thought much about the future which was in store and reflected on the saying of the prophets and their sacred writings. Different interpretations, however, began to widen and at the same time confuse their vision of the future. Looking back upon their past the Jews were stirred by the mighty works of God on their behalf. God had called their ancestors from the condition of nomad shepherds to become a nation and to receive a divine benediction. Held as a subject people by the powerful Egyptians they had been led forth in a miraculous Exodus, made into a chosen people at Sinai and given a promised land. Set up as a kingdom despite their many backslidings God had multiplied His favours and prepared them for a 'day of days'. It was natural that the thought of this great day, a day of triumph and salvation should more and more take hold upon their minds, especially as in the later days of Israel strong alien powers had subdued them and kept them subject. So it is that the idea and hope of a Messias became predominant in their picture of the future. In the first stages of their history this idea of a Messias has been in the background. It was connected with the prophetic role, for the prophets were the representatives of God and the transmitters of his thoughts and wishes. It was not until Israel became a kingdom and the heroic figure of David became part of their national story that they explicitly conceived of a Messias who would be a king and a priest. This development is proudly expressed in Psalm 109, of which I give the translation by Rev. Eric Burrows.

Sit at my right hand
Until I make thine enemies thy foot-stool.
Yahweh shall send forth the rod of thy might from Sion;
Rule thou in the midst of thy enemies.
With thee is all princeliness in the day of thy power, in thy holy
    splendours;
From the womb of the dawn hast thou the dew of thy youth.
Yahweh hath sworn and He shall not repent:

Thou art priest for ever after the manner of Melchisedech.
Adonai at thy right hand
Shall shatter kings in the day of His wrath:
He shall judge among the nations;
He shall heap up the corpses.
He shall shatter the dead over a wide land;
From the torrent in the way shall he drink.
Therefore He shall lift up the head.

In this psalm there is a sequence of images of throne, sceptre, a sacred splendour from anointing and priesthood. If, too, we put this psalm side by side with Psalm 2, where the kings of the earth meet together against the Lord and against his anointed one, the impression is confirmed that this is a prophecy concerned with a Davidic Messias of the future.

The combination, however, between king and priest led to rivalries, and the mingling of apocalyptic and eschatological prophecies obscured the figure of the Messias. The recent discoveries of the Qumran Scrolls provide evidence of the dissension in the period near to the birth of Christ between the party favouring a priestly saviour and that favouring kingly descent. The somewhat vague idea in the earliest prophecies of a representative of God, so close to God as to be a special manifestation of God, had fallen into the background. Thoughts turned to prophets who had not died, like Elias. The misfortunes, too, of the Jews led many to think in terms of a material recovery, of a time coming when a leader would arise who could overturn the empires around them and give Israel supremacy over the earth. This would be the day of the Lord. On the other hand this day as the culmination of all that had hitherto happened could be and was thought of by some as the end of time, a day on which the Lord should judge all nations.

Another note was sounded in the prophecies to which the Jews, preoccupied with the hope of rescue from their subject state, ceased to be attentive. This note is that of suffering and the theme is that of the Suffering Servant of Yahweh. Scholars, both Jewish and Christian, accept the passages dealing with the Suffering Servant as Messianic, that is, as predicting an event which belongs to the future. These passages occur in Isaias, and they have to be compared with Psalm 21. There are four passages, chapters 1, 49, 50 and 52–3. In the first God says:

'Behold my servant whom I uphold. My Chosen, in whom I delight. I have put my spirit upon him; he shall bring forth justice to the nations . . . he shall not be extinguished nor crushed till he has put justice in the earth'. Even the Isles of the Mediterranean are expecting it. In the second passage we have the Servant's response to the prophecy. He tells of his vocation to the Isles and Peoples, for Yahweh has said to me: 'I will give thee for a light to nations: to be my salvation to the end of the earth.' The universal nature of his mission is here clearly marked. In the third passage he gives his qualifications for his mission and a description of his sufferings. In chapters 52 and 53 there is first God's declaration of the greatness of His servant: 'Behold my servant shall understand; he shall be exalted and extolled, and shall be exceeding high.' But the prophet, thinking of the servant and what he is to suffer, has to exclaim: 'Who would have believed our report?' There follows the account of the suffering and humiliation of the servant, a passage which is too well known to quote. Such suffering, he concludes, can only be explained as expiatory; the servant has taken upon him in his innocence the iniquity of his people, and because of this voluntary offering of himself he 'shall see a long-lived seed and the will of the Lord shall be prosperous in his hand'.

NOTE

Scholars have varied in their opinions as to who the Servant was intended to be. Some give it a collective interpretation and suppose that the reference is to the people of Israel or to an ideal Israel or a sacred class within it. Others take the passages to refer to an individual and they vary from Moses to Cyrus. Many of these views can be dismissed, and the debate is really whether we are to take the servant in a collective sense, as, for instance, Israel, or as pointing to one individual. The most attractive suggestion is that the Servant is at the same time the House of David and a representative of it. This would be in accordance with Jewish habits of thought and speaking, which can give a name and a person and refer to a tribe or house, thus making the chief or greatest representative stand for the race or house and embody all its ideals in his own person. The servant, then is royal and of the stock from which the Messias will spring. His role seems also to be a priestly as well as a prophetic one, and he is in a special sense the well-beloved of Yahweh. All these various roles, as we have seen, were attributed confusedly or explicitly to the coming Messias.

Looking back on his history the Jew felt that he could not be mistaken in regarding himself as belonging to a chosen people. Both the promises made by Yahweh and the actual story showed that its lot was exceptional. Some of the prophecies and promises have already been quoted. The incidents in the long record of Israel are even more striking. Of many that could be chosen to prove this the Exodus is perhaps the most impressive of all. It served to form the Hebrews scattered in Egypt into a people, and the story of their rescue from Egyptian bondage commemorated for ever after yearly in the feast of the Passover, was entirely different from the seasonable feast of spring common among the nations which surrounded the Jews. This Exodus, then, was the birth day of a nation, and though at first the Israelites must have regarded it as little more than freedom from oppression, the further acts of God in their behalf and especially the covenant made by God at Sinai with His people gave them a sense of belonging in a unique way to a God who had revealed His true name to them, given them commandments and a law and promised to be their protector and guide. The supper meal and the smearing of blood on the door-posts, the water that flowed from the rock in the desert to quench their thirst, and the bread from heaven, imprinted themselves upon their minds as sacred signs of God's dealing with them. So time passed and their infidelities to a faithful God multiplied, and as they contrasted their fortunes and religion with those of the nations around them, they grew more and more conscious both of their unique mission and of the need of a saviour and Messiah who would lead them in a new Exodus out of the miseries into which they had fallen by their own fault. The Rabbis had spoken of the Shekinah, the divine presence or glory which appeared in the Burning Bush and on Mount Sinai and accompanied the Ark of the Covenant, dwelling or tabernacling there. (The Prologue of the Fourth Gospel seems to make a direct reference to the Shekinah in the words 'dwelling amongst us', and 'we saw His glory'.) This

Presence was a pledge that Yahweh was faithful to His promises. In the Book of Leviticus Yahweh had declared: 'I will set my tabernacle in the midst of you; and my soul shall not cast you off, I will walk among you and will be your God; and you shall be my people.' But if they broke His commandments and did evil, 'I will scatter you among the Gentiles; and I will draw out the sword after you. And your land shall be desert, and your cities destroyed' (v. 33). 'Yet for all that when they were in the hand of their enemies, I did not cast them off altogether. Neither did I so despise them that they should be quite consumed; and I should make void my covenant with them. For I am the Lord their God. And I will remember my former covenant, when I brought them out of the land of Egypt, in the sight of the Gentiles to be their God.' At the time of the great exile the condition of the Jews was like that which was announced in Leviticus, but the great prophets were mindful of the Exodus and felt that God would remember His former covenant. After having declared the calamities of Israel to be due to their sins, Isaias goes on: 'Thus saith the Lord, thy redeemer, the Holy One of Israel; I am the Lord thy God, that teach thee profitable things, that govern thee in the way that thou walkest. . . . Declare it then with the voice of joy. . . . Say: the Lord hath redeemed his servant Jacob.' The same hope is preached by Jeremias. He doubted whether salvation were possible, whether the Ethiopian could change his skin or the leopard his spots; but remembering the old covenant after the liberation from the Egyptians, he prophesies: 'Behold, days are coming, saith Yahweh, that I will make a new covenant with the house of Israel; not according to the covenant that I made with the Fathers in the day that I took them by the hand (to bring them out of Egypt). That covenant of mine they broke, and I abhorred them. But this is the covenant that I will make with the house of Israel after those days, saith Yahweh. I will put my law in their inward parts, and in their heart I will write, and I will be their God, and they shall be my people. And they shall teach no more every man his neighbour . . . saying, "Know Yahweh"; for they shall all know Me, saith Yahweh.'

Both Jews and Christians agree that the story of the Jews in the Old Testament is like a drama which lacks its full significance without a final act. In this final act all that has been promised by God, much that has been prefigured, many obscure incidents, will be brought together in a plenary conclusion. The Messias or saviour or triumph has been awaited, and both Jews and Gentiles are to enter a promised land. To the Jews that ending has not yet come. Their interpretation of the story, therefore, differs from that of the Christian. To the Christian Christ is the fulfilment of the promises and the key to history. The prophets at various times had spoken of the One who was to come as a representative of God, as a priest according to the order of Melchisedech, as a prophet, as a king of the house of David, as the power and glory, like the Shekinah, as a Counsellor and Prince of Peace, as what the Targumin (the Aramaic renderings of the Old Testament) call the Memra, the Word. As Fr. Alexander Jones has pointed out, the Memra acts as the mediator between God and man. In the Memra 'redemption will be found'. 'My Memra', says the Lord God, 'shall be unto you like a good ploughman who takes off the yoke from the shoulder of the oxen.' We have seen how, as contrasted with the Greek conception, the Hebrew use of the 'word' is always dynamic. God creates by His word, and it is the 'word' which is both truth and life to the people of Israel, God's gift and saving power. It would seem as if the Memra, the Word, received its so far hidden reality and significance in the message of the Prologue of the Fourth Gospel, where we are told that the word which had been that whereby 'the heavens were made', for 'without him nothing was made, now is made flesh and gives to' those who believe in His name the power of becoming sons of God.

Christian writers have delighted in tracing types and analogies and prefiguring symbols in the Old Testament, the sacrifice of Abraham, the exodus itself, the manna, the brazen serpent, the blood on the door-post signifying salvation, the waters of the Red Sea and baptism, to mention only a few. They are so numerous that accumulated together they provide a persuasive confirmation of the Christian interpretation. Moreover they give a further distinguishing mark to a history so very unlike in its beliefs to the records of other nations. In any philosophy of history notice must be taken of this belief. Amongst other peoples in the East and in the West religion may be a potpourri of myths about the gods, and of rituals founded on the cycle of the seasons or impregnated with the sense of fate and necessity, or born from the mystical experience of liberation from the wheel of fate and time's miseries. The Jewish religion, on the contrary, begins and ends with a living God who chooses a people in order to work out through them and their history His purposes and His good will towards mankind. Historical persons and events count, and providence and history are intimately conjoined. Now, were the oracles and promises of the God of Israel confined to the single and relatively unimportant people of Israel, they could be dismissed by the philosopher of history as having little to do with what he is seeking, namely, a design or pattern of events which covers the whole story of mankind. But, in fact, the promises made by Yahweh are not confined to the Jewish people, and it is explicitly said again and again that 'all the ends of the earth shall remember and turn to the Lord; all the families of the nations shall bow down before Him'. Even in the first book of the Old Testament the universality of the vocation of the Jews is declared, for God says to Abraham, 'In you shall all the nations of the earth be blessed'. If, too, the inter-connection between the Old and New Testaments be accepted, and Christianity be the new covenant, the new divine community which is to spread to the ends of the earth and mediate between God and man, the divine revelation to Israel becomes the key to history.

It would look then as if without more ado a philosophy of history were presented to us on an open dish. The appearance is, however, deceptive. Taken by itself the history of Israel is only a small rivulet in the great stream of history. The historian will naturally turn to deal with the record in terms of social and cultural forces, bearing in mind the external influences, such as those of Mesopotamia and Egypt, its geographical situation, its access to the sea and the size of its population. These fail to explain the unique course of its history, but the historian is slow to appeal to extraordinary or miraculous factors. The philosopher of history may note these extraordinary facts and see in them the scaffolding of a philosophy. The conclusions to be drawn from this history are that the philosophy must be a religious one, that God has an end for man and has revealed what that end is and how it is to be accomplished. Such conclusions may be very valuable; nevertheless they have to be applied to the histories of other vast nations and civilizations and given a concrete meaning. And here immediately difficulties of various kinds arise. One is that in time the religious and the secular ends of man tend to separate. In the history of Israel they make one pattern, but who could say the same of the histories of Greece or Rome and modern civilizations? The Christian might answer that Israel is not to be taken by itself; it issues into Christianity, and Christianity is universal. It is true that it claims to be universal, but the philosopher of history cannot take this for granted. He sees many pages of history in which the name or ideas of Christianity have no place. He must notice, too, that within the Christian culture there is a long-accepted distinction between church and state, religion and secular ideals. Use is made of the saying of Christ that the kingdom was not of this world. If this saying summed up the attitude of Christianity to world affairs, then the philosopher of history would find little relevant to his purpose in the Christian interpretation of the Old and New Testaments. If the distinguished protestant theologian, Karl Barth, represented the main Christian tradition, discussion of this point would be closed. He holds, as we have seen, that there is no thoroughfare between the kingdom of God and the kingdom of man. But this is not the traditional belief. True it is, indeed, that Christianity is unworldly in this sense that its aim is a fellowship with Christ in a supernatural order of grace and that the consummation of this lies beyond history. But the stage on which this drama of grace is being enacted is that of history. Both the Jewish and the Christian religions are historical, and the Christian religion has by its title deeds, the incarnation and the redemption *sub Pontio Pilato*, a liaison with history. This fact does not, however, provide us with any open sesame to the problem of history; it simply puts up a sign saying that the way is not closed. The Christian can assert with certainty that Christ is the centre, the midpoint, to borrow an expression of commentators on the Bible. All things, as St. Paul says, are constituted in Him, and all is to be restored in Him. But such knowledge by faith, as it relies on divine revelation, so it is circumscribed by what has been revealed, and Christ Himself refused answers to questions which went beyond the mandate given Him by His heavenly Father. As Christian theologians know full well, the relation between grace and nature can be at times baffling; the relations between the spiritual order and the natural, the Church and the State, have given rise to many problems and disputes. The end and the dénouement of human history is beyond time. We have, therefore, still to seek in what sense a Christian philosophy of history can be adumbrated, and whether it can be hopefully developed. In any case it needs a superhuman artist to fit the pieces in a jigsaw which is ever changing its shape, as the years pass.

Chapter X

CHRISTIANITY AND HISTORICISM II

In an earlier chapter I made the tentative suggestion that a philosophy of history differed from history proper by interpreting the past in a way which could be called epical or gnomic. The ceaseless searching for significant facts and the weighing of them, while not abandoned, are partnered by poetical or imaginative insights. History, as Vico argued, is unlike science in that it is concerned with human deeds and works, what man has himself made. It is a kind of poiesis, and when the immense story of what *homo sapiens* has accomplished has to be measured and weighed, we cannot expect the same kind of truth as that open to a scholar working in some marked-out episode of a nation's past. But even if this be the right manner of trying to write a philosophy of history, it does not follow that it can be successful. We have seen a number of attempts, and though different persons will have different verdicts on their fruitfulness, no one of them can claim to be final. In the past many thinkers have rushed in to disclose a Christian version of history. The Old Testament seems to give a warrant for such an attempt, for here is the history of a nation with a mission and a message. Christianity, also, is an historical religion, both in the sense that its Founder was born in Bethlehem of Judah, in the days of King Herod, and suffered under Pontius Pilate, and because He left a visible society which has continued in time and played its part in history. So far, so good, but when we remember that the Christian lives by faith and not by complete comprehension and that the Christian Revelation can be compared to a pathway of light across an otherwise dark ocean, there is good ground for doubting the possibility of a Christian philosophy of history which will satisfy 'man's greedy mind'. In the preceding chapters I have tried to show that Christianity has two contributions to make for any adequate philosophy of history. One is that the temporal order, and the cultural values in it need not be looked upon by Christians as a waste product. The end of human life, as taught by Christianity, while stretching beyond and above time, does not entail a denial of human values. *Non eripit mortalia qui regna dat caelestia.* The second is the outstanding importance of each person, with the consequent dramatic, and cosmic quality of his choices.

Christianity, however, is more than a collection of individuals. The question, therefore, remains whether, taken as a body and a form of life, it provides a clue or clues to the historicist, who by his calling is concerned principally with societies, their rise and fall and the growth and meaning of this constant movement. The Jews constitute one of these societies. Christianity also is a society, although unlike any civil society; and just as Israel was treated by the prophets as if it were one living body or being, and described at different times by the name of one of its patriarchs or as a virgin daughter or a house or city, so, on the Christian assumptions, Christianity is the continuation and fulfilment of this chosen people and is a corporate society or community. It is composed of individuals, but these individuals, while remaining persons, undergo a change, which is as thorough as it is mysterious. The first Christian writers strained language in their attempts to describe the nature of this change. Christ himself used the image of vine branches of a vine and compared the relation of His disciples with Himself to that of His own sonship to His heavenly Father. St. Paul liked the image of a body and its members as it well expressed the unity, even though it did not serve to explain how the members of this new body could remain personal and free. He saw Christ as the Head of this body, the same Christ who had been born of the Virgin Mary and had suffered in His human body, now by the power of His active love adapting into the same risen body and life the lives of those who would take His name. This new body or society Christ wished to be coextensive with mankind: 'all those who did welcome him he empowered to become the children of God, all those who believe in his name'. To use still another image and reality, that of the Tabernacle of the Jews, Christ's humanity becomes the Tabernacle of the new Covenant in which God dwells perfectly among men, and so raises man to a new sacred status and dignity.

If this statement be a true account of the Christian teaching there can be no doubt that it gives the one practical and theoretical answer to the meaning of history. It explains God the Creator's intention with regard to His creation and the end or purpose of man's life on earth. If a name is to be given to such an explanation it should be theological rather than philosophical; and straightway the shortcomings of the view looked at from the historicist's angle become apparent. It is all very well, he may say, to appeal to a supernatural explanation which relies on a revelation from God that God wills to raise man to a new order of being. That does not belong to a philosophy of history which must rely upon empirical methods as far as possible. But, even were such a hypothesis acceptable, it leaves out almost all that a historicist wants to know. Christianity sits very lightly to the affairs of this world; it bids man look beyond this world. Human history is only a kind of larva state, and the worries of the caterpillar have no interest for the butterfly. The distinction of the supernatural and the natural is bound to reduce the natural to relative nothingness. Exaggerated as we have already seen this complaint to be, it nevertheless still has a sting. Were the views of Karl Barth in his earlier writings to be representative, Christianity would have nothing to say about history. But as we saw, even such moderate writers as Père Congar and Père Malevez do set up an unbridgeable gulf between the supernatural end of man and his human ideals and achievements. And even if we despair of human achievements and cry out that 'there is nothing worth the wear of winning save laughter and the love of friends', even these might be said, wrongly I think, not to consort with the beatific vision.

There are Christian writers who are ill at ease with this dichotomy. In an essay on *The Christian Hope* in a series of Studies by Members of the Anglican Communion with the title *Christian Faith and Communist Faith*, the Rev. Dr. J. A. T. Robinson simplifies drastically this problem of grace and nature, and in so doing he brings into closer accord human history and the Christian ideal. He bids us beware of assuming that the New Testament expression, 'the end of the world' has the sense of the extinction of this earth. It does not, he says, refer to 'any event that can be discussed or predicated in physical or astrophysical terms'. Both of the words used in the New Testament, 'aiôn' and 'kosmos' have a special sense. The end of an 'aiôn' refers to the closure of that particular stage of the divine economy which may close a former or inaugurate a new dispensation; that is to say, it designates purpose more than process. 'This age (aiôn) of which St. Paul writes is a period between the Fall and the Coming, the Parousia—system or order, ruled perhaps by an evil spirit and determined by its historical factors. Similarly by 'cosmos' is often meant a world in opposition to God, and under a management which has nothing in common with Christ. But despite appearances and despite 'the rulers of this world', spirits or men, the kingdom of God is being realized here and now, and Christians are those who have the new life now, their 'citizenship in heaven' now, and pray that God's kingdom and His will shall come on earth as it is in heaven. Their hope will be fulfilled when Christ comes again: 'The focus of the whole New Testament expectation is in the hope of His *appearing*; Christians are those who wait for God's Son *from* heaven.'

Such a view as this implies an intimate connection between history and the kingdom of God and calls to mind immediately the Marxist view. Dr. Robinson is of course aware of this resemblance and shows where he thinks Marx went wrong. 'The kingdom of God is in time—and history is moving to its consummation, not in a materialistic classless society, but to the "new city and the new heaven".' For evidence in support of this view the Acts of the Apostles are quoted which say that Christ is He 'whom the heavens must receive until the times of the restoration of all things'. Again, Christians are born into an inheritance, and by 'the power of God are guarded through faith unto a salvation ready to be revealed at the last time' (1 Peter 1, 4-5). This promise is understood by Dr. Robinson to be 'of a renovated cosmos which will include a new heaven and a new earth, an order, that is to say, in which all things, spiritual and material, shall be fully reconciled in Christ. It is a hope for history, not a release from history'. Whereas the 'figure of this world' passes away, the world of ambition and avarice of the Herods and Caesars, a house is being built up, 'a house not made with hands, eternal, in the heavens'; or to use another Pauline image, a hidden reconciliation is at work, 'unto the building up of the body of Christ: till we all attain unto the unity of the faith, and of the knowledge of the Son of God, unto a full-grown man, unto the measure of the stature of the fullness of Christ'. The image and guarantee of this reconciliation is the 'resurrection' of Christ. He rises victor over all the forces of evil, and now is able 'to subject all things unto Himself' (Phil., 3. 21); and as this resurrection was an event of history, in that the same body that was buried rose from the grave, and is also a cosmic event foreordained by God, we are bound to regard it as a factor in history, and a commanding one. History, when studied on naturalistic or positivist lines, shows no notable bias in favour of good over evil. Chance and necessity have been prominent in the past, and the future offers no certain promise or even the means of avoiding the confusions and mistakes of the past. 'All things continue as they were from the beginning of creation' (2 Peter 3. 4). But in Dr. Robinson's view, 'the Christian knows that the move that decides the game has already been played. Since the resurrection of Jesus Christ there can in fact be no other outcome to the contest. It is the period of the end-game. The enemy may go on redisposing his pieces as he wills. But the issue is now foreclosed, however delayed the finish may be. The end can bring nothing new; the final checkmate will simply translate into universal acknowledgement what is already a *fait accompli* in the finished work of Christ.'

Dr. Robinson bases his understanding of the 'kingdom of God' on texts from the New Testament, and is thereby enabled to present a view of the reconciliation of all things in Christ which is too often forgotten. Part of what he says cannot be omitted in any account of the relations of Christianity to history, and it is the more salutary in that it corrects the too individualistic interpretation of the Gospels which has been prevalent especially among the *illuminés* and those described by Mgr Ronald Knox in his book on Enthusiasm. Bunyan's *Pilgrim's Progress*, for instance, gives a one-sided, if highly spiritual, idea of the Christian life, and some, who have lived away from the world, in the cloister, have been tempted to deny 'the world' any value. Dr. Robinson by his exegesis of the word 'world', and by emphasizing both the communal and historical character of the Christian outlook, redresses the balance. Nevertheless his own view exaggerates in its turn one side of the

237

Christian message, and he goes beyond what we are justified in doing by the New Testament in his statements about the course of history and human lives. He seems to identify the victory of Christ over sin and death with a total conversion of the whole human race into the kingdom of God or the beloved community of Christ. In other words he means by victory a universal redemption, and there is no mention of the new Israel, the new body of Christ which is to serve as mediator between God and man. Such a view would have astonished the apostles and disciples, who regarded themselves as specially chosen to be the light and life of the world in succession to their head who had declared himself to be the light and life of the world. For Dr. Robinson's view to be right, we have to suppose that the Church has had no failures or that somehow or other we shall find at the last day that all without exception have streamed into it. This is to go beyond what we can deduce from the New Testament, and to ignore both difficult texts and the experience of history. The view perhaps has gained plausibility owing to the complete silence about the trans-historical side of Christianity. Christ may indeed return at the end of time and reveal what is dark to us while we are making history and travelling to our destiny; but such a return does not rule out the constantly taught truth of another life, the essential life in fact of ineffable union with the Godhead in Christ, which is the chief promise of the Gospels. 'Beloved, we are now already sons of God, and it hath not yet appeared what we shall be. We know that when it shall have appeared, we shall be like unto him, because we shall see him as he is' (1 John 3, 2). St. Peter tells us that we are to be sharers in the divine nature, and, as to this world, he says that 'the heavens shall pass away with great violence, and the elements shall be melted with heat, and the earth and the works which are in it shall be burnt up'. The passage continues to this effect that seeing 'that all these things are to be dissolved the Christian community should look for a new heaven and a new earth, according to his promises, in which justice dwelleth'.

These and many other texts have to be taken into account by Dr. Robinson, and also by such writers as Père Teilhard de Chardin and Mr. Gerald Heard, who align the data of Evolution with the Christian message.[1] Père Teilhard de Chardin,

[1] For a résumé of the views of Mr. G. Heard v. Appendix.

looks at the future with a certain benignity. Let us not be disturbed, he says, by rumours of coming catastrophe. Now that man has been placed at the summit of biological evolution, we need have no fear that it is the earth which is going to fail man. 'In one or two or three million years the Earth will certainly be ever there under our feet—and ever as habitable by reason of its temperature and its bounds as it is today.' Such, however, is not the opinion of the German Catholic philosopher, Dr. Joseph Pieper. His *Uber das Ende der Zeit*, now translated into English with the title, *The End of Time*, is, as he himself calls it, a Meditation on the Philosophy of History. To a philosopher of history the most pressing question, he tells us, is the end of history. Such a question clearly cannot be answered by the historian, nor by the philosopher, unless it be proved that history repeats itself in a cycle or be predetermined. Christianity, on the other hand, just because it is committed to the belief that history has a beginning and an end, can pronounce on the end to come. Divine Revelation gives us a history of salvation. 'It treats of a single stream of historical happening—starting with the Creation, the beginning *per se*, ending with the Judgment on the Last Day, and between beginning and end the history of the Fall of Man, the awaiting, the Logos made flesh, the agony on the cross, the Resurrection, the Ascension of the God-man. Theology, therefore, must take up the task of interpreting history, where science and philosophy come to the limits of their understanding. It does not, however, dispense with philosophy and historical observation, for the theological interpretation can grow not only clearer but also richer in content by incorporating them. Whoever accepts in faith 'the revealed prophecy of the end of history ... is able to see more and more, and, in addition, to see it in historical events and formations; he is able to perceive something about the events and formations which has an inner connection with the end of time'.

Pieper is, as his words show, confident that a philosophy of history can be written, if the Christian view of the end of history be accepted. 'How is the end of history', then, 'to be conceived?' Pieper goes to the *Apocalypse* for his information, and relies upon the explicit prophecy of 'a new Heaven and a New Earth.' This is taken to mean a 'transposition of the temporal being of the historical world into the state of direct participation in the untemporal mode of being of the Creator'. Such a transposition cannot be effected by history itself. No temporal power can avail, and therefore it must come by a 'direct intervention of the Creator'. He quotes, as corroboration of his argument, a passage from Immanuel Kant's *The End of All Things*. In the Apocalypse 'an angel lifts up his hand to heaven and swears by him that liveth for ever and ever . . . that there should be Time no longer'. If then time is to come to an end, and if, as Pieper has argued, no force within history is capable of making the transformation from this order to a new heaven and a new earth, then either there must be a complete dichotomy between the two orders or else, as the prophecies declare, the historical process must move to the end by a momentum of its own and culminate in such a crisis and catastrophe, that the 'transposition' will prove to be a 'deliverance'. 'History will debouch into its end as into a deliverance coming from outside.'

Whether the argument be considered cogent or not, Pieper is insistent on a catastrophic end. This is the burden of many of the prophecies, but it does not entail a pessimistic view of history. There is certainly to be 'a catastrophic end-situation of history', a foundering on a scale both so extensive and so intensive that salvage within history seems impossible. Nevertheless, the Christian need not be dismayed, because the 'end-situation' is not the ultimately valid one. Moreover, concealed within failure is the germ of life, and 'authentic realization may be achieved under cover', even as the redeeming act of God was concealed under apparent downright failure.

In the last part of *The End of Time* Pieper attempts with the help of the prophetical literature to give some content to his picture of the end of history. He feels justified in believing in the rise of an Anti-Christ exercising political power over the whole of mankind. This pseudo-order will deceive many. Amongst many who have sensed the coming of such a tyranny he quotes Lenin: 'The whole of society will be *one* office and *one* factory with the same work and the same wage'; and also Jacob Burckhardt, who anticipated some 'great future authority' for which an all-levelling radicalism is preparing the way.

Pieper does not hesitate to call what he has written a philosophy of history. He holds that a Christian has an advantage because he knows from divine revelation the beginning of history and the end of it. Without such an aid from theology a so-called philosophy is bound to become nothing more than a sociology of culture. Historicists tend to place their faith in progress, in the gradual development of a perfect society. Pieper is tilting against them, and that makes him lay stress on the eschatological and apocalyptic literature of the Bible, which so often prophesies a catastrophic end to history. Not all Christian scholars would accept such a literal acceptance of this type of literature, and others again would quote in correction other texts of the kind which Dr. Robinson has chosen. Pieper and Robinson have this in common that there is to be a new heaven and a new earth, but whereas for the latter 'history is moving to its consummation', and all things material and spiritual are to be fully reconciled in Christ, for Pieper catastrophe has first to intervene at the end of time. In comparing the close of history to the death of Christ and so establishing the repetition of the Christian theme of victory through apparent failure, life through death, Pieper recalls the clue suggested in an earlier chapter. But for all I know Robinson may intend the same theme, for his image of the game being played between, so to say, God and the devil, and his statement that the kingdom of God is operative now in a struggling and sinful world, are consonant with this theme. But it is not at all clear what happens while and when the reconciliation is made between heaven and earth. Robinson tells us that 'the God of the Bible is not *accidentally* a God of history', and furthermore that the 'Christian hope is not of resurrection from the body of history to an existence beyond time and history'. This would seem to mean that everlasting life after death must be temporal and historical after the manner of our life now in time. Such a view is almost impossible to maintain in the light of the constant teaching of Christianity about the after-life. It also makes it very difficult to understand the lot of those who have died in grace since the coming of Christ. According to Christian teaching they are already enjoying eternal felicity and belong to the communion of saints. They do not easily fit into a scheme according to which God has reconciled the world and history to Himself in Christ, and a new heaven and a new earth are now in process of being constituted. This new heaven and new earth are to be the kingdom of God, which will be manifested not now, but in the future, at the end when Christ returns in glory.

It should be admitted that whatever answer be given a mystery remains. If, as has been suggested in a previous chapter, history is not to be a waste product, and we carry our sheaves with us into the kingdom of God, there exists a mysterious relationship between life on earth and life to come. In the Christian tradition Christ at the Last Judgment will, in scriptural language, separate the sheep from the goats and make manifest the hidden ways of God, His wisdom and His love. We do not go beyond the book if we surmise that not only the special providence of God in dealing with each individual life, but also God's general reconciliation of history with His design will be seen and vindicated. There will be no loose ends, nothing astray. Usually this form of explanation limits itself to the problem of salvation, and would show that even sin, if repented, can be a *felix culpa*. But if we wish to include the private and public lives of all who have ever lived and press for the reconciliation of all history with the new heaven, we produce such a complicated situation that the mind boggles at it. Yet this is what Dr. Robinson wants us to consider, and perhaps it is necessary if we make up our mind to write an adequate philosophy of history. With part of this ambition many of us may be sympathetic, but Dr. Robinson seems to believe that the victory over evil will be so signal that despite obdurate wills the kingdom of God will include all human beings without exception. Previous writers on this subject, such as St. Augustine and Bossuet, took the world as they knew it for evidence and the Christian Church as the foundation and centre of their theories. As we see now, that world was too tiny, but they were wiser than some later philosophers in beginning with the Christian Church. This must be the correct method for a Christian historicist who believes in divine revelation, for he starts with what is certain and may proceed to speculate on firm grounds. If, on the other hand, we begin with the supposition that all history and all nature are to be reconciled or restored in Christ, we leave the field of revelation and lose ourselves in speculation. What the Christian knows by faith is that Christ is the one mediator between God and man and that He has opened the way to happiness to all mankind. We know also the nature of this way, for His mediatorship continues in time in and through the extension of Himself in a living community or body of which He is the head and life-giving spirit. It follows from this that we cannot say without qualification that all mankind is reconciled and that history has become the story of this reconciliation. On the contrary, Christ's victory consists in this, that there is ever offered a certain way of happiness to be accepted or rejected by the free choices of man. We may speculate as we wish about the response to this offer, be optimistic or pessimistic, but we have no certain knowledge. If our cast of mind be empirical and we consider the place and influence of Christianity in history we may be pessimistic. If, however, we take certain texts and amplify them from our knowledge of God's providence and love, we may feel confident that somehow or other God will be all in all. Speculation along these lines may provide insights even though the material for a definite conclusion may be wanting, provided that a foundation for such cloud-capped thinking has already been laid. What can lead nowhere is to start with such speculations.

If, then, we begin with what Christianity claims about itself, we have first an historical figure, Christ, who taught what has been inscribed in the early Creeds. These Creeds have nothing to say directly which helps to a philosophy of history. The articles of these Creeds affirm the divinity and humanity of Christ, His birth, death and resurrection, His founding of a Church, the communion of saints, the forgiveness of sin and life everlasting. These doctrines do not at first sight offer promising material for any theories of history. They are doctrines of salvation and look beyond the present life to eternity. It is important to recognize this, for it saves us from asking wrong questions and getting answers which, however attractive, are adventitious. The Christian religion, however, like that of Israel, is wedded to history, and this does open up the possibility of discussing its relation to history. Just as the Jews intermingled with Egyptians and Philistines, Syrians and Romans, so the Christian Church is connected with the later world's history, and has influenced it and showed a standpoint with regard to it. While in Christian literature there is always the refrain that we must bid farewell to all that is lovely, that very loveliness is praised and understood. A prayer of the liturgy begins: 'O God, who has wondrously established the dignity of human nature, and still more wondrously refashioned it . . .' and this includes the body as well as the soul. The article of the Creed, 'I believe in the resurrection of the body', might furthermore, be stretched into meaning a recovery of the temporal, seeing that our temporal experience is in and through the instrumentality of the body. The risen body will have an identity with the body of our present experience because of the permanence of the self and the structure or configuration of the self. To carry the idea still further, we may fancy something analogous in experience to a recording set, so that what is past can be revived and played again. Be this as it may, human experience is the material of the supernatural order, the new life of grace in kind. The new life does not lie alongside or above what is human and temporal; our humanity is neither lost nor diminished. Constantine the Great swore that before the battle of the Milvian Bridge he saw the sign of the Cross in the sky. His victory, however assisted, was an event in history and in the development of Christianity. St. Louis and Fra Angelico were examples of Christian living, and the one has his place in the history of France, the other in the history of art. The works and actions of human beings are the meeting place of the kingdom of God and the kingdom of man.

Christ, therefore, continues in the world and in history. He abides in His visible body, the Church, and in the individual by grace. Theologians have been wont naturally to dwell on the specific aim of the Christian religion and separate it from all that man could accomplish left to himself. They are very conscious that the supernatural end is their concern, and consequently they have tended to leave it to philosophers to study the purposes and end of secular society and what man is capable of becoming when left to his own initiative and strength. If the philosophers were agreed in their conclusions on this subject, we should be much nearer to composing not only a Christian view of history, but a textbook for all the nations. Unfortunately there has been the widest discrepancy in their views! From a Christian point of view this is understandable, for Christianity holds firmly that there never has been a model specimen of human nature; man as we know him has a fallen nature. Wherever, too, we consider human ideals, we are checked by the fact that there are two stages in the life of man, the temporary one enshrined in history and an immortal one, and if we lay too much emphasis on the latter we rob history of all vitality. This, as we have seen, has been the mood of the Eastern religions, and has not been absent in Christian thought. But if, out of an amalgam of Plato and Aristotle and Locke and Leibniz and Kant and Hegel, we cannot discern a clear pathway to human perfection and a city of happiness at the end, the majority of philosophers do attach significance to moral and spiritual ideals and, with the growth of civilization and culture, to highest common factors in the growth of them.

Now it is here that the work of Christianity in history becomes apparent, as aiding this growth and as lifting it on to a higher plane. It does now universally what the law and the prophets did to Israel. Israel, indeed, offers a specious clue to the office and the function of Christianity in history. The area covered by Jewish history is very small. It is like a flash of light in a surrounding darkness, a glimpse of a providential design, a sky which 'lights a lovely mile'. We are brought at a break-neck pace from Adam, the progenitor of the human race to Abraham, and the God strikes a covenant with his people: 'the oath which he swore to Abraham, our father, of salvation to his people, so that those who sit in darkness and in the shadow of death shall be enlightened, and their feet directed in the way of peace.' From then Israel has its own separate call and destiny. Other nations appear and disappear in the biblical story; they are usually treated as if outside the Providence which governs Israel. But the point is that in the end Israel is to introduce the Lord whose coming will affect them and all nations, and, as already shown, the prophecies reach out to the Gentiles. Christ, when He comes, breaks down the barrier of races, and Christianity has always understood itself to be the heir of Israel and to consist of a sacred people with a mission; but this time its mission is to be for the whole world. Christ is 'to dominate over all things, visible and invisible, which the Father has conferred upon him'. 'All things are to be recapitulated in Christ', for He is the head and Lord of the living and the dead, and also the key to the world's progress. The old law is abrogated and prophecy has passed into reality. Circumcision is no longer to mark the difference between the elect and the stranger outside the Temple. St. Paul is the outstanding example and exponent of this change of attitude. A strict Jew, educated in the traditions of the Law, he nevertheless proclaims the good tidings of hope and salvation to the Gentile world; he steps up to the Areopagus to preach the universality of the Christian message in a language which has been called by scholars 'a foreign body' in the framework of the Bible texts. The listening Athenians heard how the true God, whom they had sought blindly, was of necessity the Lord of all men, 'for it is he, who has made of one single stock all the nations that were to dwell upon the whole face of the earth; and one man has been appointed to give just judgement to the whole world'. The style and phrasing of this speech herald the alliance between Christianity and humanism.

St. Paul was ready to spoil the Greeks as well as the Egyptians to adorn Christian truth. The Prologue of the Fourth Gospel brings Hellenic philosophy into the sanctuary, but the conditions of the Christian community in the first centuries delayed the approach of Christianity to civil life and culture. Christians were pariahs, and their thoughts turned to the immortal life promised to them and to the expected end of the world. Nevertheless the Greek Fathers and later St. Augustine found it appropriate to clothe the Christian doctrines in the philosophical dress of the time. By this very act a tie is formed between Christianity and human systems of thought, and a Christian historicist is encouraged to look for a further collusion between history and the Christian promise. We shall not, however, find many forerunners before the nineteenth century equipped to treat of the subject. The early Christians and the medieval writers were all too ready, indeed, to find analogies and figures and symbols in ancient history which could serve to embellish their accounts of the Christian faith. But they belong to the genre of story-telling. Even in biblical exegesis the over-readiness to pick out foretypes and prophecies in the Old Testament has led to a reaction against this habit. This kind of exaggeration, moreover, went with a lack of the historical sense. History, as we now understand it, is a late product or experience. When Hegel announced that 'being was becoming' he summed up in an exaggerated form a relatively new phase of thought, which dominated the nineteenth century and fathered the theory of evolution, the pragmatical philosophies and modern history. The past was seen now in terms of 'becoming', and interest centred on the genesis of religion, philosophy, history and science. In history the difference between modes of thinking and of culture and the gradual growth of institutions was marked. Until this momentous change occurred a static conception of mankind prevailed; the present was read into the past; no one asked himself what kind of a man Adam would have been; it was sufficient to look at the ceiling of the Sistine Chapel. Noah was as well informed as a Seneca, and more fortunate in length of years. There was no reason why a disciple of St. Paul should not have been Bishop of Athens, founder and Bishop of the Church in Paris and writer of a metaphysical treatise on the Divine Names. This same indifference to change and growth in time led also on occasions to the misapplication of texts from past writers. If the book of Genesis mentions the words 'soul' or 'spirit' or 'justice', it was taken for granted that the word had remained static in meaning throughout the centuries. Such an outlook stood in the way of constructing a philosophy of history.

Nevertheless, as Père Daniélou has pointed out,[1] Christianity had within it from the beginning the means and opportunity to free itself from the static conception of history. Its own novelty postulated a change from the past. As Daniélou says: 'The greatest criticism that Celsus could make of Christianity is its novelty, which comes to upset the ancestral practices of the traditional religions.' So deeply convinced, however, were all at this period of the unchanging nature of history that a genius like Origen, when defending Christianity, chose the argument that the role of the Incarnation was to restore the pristine perfection of creation which had declined because of the Fall of man. 'Likewise, for Eusebius, Christ did not bring a new message; he came merely to re-establish in its purity the religion of primitive humanity, which had been provisionally replaced by Judaism.' The Hellenic world made a sharp distinction between 'divine things', which are everlastingly the same, without beginning or end, and lesser realities which are corruptible, and therefore must end even as they began. Confronted with the Christian belief in the Incarnation and in the advent of realities which had a beginning in time and yet are to last for ever, the wise men of the time were shocked. St. Augustine was well aware of this climate of opinion, and it is with it in mind that in the *De Civitate Dei* he loosened history from its old fastenings and initiated the idea that history is

[1] *The Conception of History in the Christian Tradition*, by Jean Daniélou; *The Journal of Religion*, Vol. XXX, No. 3, July 1950.

constituted by the great creative decisions of God, such as the creation of man, the covenant with Abraham, the Incarnation and the Redemption. Novelty is thus introduced into history, and what is introduced at a moment of time can remain permanent and incorruptibly the same.

Christianity, therefore, brought something new to history in its revolt against the conception of an immobile history and reality. Kierkegaard, in so far as he denounced Hegel and essentialist philosophies, was only following in the footsteps of the first Christian writers. The universal and the unchanging exercise a dread fascination for the philosopher. Even today, so we are told by Raymond Aron: 'The intellectuals cannot tolerate the chance-event, the unintelligible; they have a nostalgia for the Absolute, for a universally comprehensive scheme.'[1] Père Daniélou has brought to light the struggle which the Christians had to make to vindicate the value of the singular and the novel event, of new beginnings which could last perpetually. Here they had had to face the opposition of the Hellenic world. But, as he goes on to say, they had to meet a different kind of criticism from the Jews. Both the Jews and the Christians accepted the institutions of Judaism as of divine origin, institutions like the Law and the Temple. The Jews regarded them as holy, and the question arose, how can what is holy and good be abolished? What is good cannot cease being good, and yet the Christian claimed that it had been superseded. Puzzled by this problem some Christian apologists, like Justin, took the desperate line of answering that these institutions had not been good, except in so far as they admitted of a spiritual sense. 'Irenaeus was clearly the first who discovered the solution by showing that, again, to the dismay of reason, the temporal aspect, the kairos, should enter into the value-judgments to be brought to a reality. Thus, on the one hand, it is necessary to affirm that the Old Testament is good and that it is the work of the same God as the New. But at the same time the realities of the Old Testament were provisional. An effort must not be made to keep them when their time, their kairos, is over. The sin of Judaism is a sin of anachronism; it consists in wanting to arrest God's plan at a moment in its growth, to maintain out-of-date forms. The Old Testament, says Origen, following Meliton of Sardes, is like a rough model.

[1] *The Opium of the Intellectuals.*

It was necessary but is no longer useful when the statue is there. "It is like a lamp; absurd to keep it lit when the sun has risen." '

From this it is clear that the early Christian thinkers by having to wrestle with criticisms from Greek and Jew became aware of the true nature of historical events as against philosophic concepts, and, secondly, of the nature of development or growth in history. They were already relating all the past to the unique series of events of Christ's life and subordinating them to the Christian theme. They were also stimulated but also baffled by another element in the teaching of the New Testament, namely, the eschatological. As we have seen, the promises of the Old Testament were fulfilled in Christ. Time had completed its function; the day of days had come, and as the Baptist had declared: 'all mankind is to see the saving power of God'. But in fact time had not stopped, nor had the power of evil been chained up. The world was continuing with evil still rampant, and apparently even more triumphant. The answer which became in one form or another the official view of the Church is summed up by Origen. He argues that eternal life has begun, salvation has been given, but the full glory of it has been delayed until the end because of the rejection of Christ by the Jews. 'The Parousia was fulfilled in the humiliation of Christ, but there is another which is awaited in Glory. This first Parousia is called the shadow by the Holy Scripture in a mysterious text: In the shadow we shall live among the nations. By this we understand that many things are shadow in the first Parousia.' He compares the time-epoch of the Church in relation to the Second Coming to the time-epoch of the law of Moses in relation to the First Coming of Christ. 'The Apostle says that the Law is the shadow of good things to come. Thus those who were under the Law were under its shadow. But we are no longer under the Law, but under Divine Grace. But although we are no longer under the shadow of the Law, we are, however, under a better shadow. Truly we live in the shadow of Christ among the nations.' One vital difference, nevertheless, is that under the shadow of Christ, eternal life is already present, and Christ is gathering up the spoils of victory.

This interpretation, however, in its very solution of a difficulty, lent itself to an abuse, which delayed any interest being taken in history. As the times remained dark, Christians turned with hope to a Second Coming. This expectation was so strong among the early converts that, as we know, St. Paul had to write cautioning them. Though the fact was certain, the time was uncertain, and so there was no excuse for idleness. This expectation persisted and led to all manner of guesses about the hour and nature of the Parousia. Some working upon the prophecies, especially of Daniel, placed the Second Coming in the year 500, others, including St. Augustine, were tempted to conjecture the year 1000. Interest in the millennium overshadowed the age and remains, as the tenets of some modern sects prove, perennial. Today, however, the general Christian view is that the Parousia awaits the preaching of the Gospel to the entire universe. Only when the voice of God has been heard throughout the world and the visible Cross has been planted in every land will 'the end come'.

This sense of mission, of a work to be done, brings with it, also, a sense of sacred history. The doctrine of the Parousia for a while took men's minds away from history, but disappointment brought them back to a new understanding of it. The certainty of the Parousia gave meaning to what had to be done before the end and made time important. Moreover it increased the significance of the mysterious interim between the First and the Second Coming. If all that preceded the First Coming of Christ was preparatory to it, as the soil is prepared for the seed, all that followed the coming is the sowing of the seed and the gathering in of the sheaves. The Redemption had for once and for all been accomplished; the Christ life, the *annus Domini*, had begun, and time had now become a divine contrivance for unfolding, like a fan, the many-splendoured beauty of the God-man and for changing civilizations into the people of God, rank after rank of Christians. In a way, nothing new could ever happen again. Perfection had been exhausted in the divinized humanity of Christ, and therefore in the Christian era all new discoveries in science or art or philosophy had to be integrated into an unchanging truth. This meant that a special importance had to be attached to the notion of growth, and the Christian philosophy of history must work with this enriched idea of growth in mind. As Christ exists yesterday, today and for ever, so eternal life is compresent with daily happenings and gives them somehow or other an unrusting patina. This, however mysterious, does fulfil a fundamental human need, the need for a family and corporate continuity. The Pagans expressed this need in the devotion to ancestors and worship of them or in the religion of the household gods. In the Church, looked upon as the extension of Christ in time, this need is met and the ideal embodied. The past flows into the present, and the dead still live in the communion of saints. 'The Mystical Body of Christ unites all ages into one company, and I can talk to Augustine, not as to a memory, but as to a man. The Incarnation did not destroy time, but raised it to an altogether new dimension. When St. Paul speaks of the "life of Christ" he usually does not mean the thirty-three years Our Lord spent on earth. He means, as Mgr. Knox has said, an "energy" poured out on the world, filling all times, and transcending each one of them, uniting together the whole course of mankind, making the Franks before Tours the companions of the heroes of the Alcazar. The Catholic holds his youth against an ageing universe; he begins his eternity while still a wayfarer within a world that passes.'[1]

Reflection, therefore, on time as a function of change and becoming has promoted a new interest among Christian thinkers as to the nature of the Church's development and its relation to general history. Moehler's and Newman's analyses of the meaning of development within the Church are an indication of this, and on a world scale the effort also of Père Teilhard de Chardin to reconcile Christianity and a general theory of Evolution. The Christian is better off than most other modern or contemporary philosophers in tackling this problem of development, for he unites the conception of time and change with that of a subsistent being, God. Kierkegaard caught the secret of history for a moment when he said that 'eternity is the fullness of time—that word taken in the sense in which it is used, where it is said that Christ came in the fullness of time'. From this it is easy to go on to say that all history is in God's present being or presence, a sentence uttered by the Word made flesh. The doctrine of the Mystical Body adds a further note. A member of it does not celebrate the memory of the world's redemption, but proclaims the *living* Christ. But perhaps there is an excess of light in these mysterious truths, and they are not available for development into a philosophy. Much has been written, and with great penetration, about time and memory and the sense of presence, since the ideas of 'becoming' and

[1] F. Wilhelmsen in *Born Catholics*, pp. 31-2.

evolution have taken root; but the conclusions have, for the most part, been unrewarding. Perhaps some future philosopher, out of the partly mistaken and partly tentative ideas so far put forward, may with the help of future discoveries be able to formulate a convincing account of history. The Phenomenologists have tried to lay bare for us the sense of presence and of distance. Bergson set time free from our inveterate habit of spatializing it, but in doing so loosened our hold on subsistent being. Poets, like Eliot, have meditated on the moment which is still and tells that God is nigh in defiance of the novelists who have been submerged in the stream of time; Proust from his sick-room searching for his identity in past memories, Kafka, 'an old man, naked, exposed to the chill of this unhappy age, I drive around in an earthly carriage, with unearthly horses'; and Joyce, a stream of consciousness, like his own Liffey, 'sheshell ebb music wayriver she goes'. Science is brought to our aid by Teilhard de Chardin, and philosophy by Croce and Gentile.

Teilhard de Chardin constructs a theory of Evolution which is all embracing, 'regular, continuous, total', from the most primitive forms of matter to man as he is now and beyond the present condition of man to a still higher condition. Amongst many notable features of his theory the most notable concerns man himself. The factors which determine evolution in the animal world can and should be applied to man in his present state. In biology we know now that individuals form themselves into groupings, what are called species. Living matter 'fragments itself, statistically, into a certain number of agglomerations, each held together by a definite union of common characteristics'. Furthermore, by a process of mutation the species periodically divides itself and gives birth, by the appearance of a new peak, to a new species. Then after a considerable time these daughter species show a remarkable property. They set about aligning themselves in accordance with the developing qualities of a group with definite characteristics, and these successive mutations reinforce each other 'additivement'. Put more concretely this means that there is a constant grouping of individuals which are biologically close to one another; a periodic segmentation of these groupings due to chromosomic changes and the cumulative intensification in time of certain characteristics. Now man is a species, in a fuller sense than any animal, and for three reasons. He is what Teilhard de Chardin calls 'biologiquement percé', that is to say, he turns in upon himself and reflects. Secondly, because of this quality he reaches in his species to a new stage, the cultural; and thirdly, because of this new interior development, the species as a unit tends to take the form of a centred unity, i.e., a tendency for cultures to converge and form a new culture.

The situation, therefore, from an Evolutionist's point of view is this. In the growth of Life there have been various stages. Towards the end of the Tertiary period, as the consequence of some neuropyschical transformations, man, alone of the animals, crossed a stage. This had as profound an effect upon the earth as the emergence millions of years before of the first living proteins. Man, because he is reflective, begins a new form of life, not only, let us say, a new form of life, but a new world, a little world, shut in and self-sufficing, with its own rules and outside the laws which govern the formation of a species. Anthropologists have been too inclined to regard this emergent *homo sapiens* as an invariant, as remaining unchanged during the thousands of years of his existence. But in truth 'in accordance with the most certain and the most universal of the laws of cosmic substance, man has grown, in one way or another, more complex, both organically and statistically, because it is exactly the same thing for a living group to propagate itself and to ramify'. This means that another species is forming itself, and this obviously is in the line of social and cultural unity. We are seeing before our eyes that culture is embodying itself in a form which is supra-individual and quasi-autonomous. Natural evolution and cultural evolution are the same phenomenon. This throws a new light upon what is now happening in human society and upon the future. We see the growth of diverse cultural unities and their continual reaction, the one upon the other. Anthropologists study these unities with their mind solely upon particular ethnic changes. They ignore the way they tie up with each other so as to form a new order of superior degree by their convergence. Man is not merely an interesting species on a par, except in degree, with other species. He is the one species, which, because it is global and reflective, tends inevitably to knit itself together materially and psychologically so as to form biologically a new super-organism with a definite nature. Among the animals which surround us one individual is not fully distinguishable from another; it is as if the individual lived in and for the species. 'With man, on the other hand, as a result of a rapid accentuation of psychical autonomy in each thinking element of the race, the phylum tends in some manner and at first sight to separate itself into granules and even to fall apart; it is as if the individual tended to live in isolation, by itself. And so it looks as if we had reached the point where there lives on in us hardly any sense of our being a species, at any rate, so far as looking upon any one as an animal form.' Now the danger of this is that we are left in the air and disoriented, and that, at a moment such as this when we are caught in a cultural maelstrom, we are crushed and mechanized. We are between the Charybdis of isolation and dispersal and the Scylla of depersonalization. Our one hope is that there exists a psychic flux or *élan* strong enough to redintegrate each one freely and at the same time unite together the multitude of the human species into a community of persons. 'For if, for solid, scientific reasons, we come to the conclusion . . . that, far from repulsing each other, thinking corpuscles are cosmically polarized towards an agreement whereby each of them is destined to find a true completion of itself as a result of *collective reflection*,' then all the apparent materialistic and enslaving totalitarianism which seems to be going on will change and be transfigured into a welcome unanimity.[1]

In his second volume, *L'Apparition de l'Homme*, he explains at greater length what he means by this new state towards which man is advancing. Growing unanimity and co-reflection are its co-ordinates, and in the future 'certain collective acts, which are not now realizable, will become natural and beautiful'. 'At a psychical temperature, far more elevated than our own, we have no idea of what, in union with all other men, each person (without deformation or transformation) will become capable of doing. Nor, I must add now, can we have any suspicion of what in these high latitudes he will begin to see.' There will be only one science, only one ethic and only one passion, 'that is to say, one mystique'. The universe instead of crushing man by its size will be found to exalt our individual values. As he is trying to keep to the realm of science, Teilhard de Chardin does not in these pages develop any theological explanation of

[1] *La Vision au Passé*, pp. 375–8

this high work of evolution. But in other essays and in his letters it is clear that the world in evolution is the creative act of God, and that it is part of the reflective power of man to be able to see this. Moreover, in man, what went out from God's hands now begins to return to God. Man has this prerogative of reflection, and so it is that in the process of knowing the meaning of the world gradually comes to light. The world of space and time is interiorized in reflection, and the reflection leads to a common culture, and common culture leads to the hope of a complete unanimity of all men in the understanding of truth and goodness. Teilhard de Chardin argues that the very principles of evolution, which have been verified in the biological world, gives us reason for believing that mankind is converging into a kind of super-organism, which will be both collective and personal. The present time may look to be a 'melting pot'; but in fact 'man is in process of re-emerging . . . as the head of nature. The reason is that by being in this way cast into the general current of a convergent Cosmogenesis, he acquires the power and the quality of forming, in the very heart of Time and Space, a central and singular gathering-point of the whole stuff of the Universe'. 'Man gathers up, therefore, within what is without; but for this new organization or species to be true to itself and the world and history, it in turn must be centred in and round One who is the image of the invisible God, the first-born of every creature', Christ. 'All things were created by him and in him.'

This view is so all-inclusive as to bring history as well as animate and inanimate nature within its ambit. It gives a beginning and an end to history and argues that history develops on principles which are applicable to all else in the universe. Historians, however, might well jib at this assumption, and indeed the view is open to many criticisms. In order to make it valid the author has to presuppose some form of consciousness, latent or implicit, as present even in the simplest elements of nature. Such an assumption takes all meaning out of consciousness, for it has now to be applied to what is precisely its opposite. Furthermore, by assuming a strict continuity between spiritual and material processes it forces history into a pattern which experience does not justify, and it skates over the very problem which underlies history, namely, the conflict of liberty and natural processes. But if the theory cannot be taken over, lock, stock and barrel, it does assist the historicist in his task. It gives a vision, and thereby a charter to other adventurers. The unity of the plan may be too grandiose in its sweep and at the same time, like a gigantic skyscraper, too uniform. But though empirical science and history cannot be treated on all-fours, the processes of development in nature may provide analogies and enable the historicist to get his bearings. But what is most of all to the point is the confirmation from a philosophically-minded scientist of the Christian belief that history is reaching to a consummation in a new heaven and a new earth. Teilhard de Chardin sees the consummation of history in what he calls man's power of 'reflection' and in the convergence of multiple minds into a new culture by dint of their discoveries of the wonders of the universe and of history. There will come a time, he thinks, when mankind will have come together in one mind and in one love, and this condition will be sustained by the presence and conserving power of Christ, who is both God and man. The scientific apparatus he uses may be at times more an embarrassment than a help, but the Christian philosopher has found an ally, if an unexpected and strange one.

Teilhard de Chardin has enlisted evolution in the service of Christian thought. Something also may probably be borrowed from the philosophers, who have favoured the notion of 'becoming'. Hegel considered himself a Christian philosopher and pressed into his service the new notion of 'becoming'. Benedetto Croce, however, criticized him for being not thorough enough, for leaving chunks of the old static philosophy unliquidated in his system. The Absolute or Spirit stood above the process of history, whereas it must be identified with it. Kant had lit upon the truth in his 'Copernican revolution', but like other revolutionaries he had not seen the full implications of his discovery, that reality as we experience it is mainly the work of the mind. He distinguished between the world as it is in itself, which we can never know, and the world of appearance. Hegel disposed of this extra, the world in itself, and maintained that Mind set over against itself this dark reality and in process of dialectic gradually mastered it, making it its own. This was a stage in the working out of the Copernican revolution. But Croce accused Hegel of still living in the old world of abstractions, of keeping mind aloof, a dead deity. History gives us the final solution of the relations between thought and reality. It is in perception, which to Croce is Art, that we are in touch with the singular and the present, and in all perception there is present also Thought, the singular and the universal joining together in a living act. Knowledge is always of a situation where intuition and idea, concreteness and universality meet. This can only be the *present*, our present experience. We talk about the past and we make free of the word 'truth' in science. But scientific concepts are abstracts, a series of pseudo-ideas which are serviceable for practical or descriptive purposes. Even the past has to be brought by us into the present for it to be alive. The affairs of a Socrates or a Caesar have meaning only when they form part of our present interest and judgment. The Spirit moves on, ever gathering up into its life the past, as an individual holds in the present whatever he has formerly experienced. Even those who have never heard of Croce admit that abstract thinking has something wanting in it, that scientific concepts do not bleed, and that documents of the past need to be interpreted by the present historian. Croce argues that reality is essentially experience, and what he calls Spirit is that historical process as now lived, the spirit ever judging the past and enriching itself in the present historic judgment. What Thucydides judged, what Polybius or Voltaire or Ranke, is all dead wood, except it be alive now in my present judgment.

This idealistic approach is not in favour now in the English-speaking world, and its defects have often been pointed out. One serious defect is that it does not seem to do justice to human experience. The past actions of human persons cannot be beaten into a powder and constantly re-cooked into a new dish. Croce has retained the belief of Hegel that personal experience can be subsumed into higher unities. This might seem plausible if we play with the word, 'thoughts', and ignore the individual who does the thinking. Even when two of us have the same experience, watching a play or sheltering from a bomb attack or agreeing at the end of an argument, I can never make my friend's experience as immediate to myself as my own. If I read the diary of a man living in the seventeenth century, I may understand his story and sympathize with it, but what I feel and think can never be the same as the experience which the author has committed to his pages. If we leave the individual case and consider a scene in the forum of Rome for even one afternoon two thousand years ago, the supposition that we can do justice to what befell the individuals there by our present historical judgment loses all sense. That is one objection to the theory. Another, equally serious, is that the theory of an historical judgment, which is ever renewing itself and never to come to an end, robs history of any goal and leaves us no measure for weighing relative good and evil. Croce, as a liberal, takes for granted the ascent of man in history, though he can say nothing about an ultimate ideal (the word 'ultimate' is not permissible in his lexicon), and he is forced to rely for his sole standard on the present judgment. He did not foresee that a later judgment would decide that life is a 'futile passion'. If, however, we ignore the Hegelian and idealistic strain in his philosophy, the point he makes that in some mysterious way the past is resumed in the present chimes in with what Père Teilhard de Chardin calls the 'pretensions of Christianity' that there is 'a real and living Centre' which gives meaning to the evolutionary process.

Croce argues as a philosopher and can find no place for the transcendent God of Christianity. The Absolute, the Spirit, is nothing more than the historical process itself. Père Teilhard de Chardin argues as a scientist. Nevertheless, in an Appendix to *L'Apparition de l'Homme*, he writes:

'Meanwhile, and without for a moment leaving the plane of the Phenomenon, we cannot help being struck by the symptomatic rise, around us, of a vigorous current of mysticism, which is inspired precisely by the conviction that the Universe, taken in the totality of its operations, is ultimately both lovable and loving.

'Made explicit in the dimensions of the modern world, evangelical charity is in process of recognizing itself as nothing else, on the whole, than the love of a Cosmogenesis, which in its very roots has its meaning in Christ.

'Just at the very moment when the Weltstoff has become conscious in Man of the focusing of its forces within the reflective self, and is gathering for its final assault, this Charity reappears, rejuvenated and universal, as the type so much needed, and dreamt of, to serve as the stimulus in evolution.

'In such a remarkable coincidence must we not see an indication that the pretensions of Christianity to join together . . . the rapidly converging streams of human experience with a real and existing Centre . . . are justified? If I were not already from birth convinced of this, I believe that I would be forced to demand it.'

Here then we see what kind of support the chief aesthetic philosopher of our time and a leading writer on science can give to a Christian philosophy of history. Of the two, P. Teilhard de Chardin is far the most impressive because he believes that the evolution of the world, and of man in particular, requires for its proper understanding the real presence of a Centre, such as that of Christ, who is both divine and human. Few scientists, however, would, I fear, go so far as Père Teilhard de Chardin, and still fewer modern philosophers would be prepared to call in the Christian faith to round off their theories. Their testimony is to be taken for what it is worth, and if they do at times dream and suggest ideals beyond their competence to prove, then it is for the Christian to look into his treasure house to see if he can meet the highest expectations. What follows, therefore, is based not so much on history as on scriptural and theological sources. The historian is not asked to endorse it, except in so far as he chooses to welcome interpretations which, while not naturalistic, serve to light up the material with which he is dealing.

Theologians have followed philosophers in their appreciation of the importance of the idea of 'becoming'. Their interest, however, lay primarily in the internal growth of the Church and its main features. Secular history was not their province, and the rise and fall of secular institutions served as a contrast to the Christian society which had the promise of perpetuity. It took time for them to concentrate on the relation of perpetual sameness with development, and when critics pointed to what they called novelties or deviations they were tempted, as always happens, to emphasize the more strongly the antiquity of the so-called novelties without reference to the element of growth during the centuries. That the notion of growth or development could play a part in 'tradition' was demonstrated with genius by Newman in his *Essay on Development*. He analysed the way such a society as the Church could grow, and concluded that the chief marks of a true development were permanence of type, continuity of principles, and a power of co-ordination making for a chronic vigour. Whereas many of his predecessors had turned to the syllogism, as the instrument of truth for their explanation of development, Newman treated the Church as a special form of life, and in so doing he anticipated the modern predilection for the doctrine of the Mystical Body. By interpreting tradition in terms of an organism, composed of a head and members, of which Christ, as the Head, is ever compresent with the members, we are provided with a truth which has many analogies ready at hand to illuminate its meaning. That Christ should still be in history and living in a society which is His Body has, for instance, an analogy in the conscious experience of every individual. We have only to imagine a man who consistently brings his past experience into the present, so that what he is now and what he is saying and doing are continuous with what he has always been. To complete the analogy we must suppose that the child is father to the man in the sense that the child's vision is both fresh and true and has not to wait to be confirmed by age. The Church, so the theologian claims, is a unique society because the Pentecostal Spirit remains indwelling in it, and Christ has drawn real human beings into his own enduring life. Hence it does not look back at far-off days of Christianity as something strange and hardly remembered, faint, blurred and imperfect. Tradition is not a matter of precedents, as in a court of justice; it is not a weight from the past oppressing the present heir. It is rather the self being true to what it is and ever shall be. A thousand years or a hundred days are the same to it, for at every living moment the perpetual memory is drawing from its treasures what is both 'new and old'. The exercise of that life is what St. Paul called 'living the truth in love', and the force of that expression is explained in his next words: 'and so growing up in Him, who is the Head, Christ'.

This view of Christ is, no doubt, what Père Teilhard de Chardin had in mind when he wrote of Christ as the Centre and of 'une Cosmogenèse christifiée', though he extends the view beyond the Church to the whole universe. What he says is supposed to be a superstructure demanded by science itself, whereas the theological statement is totally independent of science and even history. That does not, however, prevent it from being fertile, and it is permissible to pass from theological certainty to conjecture in accommodating it to the world and to history. A liaison exists in that the Christian religion is historical through and through and reaches out to all nations Furthermore it has in every stage of its existence appropriated to its purposes the contemporary ideas, arts and organizations, and in turn breathed its own spirit into those native forces. Perhaps in this cross fertilization we can find a clue to that Headship in all things of which St. Paul wrote.

Headship connotes authority and power, and within the Church these two are fully and directly exercised. But from time immemorial a distinction has been made between the spiritual and the secular power, a distinction which is derived from the answer given by Christ to the question about the Roman coin: 'to render to Caesar the things that are Caesar's and to God the things that are God's'. Already by A.D. 495 Pope Gelasius guaranteed its independent authority to the secular power, declaring that 'the spiritual power should keep its distance from the entanglements of this world, and, fighting for God, it should not become involved in secular matters; while in its turn the secular power should take care not to take over the direction of divine matters'. Now in extending the Headship of Christ to the world no disavowal of a proper and independent secular authority is intended. The world is created by God, and belongs to Him, and all power and authority are derived from God. The Headship, which St. Paul had in mind, is of another sort. He realized the uniqueness of the figure of Christ, 'the true likeness of the God we cannot see; his is that first birth which precedes every act', and 'in him all created things took their being'; and so it is in the subordination of all things to Christ by love that he sets His Headship, for it was God's 'loving design, centred in Christ to give history its fulfilment by resuming everything in him'.

This great Pauline conception was not at first developed. The time was not ripe; the world was too small a place. What lay outside the Pillars of Hercules or Ultima Thule was mythical—Isles of Atlantis and Cathay. The age and elements of the world were unknown, man's pedigree short, and the universe looked at through pre-Copernican spectacles. Now, on the other hand, we have some idea of the dimensions of the universe and of the nature of its constituents, and something of the history of man during the thousands of years since his origin has been revealed. Instead of the few races of barbarians outside the Greco-Roman civilization and Christian Europe, the millions and millions of human beings, all images of God, who have existed before and after the coming of Christ, parade before us, forcing us to ask ourselves how they enter into the 'loving design' of creation. The early Christian, so far as the world was concerned, lived in the catacombs, comforted by the Presence of Christ, and this state of mind persisted so long as the world and universal history remained a closed book to him. The modern man is out of the cave and can look down, as it were, from an aeroplane upon the kingdoms of the earth, and with this new outlook he is in a position as never before to study the meaning of Christ's headship over all things. The material for such a study is ever increasing, and perhaps there are already pointers to an answer. An answer, premature, as I think, and too narrowly apprenticed to scientific evolution, has already been suggested by Père Teilhard de Chardin. Saints have called man the high priest of nature, because he can do what nature cannot do, that is, recognize its own beauty, and so voice its mute magnificence in a song of praise to its creator. We have learnt from science the intimate connection of man's body with that of the primates, and as we make discovery after discovery of the wonders of the universe and of its size and duration, man's position in it tends to diminish. No longer the showpiece; only a tiny outcrop at the end of millions of years. And yet the truth is the opposite, for it is man who has slowly built up this new world of knowledge, putting the disparate together and tracing out processes which give meaning and unity to an otherwise senseless world. If we take away mind, there is left nothing which could be recognized as true, beautiful or dynamic. The Signs of the Zodiac, the Milky Way and even the satellites have their name taken from them; gone are the moon-goddess and the months of the year, the names of the flowers of the field, and the virtue of fire and water. The circulation of the blood, the nervous system, the pharmacopeia are unrecorded, and we are left with blobs of matter, processes, death and life to which one can hardly attribute meaning, law, order or unification without implying mind. It is not surprising that at various times philosophers have plumped for a form of idealism, according to which the material world is nothing but latent mind. Without the belief in God it is easy to fall back upon such a supposition.

This supposition, however, is ruled out by our certainty that the human mind discovers and does not create. Man is at home in this world and finds an affinity with inanimate and animate bodies. He turns the world outside in, for it is in his own mind that the world of things takes on a meaning. What is remarkable is that as he grows, so too does the meaning of the world grow, and that it takes man a long time to discover himself and his own past history, the length of his existence upon the earth, his relation with the animal kingdom, the immensities of the universe and the dynamic processes of nature, which only within the last century have been co-ordinated in the theory of evolution. Moreover time has conditioned his knowledge of the surface of the earth and his ability to make acquaintance with other races and to feel that there is one race of man, which should possess the same rights and liberties. This growth has been one of understanding and unification, partly forced on man and partly freely chosen. Means of communication have multiplied, and the forces of nature have been so put at the disposal of human living that men have been forced to come together in ways undreamt of by our ancestors. Such, indeed, has been the success of this internationalization that one part of the world would introduce a form of collectivization, while another holds that democracy is the key to peace and prosperity, and both pay lip-service, at least, to the ideal of United Nations and United Culture. But these ambitions tend to conceal the real nature of the development which is taking place. The mind of man has during the centuries, and more recently at an accelerated tempo, conceived within itself a more and more adequate image of the nature of the universe, of the history of man in all its ramifications, and man's own make-up. This knowledge is being shared by large populations, and now that the unconscious factors of our behaviour and the relations between mind and body are so sedulously studied there is every reason to conjecture a still greater unity of mankind in its experience and in its hold on truth.

Such an extraordinary series of coincidences seems inexplicable unless, as some Evolutionists have unconsciously done, there be introduced a dynamic power or mystical and purposeful *élan* into the picture of progress. Mr. William S. Haas, as we have seen, gives a favourable account of the tendency in the East to look for a 'pure consciousness', a spiritual unity to our experience; and so disheartened has the West become that it has been turning a favourable ear to the wisdom of the East and to the evidences of the power of mind over the body. A

modern sage, such as the late Sri Aurobindo, is as conscious as
the Western thinker of the mysterious convergence of mankind
through growth in science and in techniques. He accepts a kind
of cosmic evolution, with Spirit making a progressive self-
manifestation in nature and man. 'Man has to reach a full
intellectual life. But this is not the end; he has to evolve into
something higher.' Western thinkers have been inclined in the
past to put their trust in man's own powers to reach to a peace
through completed knowledge and a concord of wills. The
frustrations of recent years have brought them down to earth,
and it is dimly seen that the unification they have sought has
no clear form and, that it cannot match the past with the
present, hold out any hope of ultimately overcoming evil or
bring the dead back to life, to share in the good days to come.

If we could accept the optimistic view of the evolutionary
process and foresee the emergence of a new form of consciousness, a kind of semi-species, which would resemble symbiosis
on a higher level, then the function of Christ as the Alpha and
Omega of the world-process might be manifest. An argument,
too, could be drawn from Jung's hypothesis, if we free it from
its subjectivity, an argument to the effect that the collective
consciousness starts with archetypes, which are invariably pre-
images of the Christian symbols, and that man is moving to a
super-consciousness integrated in Christ. But such theories go
far beyond the data, and create as many difficulties as they
attempt to solve. At the same time they do pinpoint certain
characteristics of the world and trends in history, and give a
picture of the universe vastly different from that envisaged by
Christian thinkers of the Roman Empire or Medieval Europe.
They emphasize, too, the notion of unceasing growth and the
phenomenon of increasing fellowship in mental and spiritual
activities. To realize this latter we have only to compare the
narrowness of mind of a primitive tribesman or the indigenous
habits of townsmen and illiterate villagers in past ages with the
reading public now. Modern man, even with a minimum of
education, shares the ideas around him from a common treasury
of the past and of the present, a coherent, if confused, wealth
of historical, scientific, social and religious thought. But such
a community of thinking men, such a new form of humanity,
does not justify us in predicting the evolution or emergence of a
superior kind of co-consciousness or a spiritual experience of

communion, which the practitioners of yoga tell us is possible.

More than half a century ago Fr. Gerard Hopkins anticipated Père Teilhard de Chardin in thinking of the humanity in Christ as comparable to a species in itself. But whereas the one works out his view from evolutionary premisses, the other relied on the logical and philosophical ideas inspired by Duns Scotus. Hopkins is not thinking of a future race, but of Christ as the 'first born among creatures', from whose completeness, pleroma, all are filled. This 'Pleroma' he calls the 'burl of being in Christ, and for every man there is his own burl of being, which are all "by lays" or "byfalls" of Christ's and of one another's'. Hopkins is here, in his Note Book, meditating on man's co-operation with the life of grace, but the primacy he attributes to Christ extends to all things, to His leadership over them and compresence with them. All things are 'charged with love, charged with God, and if we know how to touch them, give off sparks and take fire, yield drops and flow, ring and tell of him'. He also gives the image of a kingly procession, to which human beings are attached. Van Eyck's *Adoration of the Lamb* portrays the supernatural society gathered in adoration, whereas a suitable illustration for the procession of the universal Head is Benozzo Gozzoli's *Journey of the Kings*, with its long winding cavalcade, all manner of men and shining youth, horses and sumpter mules and dromedaries, dogs, birds and flowers and a landscape where earth has become the Garden of Eden. Images may help, but it is rather analogies which are required to endow with meaning the Christian ideas of headship and compresence. The Greeks provided a prefiguring symbol of reality in the presiding presence in the fields of the goddess Demeter. Examples from everyday life and human experience are also enlightening. There are qualities or attributes or real objects which keep their identity and nevertheless are enriched by time and contacts with time.

The nature of human love has been, for instance, unchanging. Each age repeats the same phrases about it, but these, despite what the logical analysts are forced to say, are not clichés or platitudes. We shall go on to the end of time enriching our knowledge of love, and yet what the author of the Song of Songs or the Bhagavad-Gita knew or Plato or Jacopone da Todi or Shakespeare, has not been surpassed or changed by modern experience and thought. The volume of love can be summarized in one word, but the long history of mankind is not sufficient to state its wonder. It has been said, again, of a great work of art that every age adds something to it without mutilating it or even changing an iota of it. Mr. T. S. Eliot has admitted that readers find in his poems new meanings where 'new' must signify that the meanings are also old as contained in the words of the original poem. It is almost a commonplace to say that every generation, possessed as it is of its own special zeitgeist, adds something to the *Aeneid* or to *Hamlet* or *The Tempest*. Lastly, to show how a person can incorporate into himself what is scattered and passing and give it a meaning and an identity, we can take as an example the lover of an historic house or city or country, such as France. Each of these has a history and acquires a kind of pseudo-personality. That history stamps its character on the lover of it, so that usually we can tell a Frenchman from an Italian or an Englishman. But this character can be enlarged, for what we love we become. A man can so fall in love with his country that it lives again in him. He breathes his native land, and enacts its manifold story, renewing without change what is old and past. The theologian tells us that the world was made for the glory of God, and he means by this statement that God, who cannot receive any addition to His being, nevertheless can acquire some extrinsic 'glory' by the creation being His and by its perfection. Here is identity without change, and something else, and it is worth noting that, as already mentioned, the presence of Christ in time has 'glory' attached to it. We might, therefore, infer that the compresence of Christ with time and history has the result that history, in so far as it can be, becomes Christ's glory.

This idea, however, is bound to be vague and to remain so unless it can be clarified from what we learn on divine authority about the nature of the Christian Church. One unique characteristic of the Church is its combination of most intimate union between its members and its Head and the increase of freedom and personality in each of its members. Love by its very nature seems to draw persons into union and give them new life, and here before our eyes we are presented with a vision of a perfect community. If there be any meaning in the concept of progress or evolution such a vision should be of both theoretical and practical importance. Anthropologists, like

Malinowsky, have noted the passage of mankind from early tribal consciousness to individual freedom and onwards to a free society, and Gerald Heard sums up the ascent of man as 'from group consciousness, through individuality, to super-consciousness'. Historians, for the most part, are prepared to admit a kind of spiral movement, a *tâtonnement* towards a universal society; and in that progress the discoveries of a larger and rounded world, of the variety of living creatures and their interconnection, of chemical and electrical forces and radio-activity in nature, and other worlds without number, and above all of *homo sapiens* in all his ramifications, keep step in a mysterious fashion with man's capacity to use such knowledge for the better appreciation of human welfare and unity. Almost, therefore, without his willing it, man has been forced to unite, to form into nations and leagues, through the pressure of events. Science knows no borders, and medicine is to be a common possession, and what with economic and social inter-dependence and the threat of nuclear arms, an international society is in prospect.

So serious has the present situation become that peaceful co-operation is felt by many to be a decision of life or death. But in the national and international developments of the last hundred years one problem has come to the fore and looms larger than all others. States have grown in size, and the larger they grow the more widespread and intrusive do their activities become. The small shopkeeper and the small business man are driven out, private property is taxed out of existence, and the state has to manage business and banking and education and feed a nation. The state, therefore, takes charge of the lives of its citizens, and as the state exists in order to promote the personal and free life of its members, the while it is forced to take over so much power, an acute problem is created. There is the state on the one hand, with plenipotentiary powers, and the individual citizen, on the other, with his rights and his own personal life to develop.

Marx provided one form of solution to this problem, a solution embodied in the Soviet system. To its critics this system appears more like a tyranny of one party, the state, than a fair distribution of powers and rights. The Communist retaliates by saying that the present régime in Russia is only a phase which precedes the coming of a classless society; nevertheless in that society there will still be no room for the free and personal life for the citizens. Freedom is here no more than a knowledge of necessity. But though the rest of the world is repelled by such a picture, it has to admit that everywhere under the pressure of economic and social forces, the independence and self-determination of the individual are in danger of finding less and less scope. The image of the modern state as a Leviathan looms up, and there, growing alongside it, is the Christian visible society, the mystical Body of Christ. Both, at the present time, as a result of the tide of events and the spirit of the age, are vividly conscious of their corporate nature and of the need for harmony between the parts and the whole. Communism has chosen its own fate, but the welfare of the rest of the world depends upon some approximation to the model of a Christian society.

There have been many cries of 'Wolf! Wolf!' in the past, and if the present crisis were of that order, all the philosopher of history would have to do is note it and pass on. But its scale is much larger, and there are many signs that mankind is at the cross-roads, and one direction may be catastrophic. The other, though it does not promise happiness, moves towards an ideal of a universal society, where peace will be compatible with freedom. It is not accidental that the Church within recent years has shown a quickened interest in its nature as the Mystical Body and encouraged the liturgical spirit. In this community 'the Whole', as Teilhard de Chardin says, 'is not the antipodes, but the very pole of Personality'; or in Pascal's words: 'All is one, one is in the other, like the Three Persons.' This ideal of humanity has been developed by Christian thinkers *pari passu* with the growth of a so-called ideal for humanity, and this Communist version has been expanding so as by usurpation or advocacy to embrace a large section of mankind. Were it to succeed in its aims the official philosophy of history would become Marxist, as the world of the Roman Empire was seen for a short while to become Arian. A Christian society of one form or another is the alternative, and this would be a step forward for humanity, seeing that it would be based on freedom and co-operation in one community. Suggestions as to the form it might take have been made, for instance, by M. Maritain, and, as we have seen, by Père Teilhard de Chardin, but no suggestion can be taken seriously which does not allow for tares in the wheat and conflict with evil.

Evil is often personified in the Old Testament, and in reading the New Testament we are made aware of a drama, a mysterious combat between Christ, the Son of Man, and the Adversary, Satan, and the spoils of combat are the world, man, and all that goes with man. The work of God, interrupted and debased by sin, was to be brought back into the divine keeping by Christ. Two notions are present here; one that creation is wholly God's and all of it is meant to manifest His glory; the second, that it has to be won back by love from its subjection, through man's rebellious will, to the Prince of this world, the Apostate Custodian of the 'city of man'. Now of these two notions it is the second which has preoccupied the attention of one school of theologians. They give as the principal motive of God becoming man God's loving will to repair the evil of sin. Sin has brought a copious Redemption, a supreme counterstroke of love. Another school of theologians lays more stress on the first notion. The Redemption, as is evident, has for its context the evil wrought by man, but the surpassing privilege, given to man, to have God share His human nature in the Incarnation is not just a result of sin. Whether sin had been committed or not, it is likely that an event, such as the Incarnation, which crowns creation, was intended from the first, as the primary and final purpose of all else. Those who support this view can quote many passages from the New Testament in its favour. The Epistle to the Hebrews begins by saying that God has spoken to us through a 'Son whom he has appointed to inherit all things, just as it was through him that he created this world of time'. No doubt a distinction can be made here between Christ as the Word, and the Word in the flesh, but it was in the flesh that the Son spoke. Similarly in the Prologue of the Fourth Gospel a close connection is kept between the Word, through whom 'all things came into being' and the Word who was made flesh. In the Epistle to the Colossians, as in other places, there is an explicit assertion of the pre-ordained Lordship of Christ over creation, for it is after referring to the Son of God, who brought us redemption in His blood, that St. Paul declares that 'In him all created things took their being, heavenly and earthly, visible and invisible. . . . They were all created through him and in him; he takes precedency of all, and in him all subsist.' In the vision of the Apocalypse we see further how it is through conflict with Satan that all things are brought back into subjection to their true head. The vision ends with a 'new heaven and a new earth', even as St. Paul tells the Corinthians that at the end when He has 'brought to naught all other rule and all other authority and power', Christ will 'surrender the kingdom to God the Father'. The images used by the sacred writers vary, as no one of itself suffices to cover this passage of the creature into the new order constituted in Christ. There is to be a new and 'perfect manhood', a 'maturity which is proportioned to the completed growth of Christ' (Eph. 4, 13); for 'he will form this humbled body of ours anew, moulding it into the image of his glorified body, so effective is his power to make all things obey him' (Phil. 3, 21). The Apostolic writers had in mind the extension of Christ in the Church, His Body, for the Church is 'His Body, the completion of him who everywhere and in all things is complete'; but the claim and work of Christ extend without limits, since it is God's 'loving design, centred in Christ, to give history its fulfilment by resuming everything in him, all that is in heaven, all that is on earth, summed up in him' (Eph. 1).

These texts can be said to support the view that the Headship of Christ is the governing idea in the divine act of creation. If it be accepted, the Christian philosopher of history is provided with a title-page and perhaps with a cipher. Gerard Hopkins, following the line of thought of his favourite Duns Scotus in his own distinctive way, manages, not, indeed, to give shape to history, but to throw light on its ultimate worth. He saw in a well-known text from the Epistle to the Philippians the epitome of Christ's vocation as God-made-man. The text is to this effect, that though He is divine, the Son did not see, in the rank of Godhead, a prize to be coveted; He dispossessed Himself, and took the nature of a servant, and accepted an obedience, which brought Him to death. 'That is why God has raised him to such a height and given him a name above any other name; so that everything in heaven and on earth must bend the knee before the name of Jesus. . . .' Hopkins does not delay to distinguish between the Godhead and manhood in Christ, but boldly, using St. Paul for justification, presses the relationship of Fatherhood and Sonship to the extreme. In the mystery of love of the Father and the Son the second Person of His own accord adopted the role of a finite being. By nature equal to the Father, love drove Him to seek a means of expressing His filial love and homage, and this He could do by 'becoming obedient' and offering in and through Himself the infinitely distant but real praise and service of the finite. Sin made the self-sacrifice one of shame and death. The fruit, however, of this filial obedience was that the Son was given a new name, and everything in heaven and on earth was made subject to Him and became part of the praise and glory given by Christ to the Father.

This theory may sound fanciful to some, and, whatever its value, it is enveloped in mystery. It stimulates the mind, however, by finding room for finite values and intimating how they can add extrinsically to the divine perfection and glory. Finite values are incommensurable with infinite perfection; so too time with eternity. But though the finite and the temporal are of no account relative to the divine perfection, they, nevertheless, have a distinct, positive value of their own, each in its own kind. The soul of man, for instance, is an 'immortal diamond'; there is the 'momentary grace of mortal man'. There is loveliness everywhere from the highest to the lowest creature, and each draws its desirability from its very limitation. Thus childhood, youth and old age are each the object of affection, and even poverty and suffering can reveal unexpected beauties. The Japanese in their art have made a virtue out of the poverty of their materials, and have been known to create a flaw in an otherwise too perfect bowl or vase. The simplest song can be at times as moving as the opera; and there are many who are happier among the Giottos and the Masaccios than in the midst of the rounded riches of the later Renaissance. The joy of living itself seldom lies in smoothness of activity. It is to be found rather in hardship overcome, in adventure and in sacrifice; and memory has a bitter-sweet flavour, as it dwells on trials endured, on friendship and on the loved faces of the dead.

The quality which marks off all such experience is inextricably woven with time and change or growth, and so, in its frailty and finiteness, it cannot be lived except by those whose nature it is to change. Eternity is a never-changing now; it has no before and after. Pure spirits, such as the angels, so the philosophers tell us, do not grow to be themselves in time; they are complete from the first moment of their creation. Variety comes into their acts, however, because the inexhaustible riches of God's perfection cannot be taken in at one glance by them. But in each glance such spirits bring to bear a full knowledge of themselves and see *à travers* their own nature. Hence they do not require time or growth for the knowledge of what is not themselves. Human beings, on the other hand, do not spring up full grown; they are and they are not, being persistently themselves, and yet all the while coming to be themselves; and so their experiences are as compact with time as a piece of music, such as *The Magic Flute*. Such a condition of being, therefore, is man's very own. (Animals change but are not fully conscious of it and of their predicament.) The limitation increases the number of imperfections possible, but it also begets a unique kind of experience, which is positive and precious. As imperfect in its kind God does not share it, though theologians teach that whatever good there may be in it it is enjoyed by God in an eminent way. In the language of St. Paul the Son of God humbles Himself, dispossessing Himself of His rights, in taking the form of a man, and this makes the suggestion of Hopkins not so far-fetched, that the Son wished, so to speak, to bracket His equality with the Father in order to bring to Him the filial and creaturely worship of the poor but precious finite.

Some may think that the distinctions between the divine and human nature in Christ are too blurred in this explanation. All the same, the motive presented does correspond with what we feel to be the exigencies of love; for this motive is the core of many a well-known love-tale and has its type in the fairy stories, where the Prince disguises himself and heroically serves his beloved. The fleeting values, also, of time and history are rescued from oblivion, and in the human nature of Christ are made part of the filial love of the Son for the Father. The splendour of Christ's own human nature is such that it needs an embodiment in history, for the myriad capacities of the species, man, to be realized and to shine in a divine setting. Always intent on finding ways to express God's sanctification of man in Christ, St. Paul wrote of corporate unity and the indwelling of the Holy Spirit, what now are called by theologians inhabitation and incorporation.[1] St. Paul told the Ephesians that the 'love of God has been poured out in our hearts by the Holy Spirit, whom we have received'. From these and other texts

[1] For the form of this distinction I am indebted to the Reverend Cuthbert King, S.J.

the work of sanctification is attributed to the Holy Spirit, and by sanctification is meant the sharing of the divine nature, so far as this is possible to an unassumed human being. Incorporation is often used as an alternative or synonym for inhabitation. The word, however, while closely associated with inhabitation refers directly to the sacred humanity of Christ. It was through His humanity, the 'flesh', that He reconciled man to God, and it is by partaking in this humanity, becoming members of the Body, of which He is the head, that we enjoy the fruits of His Redemption. As we have already seen, Christ, according to the Christian faith, lives on in time in the sacred society of which He is the head, and so closely are the members united with Him that they are said to be incorporated into this society and to have a function with it.

The humanity of Christ is personally united with the Godhead, but as human it is of itself finite, and it follows that incorporation into it does not of its own accord and directly produce union with the Godhead. That union comes rather from the work of the Holy Spirit, its Inhabitation. Although, owing to the one Christ being both God and man, this distinction might be said to be one without a difference, it is worth while pointing out the difference of the two functions. If the direct function of the sacred humanity is to make us members of the Body of Christ, incorporation suggests that the purpose of God in the Incarnation is to draw up what is human into the Christ-act of adoration of the Father. What is human nature reaches its absolute perfection in Christ, God and man, and this sacred humanity 'draws all things to itself', and makes of what is temporal and finite, growing and various, an increment or instrument of the Son's filial love—a glory incomparably below what belongs by right to the Trinity, but infinitely acceptable as belonging to the Son and as a love-offering of His. If this be so, then the Incarnation ennobles all that is lovably human, and the perfect human nature of Christ is not only a model but a life-giving agent, converting into its own condition all that is amenable in human experience and reorienting even 'the elements of the world'. What is passing and seems of no account in comparison with the everlasting perfection of God acquires a new dignity, and is sanctified in its own precise and limited being. As the object of the sacred humanity is also to 'give life more abundantly' and not to destroy, the infinite variety which makes up human experience, the expectations of youth, the struggles of maturity, and the memories of age, 'the summer flower' which 'is to the summer sweet', those 'blenches which give to the heart another youth', are all caught up, as it were, in a stillness which does not fade. Not only personal experience, but the historical movements, which must have some law and meaning, however elusive and vagrant they seem at times to be, take their place in the expansion of the Sacred humanity throughout the ages, the dry wood turning into the green.

That something of this kind is happening is the belief of those who accept in full the promises of Christ. The historian, however, may well retort that such a belief is immaterial to him; and again the philosopher of history may complain that his main work still remains to be done. Certainly the historian must stick to his empirically formed judgments. With the philosopher there is more licence as his certainties, we have argued, are of a different kind, and he can seek help from the poetic and gnomic, from epic and myth. He has, that is, to use a special form of interpreting, and the Christian may claim that, even if he is not able to predict or lay down laws, he can at least see more in history and point to the destination intended by God for man. Here the viewpoint and the interpretation are important, as, for instance, in the difference between an El Greco and a Goya in their attitude to death; Goya sees it in its horrors, in the brutal extinction of human life, whereas in the scene of the Death of the Count Araoz the close of a human life is depicted in all its worth and vanity, and at the same time the majesty of the figures and their Christian reverence lead the mind on to what is above, the entrance of the dead Count into immortal life. This counterpointing of El Greco is still better exemplified in the Old Testament. Here is an historical narrative, and coexisting with it is another theme. We have the story of Abraham having to take 'his only begotten son, whom he loved', to offer him in sacrifice, of David weeping for his ungrateful child Absalom. They are live figures, and they are also anticipatory symbols. The people of Israel and Jerusalem have their tiny place in the struggle to power of the races around them, but their deeds and the city are charged with significance like no other. Looking back we can see this, and to what purpose they were being led on. The Jews themselves at the time were made conscious of their high destiny, but they misinterpreted it, and even the prophets spoke in the dark. The Christian historicist is also confident that history revolves round Christ, but like the Israelites he is living in the midst of that history, and not at its end, and he has not even the special light of the prophets to enable him to see something of what is to come. No doubt that with the past centuries of Christianity before his eyes he can say:

> *'It seems as one becomes older*
> *That the past has another pattern, and ceases to be a mere sequence,*
> *Or even development.'* (*The Dry Salvages*)

There is a presence in history which makes it more than mere 'development'. What is new is written as in a palimpsest on something already and indelibly there, which enlarges the meaning indefinitely. 'Apprehensions are God's introductions, extended inscrutably' (Emily Dickinson).

'Truly fortunate is the Christian philosopher', a neutral historian might say with sarcasm or in envy, 'at having such a privileged outlook'. But if it give him a deeper insight into the drama of history, as a solver of crossword puzzles is more fortunate if the puzzle be in his native and not in a foreign language, he is also at a disadvantage in that the problem as he sees it is far more complicated than it is for the historian or other philosophers of history. If they decide to explain history in terms of economic determinism or biological analogies or Yin and Yang, they make their task comparatively simple; but the Christian philosopher, as already shown, lays immense emphasis on the importance of every individual. Each has a cosmic significance. Then, too, he tries to join together the everlasting and the temporal and to interpret the Divine Mind beyond what has been definitely revealed. He is too near the Burning Bush for comfort. Furthermore he takes seriously that factor in history, man's freedom, and what is worse he has to try to come to terms with evil, moral and physical, and the apparently irreparable damage caused by sin.

If we confine ourselves to the sacred society, the Church, the case for a supernatural intervention in history can be made out. But the philosopher of history cannot be content with this. He leaves to Christian apologists the task of showing the unique character and function of the Church. It is of the world outside it he wishes to make sense. He is aware that there are those who say that the 'world is as replete with misery as the bowl the beggar raises'. Or is he to be content with the view of Dr. Edwyn Bevan that 'the passage of humanity appears, not as a passage along the line of earthly history to an ultimate goal upon earth, but as a passage *across* the line of earthly history'? From the texts quoted in preceding pages this view, while rightly emphasizing the other-worldly nature of the Christian hope, does hardly justice to history, for 'he who has gone up high above all the heavens' is 'to fill creation with his presence'. This 'presence' it is which invites us to believe that human experience which is a succession of moments, coming to be and passing away, can be kept alive, not as by memory, but in the abiding presence of Christ, reaching 'his full stature' in His Mystical Body. What, however, of the other disconcerting element in history, the interminable clash of wills, the struggle for existence, the setbacks and the suffering? So grave is this aspect of human life that the Eastern religions have tended to call everyday experience an illusion and to seek for an escape into a higher condition of being. Christianity has been tempted at times to adopt this formula of 'contempt of the world' and 'flight'. The main tradition, however, has for its tessera the confronting of the unresponsive and hostile and the turning of it into a friend. So traditional is this habit of mind that it has given rise to a new system of philosophy, whose rubric is the 'dialectic'. Opposition, it has been recognized, is not the same as contradiction, nor does it lead to a stalemate. It is the secret of development and of fertility. Vital functions degenerate if they do not meet resistance, as the wings of a bird need the resistance of the air for their exercise. Such an explanation helps us to understand how some of the resistances in history, the struggles, in which the good is checked, thwarted and for a long period victimized, may help to define the process wherein the kingdom of God is being established.

This explanation, nevertheless, falls down when applied to the specific human evil of wrongdoing and sin. The historian can ignore this. He reads of a man who robs another of his rights and his lands, and in time his descendants become among the most honoured of their country. Pirates found cities, and unscrupulous financiers have monuments put up by Governments which have grown rich by their bequests; dynasties have bloody beginnings, but the historian is more properly concerned with their causes and their after-effects in the period he is studying. Poets and playwrights, also, often take some story from history and dramatize the consequences of evil. They can break away from historical fact, and smooth out evil or exaggerate its effects for the sake of artistic unity. They dwell on evil more than the historian, and can sense how indelible and humanly irredeemable it is: 'All the perfumes of Arabia will not sweeten this little hand.' But they are at liberty to take the sting out of it and make it a medicine of hope: 'Nothing is here for tears.' But life does not provide such consolation, and a Christian philosopher of history has to reckon with evil and not ride off with a theory of poetic justice or an historical explanation. He is aware of sin as the undoing of man, as a sore which festers and saps the character. This is bad enough; but far worse for any theory is the fact he has to accept that it was one of the first followers of Christ who sold Him for thirty pieces of silver and then went and hanged himself.

I have already suggested the beginning of an answer to the problem of why the individual is so afflicted by misery and calamities, despite the bright dawn of redemption and joy promised apparently both before and at the coming of Christ. The answer applied to individual life is applicable also to the whole society comprised by the Church and also to mankind in general. The rejection by the chosen people, abetted by the ruling power of Rome, of the Saviour of man meant that the mode of Redemption and the course of history had to be one of suffering and of victory through apparent defeat. The Cross became the symbol and pattern of the new way of life. The Church itself, as the Mystical Body of Christ, the extension of His humanity upon earth, has 'to fill up what is wanting in the sufferings of Christ'. It grows in every generation by incorporating into its life all those who will to abide in Christ, but in its external history it is subject to setbacks and human weakness and affliction. Christians touch fire, and, unlike the children in the fiery furnace, their fingers are burnt. They form outposts of Christianity in Japan, Paraguay and China, and their work seems to come to nothing. Even in the first days St. Paul has to upbraid his converts for laxity and for scandals, and there were times afterwards when the world foresaw the rapid collapse of the Church. But there has always been present 'the substance of things hoped for', and 'He who is within is greater than he who is in the world'; so that when things look their worst and disaster seems imminent victory is never more sure. Such a philosophy of history, so to call it, has already been expressed by Newman: 'The whole course of Christianity from the first is but one series of troubles and disorders. Every century is like every other; and to those who live in it seems worse than all times before it. Troubles have ever been; they ever shall be; they are our portion. "The floods have risen, the floods have lifted up their voice, the floods lift up their waves. The waves of the sea are mighty and rage horribly; but yet the Lord who dwelleth on high is mightier."'

This view, in the light of the intractable and vicious character of spiritual evil, needs supplementing. As sheer evil seems both indelible and irredeemable, a shadow lies across any Christian interpretation of history. No wayfarer in time can fully solve the problem created by such evil, but the Christian philosopher can point to where the answer lies. To do more than hint at it would, however, involve a departure from history into pure theology. Human experience shows that the idea of standing proxy for another is not far-fetched. A friend can take another's place, parents stand for their children, and there were cases in the late war in prison camps when an older man or woman took the place of a younger before a firing squad or queue to an incinerator. Such substitutions lead the mind naturally to the ritual of the scapegoat, a ritual which even in its crudest form intimated a sublime hope. It was a symbol of substitution, of the transmission of the sins of a people to some object, which was given over to the gods or to Yahweh as an expiatory victim. 'All we like sheep have gone astray . . . and the Lord hath laid on him the iniquity of us all.' In the Christian belief only God can make sin to be as nothing, and evil is turned into good by the Son of God taking upon Himself the guilt of mankind. Such a belief is beyond historical comment, but it is relevant as supplementing what has been said about Christ as the consummation of history and the recapitulation of all things in Him. This redemptive virtue, which is so vividly described by St. Paul in the words: 'He condoned all your sins; cancelled the deed which excluded us, the decree made to our prejudice, swept it out of the way, by nailing it to the cross', is the obverse side of the 'loving design, centred in Christ, to give history its fulfilment by resuming everything in him, all that is in heaven, all that is on earth, summed up in him'. As time moves on Christ grows to His 'full stature', ever present and healing and giving life. Each individual, in his own way, who belongs to the mystical Body, exercises this redemptive virtue. Claudel in his book on the Canticle of Canticles grows dithyrambic on the cosmic powers at the disposition of a member of this mystical Body: 'The whole of creation, visible and invisible, all history, all the past, the present and the future, all the treasures of the saints, multiplied by grace—all that, is at our disposal as an extension of ourselves a mighty instrument.' Allied to this, and, in fact, the obverse of it, is the power of carrying the guilt of others, of rescuing what has fallen and bringing what is dead back to life.

Such a redemptive power belongs to the mystical Body of Christ, but it serves as a paradigm of a society which is in process of formation in history. Giorgio La Pira, the Mayor of Florence and founder of an annual International Congress to promote cultural unity, has for his belief that 'present things are truly a sketch for that future reality, the risen human being, the risen human society (the heavenly Jerusalem), the risen Cosmos (a new heaven and a new earth), and the new earthly reality must be formed on this heavenly model. Time has to be considered for what it essentially is—for what God intends it to be, which is a preparation for eternity'. A Christian philosophy of history is adumbrated in these words, and they correspond with what has been suggested in these pages in terms principally of 'incorporation'. Incorporation refers directly to the development of the sacred Christian society, and it is only by an extension of its meaning and by inference that we can apply it to history and nature. The attempt so to extend it is justified by a consideration of God's loving design in creation, and by pressing various texts about the primary and plenary Headship of Christ over all things. Growth needs time, and history is the temporal record of man's development. God becomes man at a definite moment of time, but all the stages of time are required for that perfect humanity to reach its 'full stature' and exhibit the infinitely various values of which man is the bearer and producer. In the process of time each age has shown a distinctive form and quality. We cannot now recover the directness and simplicity of primitive sculpture and painting, its innocence of eye and fondness for symbols and its sense of the numinous. But as the world has grown older, what unbelievable advances have been made in knowledge of all kinds, in the physical sciences, in psychology and archaeology and kindred studies, in social planning, in the understanding of our own body and its health. There is an immense and ever-growing stock-pile of knowledge, which is being put to use in multiple ways to improve social conditions and bring men and women in all parts of the world closer together. No longer is it possible to bear with equanimity slavery, ignorance, cruelty and injustice because of the growing sense of personal responsibility and the sacredness of liberty. With the now slow, now quick, accumulation of this knowledge, intellectual, moral and practical, have come diversities of joy, laughter, play, effort and aspiration. The genius of one age and place cannot be transplanted to another, no more than the snowdrop to an Andalusian summer soil. If Don Quixote and Sancho Panza journeying together think their own thoughts and dream their own dreams, how much more so is this true of a Polybius and a Vico, a Praxiteles and Giotto, a Dante and a Dostoevski, a Jerome and a Thomas More. The experience of every individual is unique, and yet a magic wand is waving what is scattered and conflicting into a common consciousness and devotion. This, Teilhard de Chardin would have us believe, is the summit of evolution, for with the coming of reflection there is a new centre within man, a Noosphere where all minds converge and meet. To explain some of the phenomena of the unconscious mind, some psychologists favour the theory of a 'collective unconscious'. Corresponding with this on the highest level there is or is coming to be a super-consciousness. Yeats complained: 'How small a fragment of our own nature can be brought to perfect expression . . . in a much divided civilization!' Insecure hypotheses, perhaps, and dreams! But they lead the mind to the hope that our humanity at its highest, which is to be found in the God-made-Man, in whom there is no spot or wrinkle, may salvage every fresh human experience in its own perfection, and also unfold in time and in change that many-splendoured beauty, which could not be fully displayed in one language, in one short meeting with fellow-men and in one small portion of history. In other words, our experience, while remaining indelibly our own, can become also Another's, and His experience in turn, which is the ideal and model one, re-constitutes in itself whatever time and growth discover—so that in the end there will be a 'new heaven and a new earth', and God will be 'all in all'.

As we have seen, the historian reaches truth by a method different from that of the physical scientist. He takes some period of the past, gathers together as many facts as he can and tries to make a consistent and intelligible whole of them. In doing this he has to interpret human actions out of his general knowledge of human character and behaviour. His method is empirical, but the criterion is the consistency and intelligible unity of the conclusion to which he comes. The philosopher of history has also for his material human actions of the past, but the past is all mankind, and this makes his task monstrously difficult, if not impossible. His only hope is that he can discover some thread running through history or that some simple hypothesis can be verified universally. Marx, for instance, began with wages, formed an hypothesis, which he believed to hold true in economics and turned it into a philosophy which made all history comparatively simple. The frailty of human life and by contrast the power and indifference of nature, with its rhythm of seasons, preyed upon the minds of the early thinkers, and led them to a philosophy of fate, the wheel of fate or the inevitable recurrence of what has already been. The Christians changed fate into Providence, and in the light of the Christian revelation grouped all that they knew of history round it. As Christianity was an historical religion of which the history of Israel had served as a prologue, it gave a new meaning to history and opened a new way for studying it. As, however, the Christian faith looked to a heavenly city and set its joy there, it made no serious contribution for centuries to a philosophy of the temporal order. Not until the sciences had formed and sharpened their techniques, and history, partly on account of heated religious controversy, had come to be recognized, did the modern idea of what a philosophy of history should be emerge. When once, however, the importance of the notion of 'becoming', of genesis and process, had seized scientists and philosophers alike, history seemed to offer a most promising subject for treatment. The German philosophers then had their day, and the influence of Hegel can be seen throughout the nineteenth century. But with the coming of scientific evolution and the triumphs of science, it was felt that nothing worth while could be written about history which did not proceed by observation and strict empirical methods.

Today, books on the philosophy of history are constantly appearing, but they are all open to the criticism of trying to generalize and find laws of behaviour on insufficient data. Either they have to fall back on the broadest generalizations or they omit facts or force facts in applying their laws. It may be, therefore, that a philosopher should be more modest in his claims, that he should confess to the historian that he cannot compete with him and has no intention of competing with him. He is artist as well as scientist, relying, if need be, on poetic truth to make an intelligible theme out of his vast material. There is, however, an undying interest in the nature of history. The pessimists give us dusty answers, and the optimists make emotional noises about the future and progress. The Christian philosopher has no misgivings because he believes God has made known the ultimate purpose of human life and man's final destination. That however, does not give him reason to boast, for, as we have seen in these pages, that knowledge does not necessarily serve to enlighten us on the history of man as such. It may, indeed, get in the way as by-passing the temporal or by a Christian's reading into history what he thinks must or should be there, but is not. Furthermore, the Christian religion is concerned with the supernatural order of grace, which is outside that of the empirical, so that an historian might well object that the Incarnation, for instance, or the Redemption have no more to do with history than Original Sin with anthropology. Such doctrines are not evidence and do but confuse issues. The answer, so far as there is an answer, is contained in the argument that Christianity is an historical religion, and its doctrines have affected culture in all sorts of ways. Moreover these doctrines have not been used in these pages to articulate a philosophy of history. There has been no attempt to explain how and why civilizations have followed each other according to pattern, how freedom and necessity interact. Little or nothing, in fact, has been said about the matters which generally take up the time of the historicist. I have been trying to answer the question: Can Christianity make any contribution to the understanding of history? The answer, I think, lies, not in trying to correct or improve upon the historian, nor, again after the manner of Bossuet, in trying to determine the place and function of the Greeks and Persians—not to speak of the Aztecs

CHRISTIANITY AND HISTORICISM II

and the Maoris—in relation to the Christian religion. The Christian religion is concerned with the Revelation of God's affection for man and man's relation to God. Out of this Revelation we may garner something which may throw a light upon man and his slow development through the ages, and so perhaps enlarge our vision of human efforts and human achievements, even as the sheet, which Peter saw in a trance at Joppa, containing 'all kinds of four-footed beasts, and things that creep on the earth, and all the birds of heaven', gave him a better taste for the things of nature and a more generous understanding of the Gentile world.

APPENDIX ON G. HEARD

In a small volume Mr. Gerald Heard has attempted a more ambitious project than Toynbee. It is called *Is God in History?* I doubt whether it will appeal either to the historian or to the theologian, for Mr. Heard is nothing if not daring in his ideas. Indeed at first reading it might be put aside as an extravaganza, so startling and, as I think, mistaken are some of the hypotheses and conclusions. This would, however, be a mistake, for there is gold amidst the quartz. Heard takes the findings of physical science, biology, palaeontology, psychology, and history and argues that put together they show that God has shown himself in nature and history by the evidence of Falls and Redemptions. History started off under the protection of Clio, one of the Muses; it was under the inspiration of one who would give mortals insights into the meaning of man's drama. But when physical science bewitched man and natural history was considered intelligible without any reference outside itself, God was permitted to exist on condition of being an unknown being who never interfered with man or nature. This was the period of deism. But general theories of science pass through stages like those suggested by the Hegelians, and we are now in the third stage when it is possible to reassert the first simple beliefs with all the wisdom gained from changes and denials added to them. In the second phase man learnt that he was an evolving animal, that his life on this planet has been much longer than once was supposed. It has come to light, also, that there was a period, which can properly be called history, when man lived a social life without violence; and we can learn something of their psychology from the economy and gear of rudimentary pre-agricultural communities. Moreover we are now in the stage when we can begin to have a real understanding of ourselves as men. 'The discovery of the limen, the threshold between our levels of consciousness and of the subconscious it-self, is in fact the finding of that microcosm, that epitome in each individual, whereby the story of mankind as a species may be understood. The psychological growth of every infant through childhood, on to adolescence and maturity, can be understood with a new insight now that we can trace man from the close psychological collectivity that we may call pre-in-dividualism, through the acutely secessionist and destructive phase of the heroic epoch into the modern ages.'

With this new knowledge the religious tradition of a Fall can be shown to be vested with a new meaning. It does not fit in with the extreme individualistic psychology, but then extreme individualism is not a blessing and modern evidence points to a pre-individualist era, and also to an event which took place when man was at another level of consciousness. Secondly, our knowledge of ourselves makes it clear that we have a fractured consciousness. Our egotistic individualism makes us ignorant of our matrix and base. Thirdly, history supports the impression that there has been a disaster which, had there not been some remedial process would have confined us to an ever narrower field of awareness akin to madness. In fact we can turn the tables on the old historical philosopher. Whereas a Hobbes thought of our progressing out of savagery and black supersti-tion to sense and reason, it appears much more likely from the evidence that man was a mild and curious animal who passed into a ritual-ruled creature. This rule, which was by suggestion at first and not by force, became in time corrupt, as if there were some degenerative process at work in man which had been checked but not cured. When this expedient failed open an-archy began, the period of the heroes when every man does what is right in his own eyes. Once more there is a recovery or check, but the contrast between a lost innocence and the Cain and Abel relation remains with increased conflicts between societies and the increase of individual neuroses. While there-fore there is progress of a kind, gained by successfully meeting the challenge of the time, the 'very success in restoring a dis-balance on the one side tends to cause a maladjustment on the other. . . . And this perpetual oscillation, this continual rise and fall, seems the specific character of man.' Heard then mentions the first attempts of the scientific historian to explain this by heredity or other factors. The individual suffers from the past, and the question is how can he as an individual be guilty for what he has not done himself. The answer now is along the line that racial heredity affects the individual. 'We cannot find honest comfort in attempting to deny the influence of heredity on the entire individual organism, mental and physical.' Instead of doing this we must expand psychology so that it implements physiology. Psychology until recent years has been too prone to confine itself to the individual. Now fortunately we are in a better position to study both social and hereditary psychology, and they serve to make us see 'that our individuality, though authentic in its own field, as the outlook point of our present consciousness, is neither the whole of that consciousness nor indeed a wholly wholesome part of it. Men belonging to less complex and critical societies than ours have less mental trouble because their consciousness is less divided, the awareness of the totality of their psyche—and of its linkage with the life of the group—far more direct than ours. We are each one in our separate self an individual consciousness, but one that emerges. And though this tension is advanced through what is sometimes a hardly permeable filter (a threshold stamped hard) yet even with us there is continual circulation, quiet or convulsive. Our personal consciousness never ceases to be affected and largely directed from range to range of other qualities and spans of consciousness. Further, these other layers not only link us without break—if sometimes through belts of darkness—with our physique, but they join us with the subconscious of our fellows, with the life of our race, our species and indeed, at the ultimate event, with all life.'

By appealing to this new evidence which shows that the human race is far more closely united than the individualistic theories, so long current, admitted, Heard is able to get over the main obstacle which prevented modern man from allowing that he was liable for anything which went beyond his individual responsibility. He takes a further step when he argues that the lesion in our nature is deeper and more serious than even modern psychology knows. The psychiatrist tries to repair the damage caused by conflicts below consciousness. What threatens mankind is a fracture in our very nature, one that may bring about our doom. And this is due to Original Sin, which is a 'Fall into individuality'. 'The Original Sin is the wish to be separate, and is crowned by Wrong Desire becoming Wrong

Knowledge, the wilful ignorance that ends in not knowing that it is ignorant and denying all guilt. Naturally then the individual cannot save himself. For he would have to save himself out of himself.' Original Sin therefore demands a Redemption, and this must be by Grace, by the restoration by One who is guiltless and free and has the power to make what was crooked straight. 'The truly selfish will is incapable of anything but an ever closer selfishness. It must become more and more self inwound and ingrown into a final ignorance.' The question, therefore, turns into this: Can we form any conception from nature and history of how this Fall took place and how the Redemption has been accomplished? From what has been already said we have this clue that man's nature has been fractured, that he is now ignorant of his full self and personally unhappy, and that society, 'now composed of nothing but anarchic granulations, is in constant peril from inner and outer conflict'.

A human being has three sides. He is an individual with a mind and will for which he is responsible; he is also a member of a special social heredity from which he has derived his way of life, his *mores*, his quality of consciousness and his attitude to the great moral laws against violence, lust, avarice, deceit and sloth. Lastly he is a member of a biological species. Now as the rings of a tree serve to tell us the manner of its growth, and, when they are morbid in their variations, they can be correlated with unfavourable climatic conditions, so these separated layers of the self can be correlated with certain cataclysmic changes in our history. Corresponding then to the three layers, three kinds of Falls can be detected. The first belongs to subrational life. From the knowledge that we have now acquired of primitive man and animals, we are safe in saying that man must have been a wild creature, aware of his body and its physiological needs and also of his communion with his fellows. In this condition he would be a healthy animal, unselfconscious, but aware of his unity with his species. Nature was not red in tooth and claw, as the first evolutionists supposed. Most species were interested only in themselves; the teeth were not for flesh-tearing but 'for gnawing roots and nuts and for milling rough vegetation. Most claws were for digging, some for climbing, comparatively few for lacerating.' It is as they grow specialized that they show signs of greater cruelty. Now amongst the animal

287

creation man would have been 'innocent if not perfect, potentially righteous'. Nevertheless evil was present; there were specialized species which attacked others mercilessly, and there was parasitism. Hence it is fair to ask whether there was not a Preliminary Fall, not such as to make all life evil, but a backward movement when all should have been moving forward. Organisms fail to respond to the stimuli of their environment and to adapt themselves to changing conditions. There is a failure to respond to the demand of constant recovery and correction. Every creature has it in its power to make a continuous series of contact adjustments with its matrix environment. As this point is essential to Heard's theory I must quote him here at greater length. 'If this activity (of contacts and adjustments) is sustained at the right pace, the correct tempo, then there will be a steady growth in the apprehension of the organism, a steady increase of its response to an ever wider range and further depth of stimuli. The reciprocity will steadily increase. The organism will never cease receiving and giving more. Until, at infinity, the whole organism will be responding throughout the entire environment, and the whole environment will be "mirrored" or "resonant" in the organism contributing to its fulfilment which is, conversely, the fulfilment of the whole.' There would then be a parallel between the atom's ultimate span of radiation which can only be limited by the bound of the space-time continuum and the organism's ultimate influence-response to the whole. The state of living organisms today seems to show that they have fallen short of the fullness of this opportunity. It is true that an organism to accomplish this would have had to call upon an energy beyond its own power, but this we see happening in the case of yeasts, which, as Dr. J. A. Butler has shown, are apparently not subject to entropy, as they can create energy. The failure to respond brought about a decline; the organisms tended to stabilize themselves; they lost their 'immortality. and became more and more specialized, in the sense that to endure they had to harden themselves, arm themselves and fight for their existence.'

What is here described is assumed to have taken an immense period of time, and it concerns only the organism in its relation to the environment. What succeeded this decline was a schism within the organism itself. Heard describes it in these terms: 'The First Fall was a slow shrinking from further acceptance, and then a retreat. It was a lapse through a slow waning of Perception, as vitality ceased to show curiosity, that longing, however rudimentary, to reach out into apparently irrelevant experience. The Second Fall must therefore be more rapid, decisive, disruptive, a sharper alteration into Wrong Time, a deliberate intention to disregard what is still presented by Perception to the consciousness. Hence it causes . . . a disruption between soul and body, an inner conflict.' This will mean the beginning of that schism in the self which prevents our conscious mind from being in contact with the other layers of the self, with the unconscious and the common, inherited experience of mankind. 'As long as the psyche and the physique were homogeneous, that is to say two aspects of one unity, a body-mind, an integral living organism, then every change in the psyche causes an appropriate alteration in the physique and vice versa.' The psyche then *thinks* through the physique. Owing to Man's superior status in the animal world he could have used the extraordinary power of consciousness which was his to break away from the narrowing individualism caused by the first fall. That fall had broken the orchestration of nature, the symbiosis, the togetherness of all life. Mind could have served to remedy this defect. But instead man used it to intensify his separateness and self-consciousness. He did not enter into life and a happy communion with creation; he withdrew into himself and narrowed himself 'down to an identification with nothing but his personal, private, temporary physique and its instantaneous sensations'. And this led on to the Third Fall which was purely psychological. In Heard's words, 'It is a deliberate conscious contrivance of the psyche, whereby it may succeed in rejecting all reality, not even holding to a fragment. The mind now resorts to complete fantasy and uses its power of suggestion—which is a specific development by man derived out from his power of Attention—to build up a lie, a false faith with which to shut out all true knowledge.' Thus, we may say that man by these Falls, described separately by Heard, lost his kinship with nature, his environment, his species and his own full and proper selfhood. His natural paradise was thus taken from him, and instead he became conscious of his mortality, his separateness and loneliness, and was filled with mortal fear and a sense of uncertainty. But though now only a fragment of what he should be as a body-mind and shorn from his place in nature, he still sojourned in nature and could wrest from it its secrets and make a kind of home there. But when he so withdrew into himself as to make himself his own law and god, he lost touch finally with God's creation, and became a pariah. This last phase is one of Original Sin.

Each of these Falls has a remedy, but until the final Redemption they are only partial. Heard tries to trace the story of this in nature and in history. He calls upon evidence of every kind, and it would be impossible to describe it in any detail. There is the evidence in nature. In the nineteenth century naturalists had romantic ideas about health-giving nature and the simple life. But we know now that disease was present and in its worst forms from the beginning amongst animals. The fossils show disease of bone and teeth and even cancer. The vast size of pre-historic creatures was a form of hypertrophy due to a failure of energy; there is a backward pattern, and the simplicity of uni-cellular life does not develop but stabilizes itself owing to a lack of power to embrace and organize a deeper extent of its sur-roundings. The multi-cellular organisms fail even to energize their own increasingly complex life. Parasitism, a degenerative form of life, multiplies and death grows normal. The remedy to this is reproduction. Sex emerges as a counter to the degener-acy into specialization and isolation. 'The creatures had in-volved themselves in an ingrowing self-regarding pattern of life, and this was checked by reproduction. The germ plasm is, so to speak, undying, so that while the body dies the race goes on. This remedy is, however, only partial. It is at the expense of the death of the individual, and moreover, "we are born with the entail of our race's mistakes".' Acquired characteristics, if by them we mean the latest, are not inherited, but we do inherit the past and carry with us the burden of human weakness. Man, however, by virtue of his mind can learn how to remedy his defects and improve himself. Instinctive life dominates the lower animals, and it is held that the rat, for instance, is teach-able only for some three weeks. Man can always learn and so free himself from any particular form his instincts may tend to impose upon him. But it is here his temptation comes and he makes his second Fall. Free as he is to some extent from racial instinct he may so ignore his natural and racial wisdom that he relies on his own private satisfactions and ideas. By doing this he increases his loneliness, adopts a selfish point of view and cuts himself off from his innate insight. He becomes *déraciné*, an individual who is a stranger to nature, to his species and to himself. That man made this fatal step long ago is borne out by tradition and by embryology. Through the study of young children we can see recapitulated in their evolution the history of early man. For the first two or three years the child lives a healthy instinctive life, and it can choose for itself what is most in accordance with its needs both in food and play. That is to say at first the child has a balanced psycho-physical organism; it is only later that its self-consciousness gets divorced from the subconscious layers. We can argue that there is a parallel to this in history; that man at a certain moment of his evolution ceased to be in touch with the whole to which he belonged, natural, racial and social, and used his intelligence to turn inward and give all his attention to himself. History does not supply enough evidence to enable us to know when this happened, and so-called primitive races are an uncertain guide, but we have some knowledge of the remedy which was used to prevent this separatist movement from destroying races and groups. The immense emphasis placed upon Tradition is best explained by the interpretation of it as a co-ordinating power. It keeps the people bound together and salvages the wisdom of the past; it issues into codes and laws, which preserve the instinctive wisdom about diets and sex. At first sight it might seem surprising that food should play such an important part in a code, but it is in choice of food that animals and primitive man showed their instinctive good sense. Sex, too, could prove the most disruptive force in the life of a group, and therefore traditional codes lay immense stress on cleanliness and on racial purity and on reproduction as opposed to lust. Lust is individual and chaotic in its effects, whereas marriage laws and customs insure the continuation of the group and of its unity. Above all religion served to restore the wrong individualism and the infection of the Fall. Early religion, as historians have pointed out, has a close connection with the cycles of nature and with the organic unity of tribal experience. The priest-king is identified with his people and through him it is kept purified of evil and in touch with the gods, the powers of nature and the authors of the mysterious world. Notwithstanding its restorative efficacy, this priest-king society could not be more than a temporary tonic. As man grew more aware of himself and of his powers he felt the urge to exploit his own strength; and moreover the régimes became hidebound and slack. They collapsed before the 'heroes' of legend and antiquity. The Saturnian rule was succeeded by anarchy, when these heroes by violent means wrested power to their own selfish ends and by internecine warfare blotted out much of the old Tradition. Religion, too, became wild and orgiastic, depraving the old *mores* and hallowing new perversions. The Greek hero, in Heard's eyes, is a gluttonous carnivore, a drunkard, who resorts to drugs, such as nepenthe, when he is depressed. 'His pride and rages were quite ungovernable. He is a body-obsessed individual who readily becomes an addict.'

Now that he is within the pale of history Heard concentrates on the great religions to illustrate and prove his thesis. He takes China, India, and the Near East of Palestine and the Grecian world. Each of these had its own way of trying to redeem its people. The Chinese created a great Tradition which was able to survive attacks, conquests and the rise and fall of dynasties. In India the appeal was to compassion as the tie of mankind and the principle of peace. Plato felt that ignorance was the primal sin, but that it could only be cured by death and rebirth, and the Orphic mysteries seem to carry this idea a stage further. In Palestine a gospel of personal righteousness and uncontaminated worship was preached. But they could not be more than partially successful. 'They either—as we have seen with Buddhism—answered the personal problem, but did not go down to its pre-personal depth: or, as did the Hebrews, they protested against the social tragedy but could put no society in its place: or, as we shall be seeing in a moment in China, did something for society but little for man. But though none of these gospels of the prophetic epoch solved the entire human problem, by their appeal to the individual they assured that human society should be able to persist.' They all end in relative failure; Malachi promising peace if the temple dues are paid; Buddhism becoming ritualized, and the two main systems of China leaving the human and social problem unsolved. Man had to descend still further into delusion and false faith before the full redemption could heal him. In order to give proper scale to this, the Christian Redemption, Heard darkens his picture of man before its occasion of redemption. Nothing else can save him; the whole of society is corrupt and the Tradition has corrupted. China and India had served their turn in checking evil, and now the West, which had for the most part remained backward, the last, was to be first. In the West the defences against evil had crumbled. The Mystery religions were degenerating into drunken, sex-ridden orgies. Its thought had become materialistic, its emotion sensual; its white magic was turning into black; its heroes handing themselves over to the devil. Therefore there had to be a salvation not only of the soul, 'but of body, soul and spirit, individual, social, racial. Man was too shattered to recover of himself. A new creation was needed, and the Redeemer must combine the Logos, the Creative principle which has inspired all life . . .; the historic individual; and the post-historic being, "yesterday, today and for ever", that assures a continuous aid to successive generations of men.'

The remainder of Heard's book gives his interpretation of Christianity, its supreme salvific power and the reasons for its comparative failure. His view of the Christian religion is so singular and personal that there is no need to say much about it. It seems to omit the supernatural element altogether; that is to say, its function is to restore man to his integrity and give him that creative energy which makes him one with himself, his society, nature and God. But of the specific quality of this religion, as described in, for instance, the Fourth Gospel and the Epistles of St. Paul, there is no mention, and perhaps no comprehension. The relation between man and divinity seems more Gnostic than Christian, as if man and the energy of the Universe were a participation of the divine life. He uses truly Christian terms when he says that the Redemption must penetrate deeper down into diseased nature than any previous remedy (though orthodox Christianity does not admit that nature is corrupt), and that this Redemption must come from outside that nature. But he defines the aim of religion as the power to create 'those liberating realistic conditions of challenge in which human character can grow'; the social structure is to be one in which 'the optimum pressure of stimulation shall be applicable to all according to the varying individual capacity and power of response. In brief, this is to create those conditions of freedom wherein the maximum of creative choice is presented.' In another place Heard sums up the Christian story as the union of an historic drama with an aeonian myth. The Gospel story is founded on fact; it is real. But it is also the true life, with its power of restoring the dreams and ideal of mankind. It is 'the infusion of the eternal Creativity into Time, an offer to meet man's bankruptcy'. But this eternal creativity has not been allowed to work perfectly because the Christian Church mistook the nature of history. This is one of Heard's most original contributions. He holds that each age lives the new redemption and is not tied to the past in the way in which he thinks the Catholic Church is. The Catholic Church relies on the deposit of faith, once given, which cannot be added to. Hence its doctrines are statements of what was once and for all revealed. No, says Heard, that is a misunderstanding of the creative activity of man and of history. 'The dichotomy between contingent and eternal is false. The temporal is the eternal (the total instantaneity) serialized.' Every moment, every age is unique, but that does not mean that it is severed from the past. We cannot, however, suck out from it what it contains if we try to make it just a repetition of the past if, as is said, we try to relive the past. That cannot be done; we cannot even go back in history so as to be sure what the event meant to those present to it. For the dogmatists 'the first century should remain like one of those pools of petrifying water into which flowers, lovely in their transitoriness, can be dipped to come out dull unchanging stone'. 'Men increase dogma as they lose experience.' Our lot is more fortunate, for time gives us the chance to continue the ideal and historic theme in our own creative experience, and in doing this we discard what belonged to the past and only to that past, the while we renew in a new environment and with appropriate adaptations the eternally significant.

Such a theory postulates a special view of history and historical development, and Heard provides one. This view emerges from his criticism of the historical outlook which governed the Modernist movement and the judgments of anthropologists such as Frazer. They took for granted that they were looking back on the past from some sure vantage ground. They thought that they possessed objective truth and by its standard could fix down the ignorance and errors of that past. But now 'we have changed all that'; there is no such privileged position in science or in history. Our present judgment is, as past ones were, a construction. In history it is, moreover, a limited construction based on selection from an indefinitely vast collection of evidence. Again our very consciousness is marching on and

showing signs of development. Each stage has its own appropriate insight, but it is not the end of truth. 'We are a sweeping
stairway, from each step of which there was a consistent outlook.' Our mechanistic habit of mind has led us wrong, and
made us interpret history as if we were dealing with an inanimate object. A play like *Hamlet* does not proceed like a series
of mathematical tables. In the latter it is the conclusion alone
which is of importance; in *Hamlet* the last line is not everything.
Every part of the play has its own significance and has to be
rightly appreciated if we are to enjoy the play and understand
it at its end. So too with human life. Every human experience
has its own value, its own vision. They renew, each in its own
fashion, the theme of truth, and like the varying versions of the
Prize Song in *Die Meistersinger*, they lead up to the finale and
keep their own authentic beauty. This, so Heard thinks, is the
only way in which a philosophy of history can be constructed.
To make his view complete, he adds that there must be both an
eternal Mind which 'sees in the serialized symbols which we call
historical happenings the constant expression of the timeless
idea and a temporal series'. The idea is never fully represented
owing to the intractability of the material and so is extended
over into time. But these two aspects must always be kept
together. 'As the new physics has done away with the dichotomy, matter and energy, and indeed energy is seen as the basic
thing rather than matter, so too with history. On the one hand
we have the dominant seminal ideas (in prehuman history the
entelechies of the life pattern: in human history the mythoi that
have shaped the social heredities). And on the other hand we
have the actual, incidental, episodic behaviour of man. But
these are not two opposed things; they are two aspects of one
process. And as the idea behind a design is greater than the
means through which that idea is partly rendered, so the
mythoi are the cause and factual history is the consequence. The
specific economic aspect of history is the intractability of the
medium whereby the texture of contingency is given to the
actual work of art. We must then look upon the mythos as
racial history as it strives to evolve an ideal. It is the theme
which imposes the behaviour pattern on those who, because
they are in "subconscious" touch with it, feel an inherent
requirement that they should fulfil it.'
The myth is history, 'is the blueprint in the minds of men

imposing on them the obligation to translate it into historical fact. Yet we must also consider the possibility that as no human infant has as yet been born at the highest level of its embryonic promise of mental capacity, so no emergence into actual history may yet have manifested the mythic ideal, the full Promise.'

This attempt of Heard's to work out a religious pattern in history has not been received with much favour. He has been accused of mixing fantasy with science and abusing historical method. The historian, so most critics think, should confine himself to the sequences which he can detect in the past by means of evidence. He has no right to pontificate on what might have been if physical organisms or men had behaved differently. There is no denying that Heard does make arbitrary assumptions at times and play with terms. He has also far too much confidence in the hypothetical excursions made by scientists into the unknown. What happened tens of thousands of years ago is treated with the same certainty as a contemporary fact, and we are supposed to believe, for instance, that primeval organisms exercised a freewill which animals we know do not possess. Nevertheless there are merits which should not be ignored because of the defects, and in a curious and contagious way he makes us feel the endemic disease of man and the symptoms which might herald a cure. If he mingles together far too rashly history, science, morals and theology, fact and fancy, certainty and provisional hypothesis, he avoids the narrowed specialism which cannot see the wood for the trees. Like Toynbee he attempts to find a shape in history, and his theory of growth by response and adaptation to the environment is not unlike that of Toynbee's. Toynbee keeps to recorded history; Heard in one short volume is far more ambitious in that he embraces all living things. To some such a bold idea may seem preposterous, but there is an undying desire to fit all the pieces of the universe into a pattern and so give a meaning to it, and in these days when confusion is mounting up and chaos stares us in the face, Heard is voicing the desire of multitudes in calling for an answer. For that reason alone his thesis should be examined with a certain sympathy. Since the time of Descartes the ego has come more and more to be identified with self-consciousness. This no doubt gave a new impetus to philosophy and science and sanctified human reason; it tended also to split the human personality and to make all that was non-rational a stranger to the self. It created also a breach between the human self and nature, between consciousness and objective reality. Strange new problems came to the fore such as, how do we know a world different from ourselves? The self, that is, by making itself into a kind of djinn or spirit hovering above the real world, lost contact and communion with that world and our own nature. Reason had become disincarnate, the ghost in the machine, and each self-consciousness inhabited a world of its own. This dire situation is being to some extent righted by the discoveries of the new psychology, though, it must be admitted, the recognition of our psycho-physical self has been blurred by some of the new theories. Heard is in harmony with this new trend in his insistence on a wholeness in man which embraces the non-conscious as well as the conscious. This is what he means by the fracture of the self which has to be mended. Again we are closer to the life around us than the doctrine of self-consciousness would allow us to believe. Much in us is consonant with nature; we have a kinship with it, and we take up into our own special rhythm its rises and its falls. And if we have this kinship with all life we have a much closer union with our fellow-men, and no account of individual life, its weaknesses and its powers, can be complete without an understanding of this brotherhood. Heard uses this truth to stress the continuation of original Falls in successive societies and individuals; it is important also for a proper understanding of history. If instead of myths he had written of 'truths', truths which are not stones or dry formulae but ever open and inexhaustible, much that he says would be both traditional and fresh. In one place he throws off some remarks on history which outweigh all his defects, so valuable and informative are they. He starts with the image already quoted of a 'sweeping stairway, from each step of which there was a consistent outlook'. Each generation, that is, mounts a step, or as I should prefer to say, a series of steps, and looking down sees the past and the world from a new angle which is its own; and this glance has truth, even if it be not the whole truth. He then goes on to say that we have to approach and understand life not in terms of mechanistic science, but in terms of art. A play, for example, such as *Hamlet* is not a process which depends for its meaning on the closing lines. Every passage and every scene in it has its own intrinsic worth and by its own significance constitutes the play. 'Every part of it is needed as a whole experience, as an instant timeless apprehension.' Heard draws from this the conclusion that at any moment in history there is an experience of truth, an insight into it which is unique and therefore cannot be repeated. The final vision, the whole which will be then completed will consist of the gathering up of these separate, constituent insights into one. As a corrective of the usual account of history and a too mechanistic theory of evolution, this theory is of the utmost value. It is quite true that every man and every generation has to behold the truth and is not cut off from truth because the end of the world is a long way off and many things are yet to be discovered. But it is a pity that Heard should spoil his suggestion by carrying the analogy of human life and art too far and so involving himself in some confusion. It is not at all clear, for instance, how a partial insight can be at the same time a constituent of the whole truth. In a play a scene can have its own beauty and also contribute to the plot and the finale. That is to say, it can be both a means and an end; but that is not to say that it is the meaning of the whole play seen from one angle, or to revert to another image, that it is a step from which the whole truth can be seen. The ideal towards which Heard is groping is that of an experience which can be both temporal and everlasting in its certainty, arrived at, shall we say, in the year A.D. 100 or A.D. 1951, and at the same time valid at the end of time. The image of a play or a piece of music serves to correct that of a mechanical process, but it does not do justice to human experience. Man is not only the spectator of history; he is also an actor in it, and he makes history. It will not do to say that he makes the most of the lines he has to recite; he is a play within a play and that play is his solitary wrestle with an angel. Whitehead with some truth called religion 'what man does with his solitariness'. He must catch hold of truth or die, and no matter what the future may have in store for other persons, his grandeur and his misery consist in making his experience and life conform to absolute truth and absolute love.[1] Heard does not do justice to man; he forgets that he is an image of God and redeemed for his own sake and not for his part in universal history. There is a sense in which as the generations pass knowledge grows and

[1] 'Whom I myself shall see, and my eyes shall behold, and not another' (Job 19, 27).

past experience can be likened to the scenes in a play, but Heard, in being content with this explanation, diminishes the status of man. He fails to see that he is always capable of truth, even of the majestic and soaring truth revealed by God, and for this reason he misses the shining light of the Christian message and is belligerently hostile to dogma and doctrine, those lighthouses of truth and safeguards of man.

As it is, much of the theology is to the orthodox mind far-fetched. Nevertheless the theologian too can pick up hints. According to the Pauline doctrine, all creation is affected by the Fall and will share in its own manner in the redemption. No one can tell how that will happen, but Heard does succeed in giving a positive suggestion based on science. Even more suggestive is his hypothesis of a prehistoric time or condition when organisms were free of the evils which now attend them, a condition of perfect balance between living things and their environment, a symbiosis which insured unity and a kind of immortality. The vexing problem of evil touches living things as well as human beings, and though Heard weakens his answer by too much fantastic guesswork, he reminds us of the mysterious interconnection of sin and death which was taught by St. Paul. When he turns to history proper, once again his interpretation may sound at times extravagant. We know too little as yet to be confident that earliest man lived in the somnambulistic peace some anthropologists assert. Jung and other psychologists believe that primitive men were co-conscious in a tribal pattern of behaviour; they were so much part of nature and of each other that it was not individuals who lived the situation as the situation which lived in them. This may be so, but it may equally be true that there are other aspects of primitive life of which we know as yet almost nothing. The coming of the heroes or ruffians, as Heard would call them, may have been a decline from the Saturnian era, in that it brought wars and separated human beings one from another. But when we consider an example nearer to our own time, the coming of the Normans, who would assert that they were just destroyers? Their monuments remain in the north and in Sicily and the Near East and bid us distrust too easy generalizations about roving men.

But, while we may well hesitate to accept Heard's version of the past, he is surely right in part of his diagnosis of the present. To combine the co-consciousness of primitive man and his affiliation to nature with self-consciousness and responsibility, to get rid of the *malaise* of loneliness and discover the way of life, man's underground solidarity and the means of redintegration, in this desire Heard represents the feeling of his age. The French poet, Pierre Emmanuel, in his autobiography, *The Universal Singular*, expresses the same emotions: 'It is possible that new symbols are in process of being elaborated among mankind, and that thousands of voices have already uttered them, that millions and millions of human souls nurture them obscurely in dreams. It is possible that these symbols are merely a new aspect to certain permanent myths of mankind, bound by an interaction whose living law escapes us, and which are the germs, or whose whole is the unique germ, of the spiritual universe. If these symbols, so long scattered like the limbs of Osiris in the shades, group themselves in a symbolic system and become harmonized under the pressure of history, once more will begin the great adventure of thought gradually raised through all the planes of human endeavour, from the womb of symbols to the extreme limit of ideas: an adventure which will be followed by many others, for as ideas become less burdened they will lose sight of the earth, and once more a split will arise, the harmony will be broken, and a new integration will become necessary. There is a particular delight in following, in the personal microcosm, the evolution of human history. A consciousness attentive to the biology of symbols, and which lives them within the situation, *hic et nunc*, perhaps contributes, in a modest but decisive way, to that unitary vision of whose coming the world feels a presentiment.' And in another place *à propos* of a universal history or philosophy of history, such as Heard has attempted: 'Pedestrian history, which goes from one nearby cause to an immediate effect, satisfies the mind only in periods of calm, when the pressure which drives man towards the unknown is relaxed. These are periods when much is learned about man, but they finish in pure abstraction: they are periods with a brief and measured rhythm, underneath which, underground, the major rhythms pursue their course. In the constitution of the earth, one might doubtless find many analogies which might illumine the constitution of history, and explain how a break occurs between a perfectly explicable past and the unforeseeable future. By studying those "great tidal waves which we call a great love, a great unhappiness, or a religious conversion", whose astonishing effects Claudel evolves in *La Peinture Hollandaise,* perhaps one might achieve an image of the radical metamorphosis which humanity sometimes undergoes. But the history of civilizations is a subject yet to be born, and comparative psychology must give way to a simultaneous vision of all times: successive civilizations are the generations of mankind, and the crisis of man are the crises of each generation. At the time, I still knew nothing of Arnold Toynbee, one of the first men of universal genius who have dared to transcend the narrow Western perspective of history, and resolutely place themselves at the centre of the human psyche: or, otherwise stated, who conceive history as the spiritual genesis of man, a genesis which has hardly begun. To reverse the whole meaning of historical research, to project the future from within the past, to initiate vast parabolas whose path, while taking full account of the single event, may express a movement whose energy goes beyond the centuries—by no other method could we be saved from the false impasse into which we had got ourselves.'

INDEX